A Mental Theater

Poetic Drama and Consciousness in the Romantic Age

ALAN RICHARDSON

The Pennsylvania State University Press
University Park and London

For my parents

Library of Congress Cataloging-in-Publication Data

Richardson, Alan, 1955–
A mental theater.

Bibliography: p.
Includes index.
1. Verse drama, English—History and criticism.
2. English drama—19th century—History and criticism.
3. Romanticism—England. I. Title.
PR719.V4R53 1987 822'.7'09145 87–10922
ISBN 0-271-00612-9

Printed in the United States of America

Contents

Acknowledgments

This work has passed through several stages, and at each I have incurred debts which I now take pleasure in acknowledging. The ideas which I develop below first grew out of conversations, in and out of the classroom, with my teacher Daniel T. O'Hara. He and David Bromwich read through an early version of what became several chapters; I found their criticisms and suggestions extremely helpful in later reworking the argument. My greatest single debt is to David Perkins, who encouraged me to continue my work, kept me at it, and read through several drafts, making a great number of thoughtful comments and tirelessly, generously leading me toward a stronger text. Jerome Buckley also read through the manuscript, drawing my attention to many lapses in style and argumentation. Vernon Shetley, A. W. Phinney, Nelly Oliensis, Brian Richardson, Kenneth Watson, and Miller Solomon read chapters and gave helpful, often indispensable advice. Joel Dando put his superior knowledge of Byron's prose at my disposal on more than one occasion, and Mary Crane also answered several otherwise desperate queries for me. Ashton Nichols and Anthony Roche, my colleagues at Auburn University, gave generously of their time, ideas, and conversation as I completed the manuscript; the epilogue could not have been written without their help and inspiration. Katherine Mosby graciously lent her sharper eye to proofreading the bibliography. For advice and encouragement at various stages in the progress of this work and its author, I would also thank Jonathan Arac, W. J. Bate, Deborah Blacker, Joseph Boone, John Burke, James Engell, Marjorie Garber, Bert Hitchcock, U. C. Knoepflmacher, Thomas McFarland, and Peter L. Thorslev, Jr.

I wish to thank the Whiting Foundation for generous support during the academic year 1984–85, during which much of the final draft was written. Robert Kiely made office space and a very congenial atmosphere available to me at Adams House, in addition to reading through a version of the manuscript and guiding me toward its eventual conclusion. The late Peter Laver gave me access, on very short notice, to facsimiles of *The Borderers* manuscripts at Dove Cottage;

my visit there was made possible by a Dexter Travel Fellowship in 1982. I would like to express my appreciation to the librarians and staffs of Firestone Library at Princeton University, Widener Library at Harvard University, and the Ralph Draughon Library at Auburn University. For inestimable help in creating a flexible manuscript and shaping its several incarnations, I thank Zack Deal of the Office of Information Technology at Harvard University and William C. Flick of the Auburn University Computing Services.

1

A Mental Theater

The Romantic critique of fixed genres did not aim simply at revising the terms or evading the constraints of neoclassical rule and decorum. Conventional boundaries were assailed as part of what Friedrich Schlegel called a "progressive" program for integrating poetry with philosophy, criticism, and manners as well as bringing its "separate species" together: "It tries to and should mix and fuse poetry and prose, inspiration and theory, the poetry of art and the poetry of nature; and make poetry lively and sociable, and life and society poetical."[1] Romantic writers developed an approach to genre at once critical and reconstructive, working in modes which resist classification—from the fragment (as with Schlegel himself) to the *gesamtkunstwerk*—and fusing conventionally distinct genres into new composite forms, strategies which artists of the avant-garde (another Romantic innovation) continue to appropriate. The English Romantics developed the lyrical ballad, the historical novel, the prose poem, the verse autobiography as vital hybrids of elements long kept apart—if not viewed as contraries—in practice as well as in theory. Shelley's subtitle for *Prometheus Unbound*, "a lyrical drama," and Byron's description of his dramatic poetry as "mental theatre" invoke the same iconoclastic program. Both poets worked at reviving the English "serious" drama from its long slumber by radically transforming it, fusing the objective portrayal of action with the subjective lyrical voice. Dramatic action would not function to portray or set off character; rather, character becomes plot as the dramatic interest centers on the history of a protagonist's consciousness.

Unlike most Romantic innovations in genre, the poetic drama has yet to find acceptance in literary history as a legitimate form. Looked at singly, works of Romantic drama have generated a great deal of enthusiastic criticism; but when studied together, the same works have been met with dismissal, marginalization, or apology.[2] Such resistance stems in part from a widespread and (until recently) largely unchallenged assumption that Romantic poetry is predominately or even essentially lyrical. Although Romantic lyrics are themselves increasingly read as dramatic or "dialogic" works,[3] critics of Romantic drama have emphasized its lyric elements to the exclusion of considering—or apparently even perceiving—its dramatic aspect, rejecting the form as static "monodrama" or accepting it as a "central" but impoverished, undramatic expression of Romantic subjectivity.[4] The tendency to diminish or dismiss the drama in dramatic poetry rises also out of suspicions surrounding the Romantic rejection of the stage. Historians of English drama are professionally uncomfortable with the divorce of drama and theater;[5] the opprobrium of the term "closet drama" suffices almost in itself to remove the Romantic verse drama from serious consideration.

Charles Lamb's paradoxical and deliberately perverse argument that Shakespeare's tragedies are better read than performed helps clarify his contemporaries' turn from the stage. For Lamb, Shakespeare's most compelling plays are (in the words of a more recent critic) "tragedies of consciousness."[6] In Shakespeare "the form of *speaking*, whether it be in soliloquy or dialogue, is only a medium, and a highly artificial one at that, for putting the reader or spectator into possession of that knowledge of the inner structure and workings of mind in a character."[7] Similarly for Byron dramatic poetry should constitute a "mental theatre," taking as its subject the human mind in all its complexity, exploring not only its outward manifestation in character but its "inner structure and workings" as well. And the Romantic poets as dramatists held with Lamb that such mental drama would emerge with most intensity through reading, which "presents to the fancy just so much of external appearances as to make us feel we are among flesh and blood, while by far the greater and better part of our imagination is employed upon the thoughts and internal machinery of the character."[8]

The positive aspect of Lamb's (and Byron's) emphasis on the reading process, which has much to do with the emergence of reception or "reader response" theory in Romantic criticism, has not been much remarked upon, unlike Lamb's negative contention that stage representation had "materialised" tragedy and "brought down a fine vision to the standard of flesh and blood."[9] Applied to the Romantic poet's disdain for the contemporary stage, Lamb's remarks evoke a by now familiar set of unfavorable conditions in the theater: monopolizing producers, a public demand for spectacle (the Drury Lane was saved from financial disaster by an aquatic dog act written into a failing melodrama), the overacting endemic to an absurdly enlarged house, and the rant encouraged by an actor's theater.[10] Whether condemned for his elitist pose and disdain for the public, or defended as a well-meaning but anachronistic reformer, the Romantic poet as dramatist is judged against his alleged "retreat" from the theater, rather than for the invention of a fundamentally new poetic form.

If we begin, however, from Lamb's emphasis on psychology, we can develop an approach to lyrical drama not as a retreat into the closet but as a foray into the minds of both dramatic character and reader. While theatrical appeal and psychological exploration are hardly mutually exclusive, neither are they inseparable; and most Romantic poets and critics understandably felt that theirs was not the historical moment for a drama that could both succeed on the contemporary stage and still recapture the psychological depth which had been missing from tragedy since the Restoration. In turning from the theater, the Romantic drama revived the "tragedy of consciousness" which, for a century and a half, English dramatists had lost sight of even when, like Rowe or (at times) Dryden, working within a professedly Shakespearean mode.

A third, and more recent, critique of the shift from stage to text in Romantic theory and dramatic practice sees the abandonment of theatrical performance as politically reactionary.[11] We are tempted, particularly since Brecht, to see theater as the most political of art forms, bringing an author's production into a public forum, directly confronting the text with an audience at once critical and susceptible to political exhortation. The Romantic turn from the stage could then signify ambivalence regarding a potentially explosive audience, an ambivalence intensified if not directly inspired by the living theater of the French Revolution, when (as Nodier wrote in 1841) "le peuple entier venait de jouer dans le plus grand drame de l'histoire."[12] The plot of Wordsworth's *The Borderers* has itself been read as an early instance of the English reaction to the French upheaval: A "sinister, subversive" intellectual leads the hero to wrongfully kill a "father-figure who might generally stand for the *ancien régime* or more specifically for Louis XVI himself."[13] This reading of *The Borderers* as an exploration of "the part played in the revolutionary crime by intellectuals" takes us far from the received view of the work as static monodrama; but it greatly underestimates Wordsworth's investigation of the politics of consciousness.

The plot of Wordsworth's *Borderers* illustrates the fusion of objective and subjective action typical of Romantic mental theater: dramatic in its emphasis on confrontation, seduction, and rhetorical struggle, lyric in its emphasis on self-consciousness. The protagonist begins as young, morally integral, idealistic, but critically lacking in self-awareness, opposed by a sophisticated and self-tormented antagonist who sees the hero as a version of his own youthful, unfallen self. Compelled by the pain of memory and by will to power, the antagonist determines on rendering the youth a mirror of his present, disintegrated self, baiting his trap with the promise of a heightened, independent self-consciousness. The temptation proceeds through a rhetorical struggle to the hero's repetition of the seducer's own past crime, one that in both cases shapes a self-consciousness radically self-alienated and intensified only by continual torment. The youth is no longer naive, but his promised psychic independence rests on the assaults of a hostile other within the self. He can in the end only become a seducer in turn, paradoxically seeking companionship through further alienation, or search for death as an isolated, restless wanderer.

My outline for the plot of *The Borderers* could, with slight modifications, describe that of Byron's *Cain* or Shelley's *Cenci;* it closely follows the first act of *Prometheus Unbound,* and the same mythos, fragmented and slightly rearranged, informs *Manfred* and Beddoes's *Death's Jest-Book.* The rather startling fact that these works have never been presented as fundamentally related attests to how much is lost when their dramatic arguments are discounted. Equally remarkable, given such correspondences, is that the younger Romantics constructed their versions of "mental theater" without reference to *The Borderers,* which remained in manuscript until 1842. The deep similarities attest to a pervasive concern with the problematic nature of self-consciousness, a shared social and dynamic conception of the mind, and to common antecedents in texts by Shakespeare and Milton, the predecessors whom the Romantics placed in the foreground of their literary genealogy. Despite a long critical tradition oriented toward "Romantic subjectivity," the Romantics themselves were deeply suspicious of a consciousness isolated from social relations.[14] In the Romantic theater of the mind, consciousness develops not spontaneously but through interaction with another; a work like *Manfred* verges toward monodrama only to reject it, less a celebration of isolated subjectivity than a critique of the false assumptions behind psychic autonomy.

The Romantic revival of Shakespearean psychological drama relied, then, on a renewed emphasis on consciousness, but equally on a dynamic conception of character as inherently unstable, changing, formed and reformed through dramatic confrontation. As the emphasis on psychic interaction separates mental theater from its received characterization as "monodrama," the dynamic conception of character distances the dramatic poetry of the Romantics from the movements conventionally held to have influenced or anticipated them: the German drama of *Sturm und Drang*, the Gothic drama, the new emphasis on character in eighteenth-century Shakespeare criticism. Although Coleridge's *Remorse* shows all too clearly the influence of Schiller's *Die Räuber*,[15] Wordsworth (like the younger Romantics) borrowed only superficially from German tragedy, valuing it mainly as a precedent for returning (in a much more sophisticated manner than Schiller) to Shakespeare.[16] For Wordsworth, Shelley, Byron, and Beddoes, dramatic poetry is a self-consciously, almost obsessively English form with its roots in Shakespeare, despite their use of German, Greek, or (in Byron) Italian dramaturgy.

The Gothic emphasis on extreme or morbid mental states and eighteenth-century studies of Shakespeare's characters similarly helped establish a climate for Romantic drama without anticipating its dynamic portrayal of consciousness.[17] Poets working directly from such trends, whether for the stage like Keats (in *Otho the Great*) or for the closet like Joanna Baillie, failed to move beyond the stable and static characterizations of neoclassical drama.[18] Baillie's De Montfort, "a sullen wanderer on the earth, / Avoiding all men, cursing and accurs'd," manifests the same sleepless agony as the protagonist of mental theater, but we see only its symptoms, not its genesis or its implication in a social context; De Montfort's unhappy consciousness is, as Baillie herself put it, "seemingly unprovoked by outward circumstances."[19] Similarly the eighteenth-century character study tends to represent the mind as an assemblage of fixed characteristics automatically producing sets of predictable behavior, such that Macbeth's inherent ambition, for example, leads inexorably to the suspension of his moral sense and predicates his resort to criminal means.[20] For the Romantics, such readings were doubly disappointing, as they both trivialize the growth of the character's mind and all but ignore the influence of psychic antagonism. William Richardson hardly refers to Lady Macbeth in his analysis of her husband, and mentions the Witches only to dismiss them. In Hazlitt's "character" of Macbeth, the "pressure of preternatural agency" and Lady Macbeth's "obdurate strength of will" are of the essence.[21]

The Romantic approach to reading Shakespeare develops integrally with the revival of Shakespearean characterization in mental theater, and one can trace a pattern very like that derived from *The Borderers* through studying the reactions of Romantic critics to Shakespeare's tragedies. While the analysis of consciousness giving rise to this pattern characterizes several of the tragedies—one thinks especially of *Hamlet* and *Antony and Cleopatra*—the Romantics found its clearest expositions in *Othello* and *Macbeth*. Milton's variations on Shakespearean psychodrama affect in turn the Romantics, who further elaborate the pattern, associating Shakespeare and Milton together with the exploration of an intensified and critically isolated consciousness.[22] As I relate these texts to individual works of Romantic drama, I will ground narrative and thematic parallels in specific textual echoes, leaving the burden of proof for the readings that follow.

Hazlitt and De Quincey both wrote essays on *Macbeth* that reflect the widespread Romantic interest in the psychological complexity and dialogical approach of Shakespeare's characterization and draw out several related motifs appropriated by mental theater as well. Hazlitt, discussing *Macbeth* in *Characters of Shakespear's Plays*, writes: "It moves upon the verge of an abyss, and is in a constant struggle with life and death. The action is desperate and the reaction is dreadful. It is a huddling together of fierce extremes, a war of opposite natures which of them shall destroy the other."[23] In "On the Knocking at the Gate in *Macbeth*," a work of self- and literary analysis proceeding from a problematic moment in his reading, De Quincey records similar reactions: "But in the murderer, such a murderer as a poet will condescend to, there must be raging some great storm of passion,—jealousy, ambition, vengeance, hatred,—which will create a hell within him; and into this hell we are to look." The violence within calls up a violence from without: "Another world has stepped in; and the murderers are taken out of the region of human things, human purposes, human desires. They are transfigured: Lady Macbeth is 'unsexed'; Macbeth has forgot that he was born of woman; both are conformed to the image of devils; and the world of devils is suddenly revealed."[24]

In these Romantic readings of *Macbeth* we find again the outlines of the pattern of psychic interaction brought by Wordsworth, Byron, Shelley, and Beddoes into their own verse dramas. One aspect arises from the concern with character interaction and to a large degree shapes the plot. This is the "constant struggle between life and death" that Hazlitt found at the heart of *Macbeth,* a struggle between characters—"a war of opposite natures which of them shall destroy the other"—that intensifies the struggle within the protagonist's mind. The first acts of *Macbeth* pit the hero against the temptations of the Witches and those of Lady Macbeth, which combine to aggravate his growing ambition. Because his struggle is waged on several fronts at once, the conflict emerges less clearly than in *Othello,* but both tragedies portray a fundamentally unequal struggle that leads to murder and self-destructive agony. It is unequal precisely because it does involve opposite natures, one naive and morally conditioned and the others knowing and amoral (though ultimately conditioned, most clearly in the case of Iago, by a confining obsession with mastery): the integrity of Macbeth warped by the ironies of the Witches, the single vision of Othello clouded by the chameleon rhetoric of Iago. On one level the struggle is waged "between life and death" because it opposes forces of vitality and destruction, but the stakes are also life and death, for an individual life—Duncan, Desdemona—hangs in the balance. When the struggle leads to murder its perpetrator meets his own destruction as well; he falls into an intolerable mental state that leads, in Shakespeare, to suicide or suicidal recklessness and, in mental theater, to either death or a loss of selfhood in eternal exile.

A second typical motif, which grows out of the first, relates to the imagery and to the general atmosphere of mental theater, and often shapes the setting as well. While the plot typically hinges on the confrontation of opposites, its progression brings about their equally violent interpenetration, the "huddling together of fierce extremes" that Hazlitt saw in *Macbeth.* De Quincey expresses his similar perception more graphically: "another world has stept in." In *Macbeth* the world of men is interpenetrated by the forbidden spirit world, "the world of devils," and the extremes merge tragically as the humans are "transfigured" by their association with the demonic realm. I have adopted the term "border violation" for such interpenetration; its application to *The Borderers* and to Byron's *Heaven and Earth* (which takes place when "the sons of God saw the daughters of men that they were fair") is immediately apparent. The "war" of opposite natures, marked by aggression, leads to their interpenetration, which is facilitated by a transgression or crime; so murder, the ultimate human transgression, grows out of the aggressive rhetorical attacks of an Iago or a Lady Macbeth. But in another sense transgression informs the aggressive struggle, for the tempter's murderous promptings can only succeed if they penetrate the borders of the other's consciousness, a violation figured in the Romantics' models by such acts as the whisperings of Satan into the ear of sleeping Eve, or the remarkable insinuation of bestial images from Iago's speech into Othello's susceptible mind.[25]

The protagonist's internalization of the struggle of contrary natures, precipitated by his seducer's literal influence, forms a third characteristic motif, that of a divided self-consciousness. Because this conflict takes place within the mind of a single character, it emerges in soliloquy much as the war of opposites emerges in dialogue. This inner conflict is the "great storm of passion" which seized De Quincey's imagination in reading *Macbeth*, the tempest in Macbeth's mind which "will create a hell within him." Here the Romantics' preoccupation with *Paradise Lost* becomes relevant, as it is Satan's inner torment, the "troubl'd thoughts" which "stir / The Hell within him" (IV.19–20), that De Quincey typically recalls in describing Macbeth, a phrase that echoes throughout the poetic dramas of Wordsworth, Byron, Shelley, and Beddoes. The character motif of a tormented, restless self-consciousness relates in its turn to the plot motifs of psychic battle and interpenetration. It arises from a struggle of opposites that takes place within the mind, described by Milton's Satan as a "hateful siege / Of contraries" (IX.121–22). And it is the same inner torment that impels the tempters of mental theater to lead their naive counterparts into murder and self-destruction, "for," as their original declares before his temptation of Eve, "only in destroying find I ease / To my relentless thoughts" (IX.129–30). Hazlitt is probably thinking of these lines when he writes of Iago, in *Characters of Shakespear's Plays*, that "his gaiety, such as it is, arises from the success of his treachery; his ease from the torture he has inflicted on others."[26] For a year later Hazlitt would attribute the same "love of power" that guides Iago to Milton's devil: "Satan is not the principle of malignity, or of the abstract love of evil—but of the abstract love of power."[27]

Let me restate the pattern I drew from Wordsworth in more generic terms: A tempter figure (in some cases a series of tempters), impelled by his own restlessly tormented consciousness, leads a naive counterpart into an act of transgression, by means of a dramatic rhetorical struggle, in an atmosphere of violently mingling contraries. The crime (usually a murder) engenders the same intolerable restlessness in the mind of its perpetrator, and a potential repetition, or series of repetitions, of the same events. The Romantics found anticipations of this plot, which I call the "pattern of seduction and repetition," in *Macbeth*, *Othello*, and *Paradise Lost;* variations of it inform the works on which I concentrate in this study (although the plot emerges retrospectively in *Manfred*, and Beddoes parodically fragments it in *Death's Jest-Book*). The manner in which these texts interact and the significance of the variations are, as a ground for developing a new understanding of Romantic verse drama, my principal concerns. The readings that follow, however, should be further prefaced by some more general speculations on the pattern of seduction and repetition as it arises from a Romantic conception of consciousness, and on how such a conception can best be approximated.

Introducing a collection of essays entitled *Romanticism and Consciousness*, Harold Bloom writes that "subjectivity or self-consciousness is the salient problem of Romanticism, at least for modern readers."[28] And modern readers, notable among them Peter L. Thorslev and Bloom himself, have written extensively on one aspect of the seduction and repetition mythos I outline above, the inner conflict leading to restless consciousness.[29] But because this problem has been studied apart from the other features of a pattern in which it is so deeply embedded, discussions of Romantic self-consciousness as it appears in verse drama have ignored the crucial dramatic context from which it emerges. Such neglect follows inevitably from the model most recent criticism relies on in portraying the development of consciousness, one fundamentally at odds with Romantic psychology.

Consider, for example, Geoffrey Hartman's reading of *The Borderers.* Its context is his thesis, in *Wordsworth's Poetry,* that the development of the imagination eventually entails an "apocalyptic" break with nature, a break which Wordsworth is precipitated toward but unable to effect, and that this ambivalence becomes a shaping force in his poetry. In *The Borderers* Wordsworth dismisses one possible mode for leaving nature behind, portraying instead "the insufficiency of a criminal or ideologically inspired separation from nature."[30] The protagonist, Marmaduke, is betrayed into committing a crime that "only confirms his new and conscious selfhood," and that leads to his assumption of a specifically Romantic burden, "doomed to eternal (i.e. generic) consciousness of self."[31]

In Marmaduke's emergence to self-consciousness his seducer, Oswald, figures as a "light-bringer," or Lucifer, who "uses his intellect to betray others into enlightenment."[32] The only flaw in this otherwise happy arrangement is that the break with nature is artificially forced; Oswald is, however, further slighted for his "deeply compulsive" nature, which Hartman relates to Freud's "repetition compulsion,"[33] as the crime he leads Marmaduke to commit is (oddly enough) a repetition of a youthful crime of his own. It is not surprising that Hartman's analysis of Oswald should invoke Freud, for his principal thesis on Wordsworth, with its emphasis on the conflict between the mind and the external world, draws heavily on Freud's economic model for psychic development, particularly as articulated in *Beyond the Pleasure Principle* (where the "repetition compulsion" is first discussed).[34] Hartman's implicit reliance on a model for the development of self-consciousness which considers primarily a single (though of course not simple) consciousness as it reacts with a depersonalized external world reflects a fundamental bias toward considering the mind in isolation from its social context, from fellow men and women.[35] His model leads to a persuasive reading of much of Wordsworth's poetry, but it is singularly inadequate to an appreciation of his dramatic poem. Hartman's reading of *The Borderers* neglects as a result its most important aspect, the dynamic interaction of its two principal characters, and hence his assertion that it is "mediocre as drama" seems inevitable.[36] Since the dramatic poem is seen as a background for the interplay of Marmaduke's emerging self-consciousness with the external world (nature), the role of his antagonist in directing (and misdirecting) that emergence is minimized, Oswald becoming for Hartman more a Socratic midwife than a Satanic tempter. From his standpoint the drama centers on the psychic struggle with nature, not on the struggle of two psyches with one another, and *The Borderers* becomes of necessity a monodrama.

The same reliance on Freud's economic model for the development of consciousness characterizes the early work of Bloom, although the terms of Bloom's engagement with Freud have often shifted. Perhaps the clearest exposition for my purposes here is his essay "The Internalization of Quest-Romance," which he begins by invoking Freud's name. "The Romantic movement is from nature to the imagination's freedom . . . redemptive in direction but destructive of the social self." "Self-consciousness" becomes the poet's necessary, if unwieldy, burden: "The quest is to widen consciousness as well as to intensify it, but the quest is shadowed by a spirit that tends to narrow consciousness to an acute preoccupation with self."[37] Insofar as Bloom reads Romantic consciousness as the field of a struggle between nature and imagination, and self-consciousness as the price for psychic autonomy, his view of the Romantics' dramatic works is limited like Hartman's to consideration of the protagonist in virtual isolation.[38] Many readings in *The Visionary Company* attest no less than *Wordsworth's Poetry* to the efficacy of such a perspective, but it is far from universally applicable to Romantic writing. Robert Langbaum, in *The Poetry of Experience*, makes use of a related model that similarly reduces the interaction of self and world to two simplified terms: "The process of experience is for the romanticist a process of self-realization, of a constantly expanding discovery of self through discovery of its imprint on the external world."[39] And consequently, for Langbaum the Romantic "lyrical drama" is "a monodrama—to the extent that only one character is unequivocally actual, with the incidents and the other characters existing as occasions for his self-expression and self-development."[40]

Each of these critics goes beyond not only the detractors but most of the apologists for Romantic verse drama as well, viewing it as a legitimate vehicle for the Romantic exploration of self-consciousness. But the "economic" bias of their models for the development of consciousness leads away from the dramatic element of mental theater. I have adapted my own model from a philosophical work which appeared midway between the dramatic writing of Wordsworth and that of Byron and Shelley. The English Romantics' profound attraction to drama grew in part out of a recognition of the social element of human consciousness widely felt during the nineteenth century, and it is in this context that the pattern of seduction and repetition and its relation to self-consciousness are most readily understood. The psychic struggle enacted in *The Borderers* and in the later works of mental theater is best approached through an influential Romantic account of the development of self-consciousness, Hegel's "Independence and Dependence of Self-consciousness" in *The Phenomenology of Spirit* (1807), a work unknown to the English Romantics but remarkably similar to the works of mental theater in its recognition and analysis of the problem of self-consciousness.

Hegel located the essence of dramatic poetry in the individual's struggle with society, and in the opposition of one individual will to another. The protagonist is not "rooted in his self-exclusive independence; he comes to his own" through "a process of development and collision with other forces."[41] His praise of Shakespeare resembles, as a result, that of his contemporary, A. W. Schlegel; both thinkers were most intrigued by Shakespeare's portrayal of psychic development through tracing the course of a passion from its inception, and in relation to the pressure of social antagonism. "The emergence of the passion that, though it implicitly accords with the character, had not erupted so far but now unfolds—this course and progression of a great soul, its inner development, the painting of its self-destructive fight against circumstances, conditions, and consequences—is the major content in many of Shakespeare's most interesting tragedies."[42] That these "conditions" are social, the "other forces" human, is implicit throughout Hegel's writings on tragedy: "the end and content of an action is only dramatic by reason of the fact that . . . it calls into being in other individuals other objects and passions opposed to it."[43]

Hegel's recognition of the dramatic aspect of psychic development in Shakespearean tragedy parallels his essentially dramatic account of the emergence of self-consciousness in the *Phenomenology*. It might be objected that in taking his account out of context one necessarily distorts the complexity of Hegel's argument; but the use of this section of the *Phenomenology* as an analytical model has an eminent tradition, ranging from Marx's adaptation of Hegel's account to his understanding of property as estranged labor, to Lacan's implicit reliance on the same model in his account of the "mirror stage" of psychic development.[44]

The drama of Hegel's account begins with his insistence that self-consciousness cannot arise in isolation and is inconceivable apart from a social context; moreover, it emerges only through a struggle with another (or rather an other) consciousness. A comparison with Hegel's model brings out a further aspect of the "constant struggle" in *Macbeth* described by Hazlitt and adapted in mental theater, that the struggle is specifically one for psychic mastery. Hegel also helps clarify the relation between the dramatic struggle and the motif of a restlessly tormented consciousness (the conflict within). According to his model, one consciousness seeks to resolve an intolerable psychic restlessness, which proceeds from the lack of a stable sense of self-identity, by demanding "recognition" through mastery of another consciousness. Such recognition relies on the subordination of the other, providing the master consciousness with a false reflection in which it illusively contemplates itself as integral and independent.

Hegel develops this metaphor of "mastery" in the influential "Master and Servant" argument of "Independence and Dependence of Self-consciousness."[45] He begins his argument by flatly rejecting the possibility of an autonomous, isolated emergence to self-awareness: "Self-consciousness exists in itself and for itself, in that, and by the fact that it exists for another self-consciousness; that is to say, it *is* only by being acknowledged or 'recognized'."[46] In dramatic terms, this means that the emergence to self-consciousness cannot be brought about in the protagonist by another character acting merely as a catalyst: "Action from one side only would be useless, because what is to happen can only be brought about by means of both."[47] The process of "recognition" is not one of simple homage but involves, as in the Romantic reading of *Macbeth*, a fight for life and death: "The relation of both self-consciousnesses is in this way so constituted that they prove themselves and each other through a life-and-death struggle."[48] For Hegel, the "conscious selfhood" and "separation from nature" that Hartman saw as Marmaduke's ultimate attainment cannot be won without such dramatic interaction: "It is solely by risking life, that freedom is obtained; only thus is it tried and proved that the essential nature of self-consciousness is not bare existence, is not the merely immediate form in which it at first makes its appearance, is not its mere absorption in the expanse of life."[49]

This phase in the emergence to self-consciousness, the phase explored in mental theater, is, however, anything but unproblematic.

As one self-consciousness attains mastery, far from becoming independent, it in fact binds itself in a dependent relation to the other. "Just where the master has effectively achieved rule, he really finds that something has come about quite different from an independent consciousness. It is not an independent, but rather a dependent consciousness that he has achieved."[50] A similarly ironic reversal problematizes the attainment of self-consciousness for the protagonists of mental theater. Along with their emergence to a heightened, conscious awareness of self, the limitations of self-consciousness, imposed by the conditions of its emergence, are revealed, limitations which arise from and are symbolized by the distorting presence of the other in a tragically violated self. The self-consciousness explored by Wordsworth, Byron, Shelley, and Beddoes in their dramatic poetry is one which pays for its emergence with a loss of integrity, and the discomforting truth they expose is the commanding presence within the self of a reflected image of the other.

Hegel's account, even in the simplified form in which I have presented it here, offers a number of provocative analogues to the works of mental theater. It is no accident that many of the same metaphors—struggle, recognition, mastery—are crucially embedded in the rhetoric of these works, for the English Romantics, like Hegel, are constantly aware both of the dramatic nature and the tragic limitations of this stage of the emergence to self-consciousness. "Romantic individualism" was so long held uncritically as a given in modern interpretations of Romanticism that it is initially hard to grasp the significance of the tragic outcomes of the works that explore self-consciousness and its attainment.[51] But for the English Romantic poets, self-consciousness is not an end in itself, and they see the quest for autonomy as ultimately self-defeating. It is a necessary phase in the greater quest for a heightened awareness, but those trapped in that phase—like the protagonists of *The Borderers*, *Cain*, and *The Cenci*—are doomed to self-division and tragic isolation. It is only in *Prometheus Unbound*, with Shelley's vision of a radical transformation of consciousness through sympathy, that the limits of self-consciousness are transcended (or rather dissolved) and the pattern of seduction and repetition broken. The other works of mental theater are concerned with presenting the struggle against those limits in all its tragic intensity.

The tension between the Romantic poet's desire to attain to self-consciousness and his awareness of the limitations imposed by that ultimately transitional state is reflected in the Romantic ambivalence toward Milton's Satan, who came to exemplify a tragically limiting, isolated self-consciousness in the allusive iconography of mental theater.[52] Southey, in his quietly influential identification of a "Satanic School" among the younger Romantics, wrote more penetratingly than he knew in defining the limitations of the Satanic stance, limitations that led to its rejection by the same poets who most appreciated the seemingly Promethean energy of Satan in the early, heroic books of *Paradise Lost*. The diabolic poet, Southey writes, will manifest "a satanic spirit of pride . . . which still betrays the wretched feeling of hopelessness wherewith it is allied"—for satanic autonomy will be inseparable from psychic torment and isolation. He will be unable to escape "remorse of conscience," and so long as he adheres to his inauthentic stance, "so long is he"—like Satan himself—"heaping up guilt upon his soul in perpetual accumulation."[53] Such is the fate of the Romantic protagonists demonically betrayed into a no less demonic self-division; a fate that Southey chose to ascribe instead to their creators.

The Romantics found in Milton models for both the form and dramatic argument of mental theater. Shelley, who found *Lear* "the most perfect specimen of dramatic art existing in the world" and *Cato* a "cold imitation of the form of the great masterpieces of antiquity," held that, as a dramatist writing in the neoclassical period, "Milton stood alone illuminating an age unworthy of him."[54] *Samson Agonistes* was, until the Romantic period, the only "dramatic poem" (Milton's subtitle) of any great stature in the language. Its basic dramaturgical pattern, a suffering protagonist confronting a succession of tormenting antagonists in a series of dialogues broken by soliloquy and choruses, recurs both in *Manfred* and in the first act of *Prometheus Unbound*, and although the three works have a common ancestor in Greek tragedy, Milton set the precedent for minimizing stage action—Johnson's unforgettable perception is simply that nothing happens[55]—and concentrating instead on intense psychological portraiture.

One might wish to consider *Samson Agonistes* a formative thematic influence as well. The state of restless psychic torment shared by the protagonists of Gothic and Romantic stage plays and mental theater alike is exemplified by Samson, plagued by his "restless thoughts" of betrayal and remorse. But whenever we can trace a correspondence between *loci* in *Samson Agonistes* and in a Romantic dramatic poem, we can usually find the same motif (and usually the same figure) more fully developed in *Paradise Lost.* With his long soliloquy on "relentless thoughts" at the beginning of Book Nine, Satan exemplifies restless consciousness for a number of Romantic writers, as many textual echoes demonstrate. Their preoccupation with Satanic consciousness helps account for the deep similarities among the works of Romantic mental theater and some of the Gothic and Romantic novels written with an early "psychological" approach.

The study of textual allusion and echo has moved in twenty-five years from the compilation of "parallel passages" ancillary to source study, through various complex, dynamic approaches taking thematic, biographical, and formal contexts into consideration, to viewing the allusion as the dominant mode of all writing, a sign of the text's implication in the intertext or universe of discourse.[56] In Romantic studies, and particularly with reference to Milton, two competing schools have emerged, both of value though working from seemingly incompatible assumptions. The relation of an echo to its source can be seen as a "field of combat,"[57] with the later text as a "psychic battlefield" on which the belated poet engages in desperate skirmishes with his Great Original.[58] Alternatively, it has been argued that the later poet confidently employs allusion to gain authority and economically enhance his own lines through implicit juxtaposition with a thematically relevant prior text.[59]

I have found both approaches useful in thinking about the proliferation of echoes and allusions to Shakespeare and Milton in the works of mental theater, and have somewhat relied on the tradition they replaced as well. The numerous scattered lists of "parallel passages" between specific works of Romantic drama and one or more of Shakespeare's tragedies at least establish beyond a doubt that the Romantic poets were conversant with and (on whatever level) responding to specific Shakespearean texts, though I will question the usual view that such parallels are evidence of pseudo-Elizabethanism. Such studies have freed me to concentrate in each case on a few particularly complex allusions or echoes, and explore the thematic interplay and historical resonance that source study usually neglects. In considering such issues, I have found both of the prevalent recent approaches—which mutually descend from Longinus's recognition that poets can derive a "divine vapor" or "effluence" from the "genius of the men of old," and that in this "strife" of emulation the later poet can be "worsted" by his predecessors[60]—provocative and sometimes illuminating. On the whole, it seems that the more outspoken a later poet is in acknowledging his use of an earlier text, the more likely is his own work to show the enrichment of effluence rather than the anxiety of influence.[61] Shelley, who openly compares his Prometheus to Milton's Satan in the preface to *Prometheus Unbound*, is able to resolve the contradictions he perceived in Satanic consciousness, while Byron, who remarks in the preface to *Cain* that "since I was twenty I have never read Milton," proves largely unable to assimilate the strong echoes of *Paradise Lost* resounding through his postlapsarian biblical drama. *Cain* and Act I of *Prometheus Unbound* are equally indebted to both Shakespeare and Milton for the model of psychic seduction and repetition, but Shelley radically reworks the model, while it forces Byron's "mystery" to a conclusion out of harmony with its revisionary sentiments.

The intertextuality that informs the works of mental theater is closely bound up with the intersubjectivity which they explore. To an extent, the relation of emulative protagonist and Satanic seducer reflects the Romantic poet's ambivalence toward his own models, and the proliferation of thematically crucial textual echoes underscores at the level of style the theme of repetition. W. J. Bate has suggested, in *The Burden of the Past and the English Poet*, that, while an effort to revive the drama lay at the heart of the Romantic movement, it was undermined by the rootedness of the Romantic imagination in the "soil of past poetry," which allowed for lyric but not dramatic expression.[62] To a degree the failure to revive the "greater genre" of tragedy in face of the seductiveness of dead voices is enacted in each of the works of mental theater, and it is significant that, in tracing the development of their central dramatic argument from the tragedies of Shakespeare through *Paradise Lost*, the topos of repetition develops along with the emphasis on self-consciousness, both reaching their greatest intensity in the post-Romanticism of Beddoes. And the pervasive theme of "border violation" can be viewed in part as reflecting the disturbing presence in the later poet's imagination of strong models and voices from the past. But once we accept the Romantic dramatists' recognition of the limitations of psychic autonomy, the failures of their protagonists to become tragic heroes, and of the works of mental theater to succeed as tragedies, can be seen as saving cautionary fables rather than as theatrical fiascos. Mental theater can be read as an enactment of the poet's struggle with his textual past, and of his realization that his imagination is inhabited by the echoes of dead voices, but it is precisely this enactment that allows him to identify and, ultimately, to challenge the confinements of what Bate has called the "remorseless deepening of self-consciousness before the rich and intimidating legacy of the past."[63] When one reads the portrayal of self-consciousness in mental theater not as a program but as a critique, one sees that the Romantic drama succeeds precisely where conventional tragedy would have failed.

At the same time that the works of mental theater acknowledge the presence of earlier texts, they exert an awareness of their own status as texts for later readers. Although "reader-response" criticism is usually thought of as a recent phenomenon, Romantic critics frequently perceived a reader's reaction as implicit in the dynamic structure of a literary text. De Quincey's essay on *Macbeth,* we will remember, is an analysis of his own uncanny psychological reaction to Shakespeare, who induces in the reader "a sympathy of comprehension, a sympathy by which we enter into his [the protagonist's] feelings and are made to understand them."[64] Hazlitt similarly felt that the unparalleled power of Shakespeare's greatest tragedies lay in their capacity to "take not only unquestioned, but undivided possession of the mind, and form a class, a world by themselves, mingling with all our thoughts like a second being," becoming "a new power in the imagination."[65] For the Romantic critics, the reader's interaction with the text does not involve surprise by sinful identification, followed by humiliation and eventual edification through a masterful author's devious constructions.[66] Rather, the reader's uncompromising and repeated struggles with a powerful text can lead to a more inclusive consciousness and a stronger imaginative stance, a dialectic powerfully described by Keats in his sonnet "On Sitting Down to Read *King Lear* Once Again":

> once again, the fierce dispute
> Betwixt damnation and impassion'd clay
> Must I burn through . . .
> Let me not wander in a barren dream:
> But, when I am consumed in the fire,
> Give me new phoenix wings to fly at my desire.

For Keats, as for De Quincey and Hazlitt, reading a Shakespearean tragedy is not a passive retreat into the closet but a heroic struggle for stronger, more empathetic powers of imagination. The Romantic poets encourage such dynamic reading in their own dramas of consciousness, through a process which Shelley called "casuistry." He found such a process at work in his own divided response, at once sympathetic and critical, to Milton's Satan. "The character of Satan engenders in the mind a pernicious casuistry which leads us to weigh his faults with his wrongs, and to excuse the former because the latter exceed all measure."[67] Shelley incorporated a divided and divisive sympathetic reaction into his own dramatic practice, as he later explained in his preface to *The Cenci:* "It is in the restless and anatomizing casuistry with which men seek the justification of Beatrice, yet feel that she has done what needs justification . . . that the dramatic character of what she did and suffered, consists."[68] As a pervasive device in mental theater, such "casuistry" confronts the reader with the danger of his or her own entrapment in the pattern of seduction and repetition, a challenge that, if met, would augment the reader's own power for a stronger, less limited, sympathetic imagination.

The Romantic mental theater is anything but what we usually mean by "closet drama." If the process of reading is emphasized, it is because the Romantics found their own response to Shakespearean tragedy strongest in reading, and because they sought to convey a similar intensity to the readers of their own dramatic poems. If this intensity has been lost on us—as it was not lost to contemporary readers like Coleridge, Hazlitt, Goethe, and Scott—it is because, misled by expectations based on a critical tradition of smug incomprehension, we have not engaged these works on their own terms; we have not allowed them to engage us. The approach to Romantic drama that I develop in this study is meant to restore some of that frightening and challenging intensity; as De Quincey wrote of reading *Macbeth,* "into this hell we are to look."

2

The Borderers and the Drama of Recognition

When Wordsworth finally brought out his early verse drama, *The Borderers*, in 1842, he emphasized that "it was first written, and is now published, without any view to the stage."[1] This was not the disclaimer of a frustrated playwright; as Wordsworth's remarks to Isabella Fenwick a year later make clear, *The Borderers* was conceived not as a stage-play but as a work of mental theater. "My care was almost exclusively given to the passions and the characters, and the position in which the persons of the Drama stood relatively to one another, that the reader (for I had then no thought of the Stage) might be moved and to a degree instructed by lights penetrating somewhat into the depths of our nature."[2] His description touches on the essentials of Romantic mental theater: the mental states or "passions" of the central characters, the psychic effect of the characters upon one another, and the appeal to the reader's engagement with a text that can illuminate hidden aspects of the mind. Coleridge, one of *The Borderers'* first and most enthusiastic readers, attested to its "*profound* touches of the human heart," which he had before encountered "three or four times in 'The Robbers' of Schiller, & often in Shakespeare."[3]

Wordsworth originally prefaced the early, unpublished version of *The Borderers* with an essay analyzing the character of its villain, an example of how integrally the development of mental theater was related to contemporary dramatic criticism. The essay on "Rivers" (the name would be changed to Oswald) resembles Hazlitt's analysis of Iago in many respects, and particularly in the emphasis on power: "Power is much more easily manifested in destroying than in creating . . . He has rebelled against the world and the laws of the world and regards them as tyrannical masters."[4] In choosing a victim for the display of his power, the villain—tormented by "that poisonous mineral of which Iago speaks gnawing his inwards"—is led, like his model, by hatred of subordination.

> Benefits conferred on a man like this will be the seeds of a worse feeling than ingratitude. They will give birth to positive hatred. Let him be deprived of power, though by means which he despises, and he will never forgive. It will scarcely be denied that such a mind by very slight external motives may be led to the commission of the greatest enormities. Let its malignant feelings be fixed on a particular object and the rest follows of itself.[5]

Following Wordsworth's allusion, critics of *The Borderers* have traced correspondences between Oswald and Iago; struck by Oswald's quest for psychic autonomy—the "Independent Intellect"—they have studied his kinship to Milton's Satan as well.[6] But understanding the complex relationship of *The Borderers* to its antecedents only begins with establishing Oswald's literary genealogy. A more direct approach to studying intertextuality in *The Borderers*—one that brings out its underestimated dramatic intensity as well—begins by turning to the relation of protagonist and antagonist.

The Borderers, like *Othello*, *Macbeth*, and the ninth book of *Paradise Lost*, portrays the demonic seduction of a naive, initially admirable hero. This tradition lies behind Oswald's first soliloquy, which reveals his designs on Marmaduke, captain of the Borderers troop:

> They chose *him* for their Chief!—what covert part
> He, in the preference, modest Youth, might take,
> I neither know nor care. The insult bred
> More of contempt than hatred; both are flown;
> That either e'er existed is my shame:
> 'Twas a dull spark—a most unnatural fire
> That died the moment the air breathed upon it.
> —These fools of feeling are mere birds of winter
> That haunt some barren island of the north,
> Where, if a famishing man stretch forth his hand,
> They think it is to feed him. I have left him

> To solitary meditation; now
> For a few swelling phrases, and a flash
> Of truth enough to dazzle and to blind,
> And he is mine forever. (551–65)

The dramatic moment is familiar. *Othello* opens with Iago's resentment when passed over for command in favor of the modest youth Cassio; the chronological action of *Paradise Lost* begins when Satan bridles at his subordination to a newly begotten Christ. A similar moment occurs in *Macbeth* when Duncan names Malcolm heir and Macbeth decides that the Witches' prophecies can be realized only through murder.[7] Oswald's resolve is equally familiar: Like Iago or Satan, he seeks revenge through misleading and mastering his victim. But another element present in Oswald's soliloquy both distinguishes his enterprise from those of his literary forebears and underscores Wordsworth's self-consciousness regarding his text's antecedents. If Oswald's plot (and Wordsworth's) repeats an established pattern, repetition is overtly emphasized at its crisis and denouement. To transform Marmaduke from a fool of feeling—a naive, compassionate hero—into a solitary like himself, Oswald contrives the repetition of a scene that haunts him continually, and surfaces (as here) even in his most confident moments. For Oswald, who in his own promising youth abandoned his ship's captain to starve on a barren island, will lead Marmaduke to abandon an old man to starve on a barren heath. Oswald expects that a repetition of his crime will render Marmaduke a subservient image of himself, but his pursuit of mastery is conditioned by an enslaving obsession with the original crime. In once more betraying his guileless Captain, Oswald will himself relive the primal scene even as Marmaduke enacts it.[8]

Many of the details of Oswald's plot are drawn, like its outlines, from Wordsworth's Shakespearean and Miltonic models. Oswald's insidious rhetoric is imaged, for example, by a poisoned ear, as in Marmaduke's belated (and projected) accusation in the early version of the drama: "What damning fiend has poisoned thee in the ear?" (*EV* V.2.68). The image recalls Iago's corruption of Othello—"I'll pour this pestilence into his ear" (II.3.353)—and Lady Macbeth's similar influence: "Hie thee hither, / That I may pour my spirits in thine ear" (I.5.25–26).[9] A related image is adopted by Oswald's tool, a female vagrant, in her attempt (perhaps unconscious) to warn Marmaduke that her story has been framed by Oswald in order to poison his mind:

> I've had the saddest dream that ever troubled
> The heart of living creature.—My poor Babe
> Was crying, as I thought, crying for bread
> When I had none to give him; whereupon
> I put a slip of foxglove in his hand,
> Which pleased him so, that he was hushed at once:
> When, into one of those same spotted bells
> A bee came darting, which this Child with joy
> Imprisoned there, and held it to his ear,
> And suddenly grew black, as he would die. (397–406)

The confluence here of dream, temptation, poisonous creature, and imminent death recalls Eve's dream in *Paradise Lost,* the product of Satan's toadlike "inspiring venom" "Close at the ear of Eve" (IV.800, 804).

Oswald's phrase "truth enough to dazzle and to blind" attests (along with several related images) to Wordsworth's awareness of the prominence of eyesight in *Othello:* "Look to her, Moor, if thou hast eyes to see"; "Give me the ocular proof."[10] Marmaduke's resemblance to Othello is in some ways as striking as Oswald's to Iago.[11] Like Othello, Marmaduke is disarmingly easy not only to delude but virtually to destroy once the deceiver has touched on his remarkable horror of sexuality.[12] Perhaps in Marmaduke's case the ambivalence stems partly from a subliminal fear of incest, since he and Idonea, his betrothed, have grown up as brother and sister; in a passage markedly reminiscent of *Othello,* he tells Oswald that their love was rooted in a shared fascination with her father:

> 'Twas my delight to sit and hear Idonea
> Repeat her Father's terrible adventures,
> Till all the band of play-mates wept together;
> And that was the beginning of my love. (92–95)

In any case, the female vagrant's story of Idonea's sexual corruption—even though it presents her as an unwilling victim—serves to fill Marmaduke with horror and self-doubt:

> No—it cannot be—
> I dare not trust myself with such a thought—
> Yet hence this strange aversion? (288–90)

Oswald's first attempt to have Marmaduke murder Herbert (who, rendering the plot more diabolical still, is none other than Idonea's father) fails, thanks to the arrival of their fellow Borderers. He then capitalizes on Marmaduke's sexual agitation by telling him that Idonea is after all more than willing to prostitute herself to the disreputable Lord Clifford, as much for her own pleasure as for Herbert's gain. Again the speech takes effect immediately, and Marmaduke (like Othello before him) assumes the pose and language of the stage malcontent. His Jacobean railings are the most stylistically anachronistic passages in *The Borderers,* and among the few which strike a false Shakespearean note. One of the most extreme includes an echo of Lady Macbeth (I.7.54–59):

> Now for the corner-stone of my philosophy:
> I would not give a denier for the man
> Who, on such provocation as the earth
> Yields, could not chuck his babe beneath the chin,
> And send it with a fillip to its grave. (1240–44)

Marmaduke's malcontentism forms, however, only one phase in the psychic degeneration overseen by Oswald. His violent reactions to the aspersions on Idonea's chastity merely weaken him enough for Oswald to more drastically—and perhaps irreparably—undermine his initial innocence. Disclaiming (still in the malcontent vein) his own powers of perception—

> if this be not enough
> To make mankind merry for evermore,
> Than plain it is as day, that eyes were made
> For a wise purpose—verily to weep with! (1271–74)—

he leaves Oswald free to interpose his own vision.

Like Shelley's Count Cenci (another literary descendant of Satan), Oswald continually anatomizes his own and others' psyches. "We dissect / The senseless body, and why not the mind?" (1166–67). But his investigations have neither the scientific method nor the detachment that his analogy implies. As Wordsworth remarks in the essay on Oswald's character, his psychic probings grow out of a wish to bury the guilt he feels for his youthful crime: "He disguises from himself his own malignity by assuming the character of a speculator in morals." But in actually reliving the crime and its results, "in painting his former self, he really *is* great,"[13] and the speeches in which he recounts his history to Marmaduke are among the best in the drama.

Oswald's original crime, which he had undertaken (like Marmaduke) in the mistaken spirit of justice, gives rise to a period of inaction and mental agony. Unable to accept his guilt, Oswald turns to a moral casuistry that fundamentally alters his relation to the social world:

> three nights
> Did constant meditation dry my blood;
> Three sleepless nights I passed in sounding on,
> Through words and things a dim and perilous way;
> And, wheresoe'er I turned me, I beheld
> A slavery compared to which the dungeon
> And clanking chains are perfect liberty. (1772–78)

Ostensibly, Oswald teaches Marmaduke that meditation revealed a state of mental slavery about him, slavery to custom and prejudice, from which he painfully freed himself.[14] But, as often, Oswald's words subvert his intended meaning. The encompassing slavery he beholds is in fact a mental bondage, never to be loosened, to his tormenting guilt. Marmaduke falls victim to a similarly compulsive analysis even before he replicates Oswald's crime. His self-anatomy begins as he seeks justification for the approaching murder:

> And yet, in plumbing the abyss for judgement,
> Something I strike upon which turns my mind
> Back on herself, I think, again—my breast
> Concentrates all the terrors of the Universe. (782–85)

Oswald plants in Marmaduke's very resistance to the murder the seed of a self-consciousness that, like his own, seems to ensure moral freedom but is actually a self-enclosing prison.

The "abyss" suddenly revealed to Marmaduke recurs as a topos throughout mental theater. Manfred, Cain, Beatrice Cenci, Prometheus, and Jupiter each encounter such an inner void: an image that conveys the absence of moral restraint, the dissolution of social bonds, the unsettling chasm that opens when the mind is led to think what has been unthinkable and psychic integrity begins to fragment. A physical counterpart usually accompanies the inner void, often signaling the approach of the crime that engulfs the protagonist. Marmaduke must lead Herbert over a dangerous "torrent" into which his guide dog, "Leader," ominously slips, suggesting not only Herbert's abandonment but the fate of Marmaduke—his human guide and the Borderers' leader—as well. Oswald stages his musings near "deep chasms troubled by roaring streams" (1805), and if his "three nights" of meditation suggest a parodic death and resurrection, his "dim and perilous" mental voyage evokes Satan's "perilous attempt" to traverse the "dark unbottomed infinite abyss / And through the palpable obscure find out / His uncouth way" (II.420, 405–7). Like Satan, Oswald finds himself in a moral and psychic vacuum, compelled to reiterate his crime.

Critics who gloss Oswald's program for Marmaduke as "philosophical" or "intellectual" murder have paid more attention to Oswald's justifications than to his acts.[15] For even if Oswald can succeed from moment to moment in masking from himself the psychic isolation and imprisonment that underlie his pretense of moral autonomy, he has no illusions regarding the fate of his disciple. He wishes to lead Marmaduke not to freedom but into servitude: "he is mine forever." In the process he tears Marmaduke from every bond but that to himself. Marmaduke's love for Idonea, his fellowship with the band of Borderers, and the deep social feelings that make him a protector of such as Herbert—"Ne'er may I own the heart / That cannot feel for one, helpless as he is" (67–68)—all disintegrate under Oswald's spell, leaving him as isolated as his mentor:

—I am cut off from man;
No more shall I be man—no more shall I
Have human feelings! (1327–29)

The self-consciousness that Oswald guarantees Marmaduke—"What is done will save you from the blank / Of living without knowledge that you live" (1870–71)—is of a kind that robs its possessor of his fundamental human identity.

Oswald's plot hinges on a belief, acquired through his self-analysis, in the power of memory to enslave. It is the dark side of the healing power of memory celebrated by Wordsworth in "Tintern Abbey," and is allied to his portrayal of the *idée fixe* in "Goody Blake and Harry Gill," both composed a year after *The Borderers*.[16] Though Oswald extols the power of thought when proselytizing Marmaduke, he denigrates it in favor of memory as he plots his second, successful attempt to engineer Herbert's murder:

> Thoughts and feelings will sink deep, but then
> They have no substance. Pass but a few minutes,
> And something shall be done which Memory
> May touch, whene'er her Vassals are at work. (1171–74)

Oswald's words are characteristically double. Memory's "vassals" are the associations that bring it into play, but Oswald knows well that the murderer becomes himself the deed's creature. He later impresses upon Marmaduke the profound inexorability of his act's psychic effect:

> Action is transitory—a step, a blow,
> The motion of a muscle—this way or that—
> 'Tis done, and in the after vacancy
> We wonder at ourselves like men betrayed:
> Suffering is permanent, obscure and dark,
> And shares the nature of infinity. (1539–44)

Oswald's philosophy invariably serves praxis. He now portrays all action as betrayal as he prepares Marmaduke for the revelation that his crime was contrived and his victim innocent. As his plot demands that the murderer feel inescapably bound to the deed, his sublime thoughts on suffering, the best-known lines in the drama, are as finely calculated as any of his subtly didactic speeches.

When they next meet, with Oswald certain that the crime has been committed, he readily admits to the deception. His justification is curious:

> Ay, we are coupled by a chain of adamant;
> Let us be fellow-labourers, then, to enlarge
> Man's intellectual empire. We subsist
> In slavery; all is slavery; we receive
> Laws, but we ask not whence those laws have come;
> We need an inward sting to goad us on. (1854–59)

The adamantine chain that binds seducer and seduced signals a number of correspondences between Oswald and Satan—and their respective temptations—which are here brought into play. Oswald's intellectual imperialism, however cloaked in Godwinian terms, is clearly Satanic. The companionship he announces to Marmaduke resembles the ironic, one-sided league Satan establishes with Earth's first inhabitants:

> League with you I seek,
> And mutual amity so strait, so close,
> That I with you must dwell, or you with me
> Henceforth . . .
> Honor and Empire with revenge enlarg'd,
> By conquering this new world, compels me now.
> (IV.375–78, 390–91)

Oswald's "inward sting," which he bestows, or rather inflicts, on Marmaduke, stems originally from Satan, compelled by the Hell that burns continually within him and finding ease only in destruction. Oswald self-delusively reverses cause and effect: The imperial urge does not demand an inner torment but is demanded by it, as the implicit parallel to Satan makes clear. Oswald's rhetoric of moral liberation rings equally hollow, for he has made Marmaduke doubly a slave: compelled by the remorseless sting of a criminal self-consciousness, and chained to the master who now takes charge. Oswald has enlarged not man's but his own intellectual empire.

The imperial theme belongs integrally to a work concerned with border violations of many kinds: political, temporal, psychic, and textual. The drama is set among the "undisputed tracks" between England and Scotland, an uncertain region where authority is provisional and action unconfined, much like Cyprus in the "symbolic geography" of *Othello*.[17] The borders of time grow as unstable as those in space. The pressure of Oswald's past crime is so great that it loses its anteriority and takes place again in the present; its original effects included the incursion of the future: "I seemed a Being who had passed alone / Into a region of futurity" (1817–18)—yet another echo of Lady Macbeth.[18] These signs of instability form only a background, however, for the violation of psychic borders. Marmaduke's will, his actions, his passions become increasingly identified with Oswald's in a merging of psyches that attests no less to Oswald's weakness than to his power.

When addressing Marmaduke, Oswald vehemently rejects compassion, pity, and "puling sympathy" (1559), and at times seems to convince himself (as his speeches have convinced more than one critic) that his independence is more than illusory. But Wallace, the "subtle" Borderer who often speaks as though he had read Wordsworth's prefatory essay, identifies his Satanic restlessness and dismisses his equally Satanic pretense to autonomy:

> Restless Minds,
> Such Minds as find amid their fellow-men
> No heart that loves them, none that they can love,
> Will turn perforce and seek for sympathy
> In dim relation to imagined Beings. (1451–55)

Oswald, however, cannot rest with dim relations; he needs tangible evidence that he is not alone. When he feels Marmaduke securely within his power and begins to disclose the plot, he allows him to see through his pretenses, or rather forces him to recognize a face that now reflects his own.

> The mask,
> Which for a season I have stooped to wear,
> Must be cast off.—Know then that I was urged,
> (For other impulse let it pass) was driven,
> To seek for sympathy, because I saw
> In you a mirror of my youthful self. (1860–65)

Oswald himself admits that not enlightened altruism but compulsion drives him to proselytize Marmaduke; but citing Freud's notion of "repetition-compulsion" could account only for Oswald's second betrayal of a second Captain.[19] Why must Marmaduke also imitate the original crime—a copy more exact than Oswald could have hoped, since he weakly decides at the last moment to abandon Herbert rather than kill him outright? Oswald had guarded his precarious sense of autonomy through years of self-imposed isolation. Seeing now in Marmaduke the mirror image of his unfallen self inspires him with a desperate wish, and with a design so fiendishly structured that Swinburne, who early recognized the drama's "poetical power," took offense at its "monstrous and morbid" plot.[20] Oswald's ultimate purpose is to render Marmaduke a double of his *present* self, a living reflection in which to behold his "independent intellect."

Wallace (in terms again reminiscent of Wordsworth's preface) remarks on Oswald's craving for power: "Power is life to him / And breath and being; where he cannot govern / He will destroy" (1432–34). The unusual form his urge for mastery takes can be more readily understood when compared to Hegel's "Master and Servant" model for the development of self-consciousness in the *Phenomenology*.[21] One must keep in mind that the account describes an early, unsuccessful phase in the movement toward authentic self-consciousness, and I appeal to it as evidence against, rather than for, the "passage toward individuation" that has been seen as Oswald's benevolent plan for Marmaduke.[22] Like the "master consciousness" described by Hegel, Oswald begins from a position not of freedom but of insecurity; in his psychic isolation he requires acknowledgment or recognition by another consciousness. But at this stage, acknowledgment emerges only through a struggle which leaves the first consciousness in a position of dominance, the second as his slave: metaphors used by Oswald himself throughout *The Borderers*. Marmaduke is the titular master, but the dramatic struggle of wills renders him Oswald's creature. Oswald hopes to gain precisely that which the "master" in the *Phenomenology* seeks: a confirmation of his independent status through the recognition which the servant, a subordinate reflection, yields him. "The goal is reached," he declares toward the end, "My Master shall become / A shadow of myself—made by myself" (2008–9). As in Hegel, however, the process proves not only unsuccessful but tragic for both antagonists.

For Marmaduke the tragedy is obvious: Bonds that foster him are replaced by a bond so stringent as to destroy his individuality. We can see now that Oswald's destruction of Marmaduke's social relations proceeds not from enlightened cynicism, nor from ordinary jealousy, but in the pursuit of total mastery, and we can identify a deep irony in his characterization of all bonds but that to himself as servitude. For Oswald, the social contract is the "tyranny/ Of the world's masters" (1485–86), a lover "one of love's simple bondsmen" (1841). He criticizes the social conscience in remarkably Hegelian terms that, again, ironically condemn his own project:

> I had been nourished by the sickly food
> Of popular applause. I now perceived
> That we are praised, only as men in us
> Do recognise some image of themselves,
> An abject counterpart of what they are,
> Or the empty thing that they would wish to be. (1821–26)

Oswald's need for Marmaduke is no less tragic. His compulsion to "seek for sympathy" with Marmaduke does not belie his rejection of human sympathy, for he seeks in fact only a servant's forced homage. But immediately Oswald finds himself bound to Marmaduke's recognition; he cannot imagine their separation. His youthful crime, rather than liberating him, began by determining his character and actions. Now he binds himself in turn to a living mirror image, one that ultimately reflects only his incompleteness.

Another of Oswald's self-exposing lectures to Marmaduke raises the topic of repetition in a different light. He is deviously preparing Marmaduke for the discovery of their league in parallel crimes:

> My young Friend,
> As time advances either we become
> The prey or masters of our own past deeds.
> Fellowship we *must* have, willing or no;
> And if good Angels fail, slack in their duty,
> Substitutes, turn our faces where we may,
> Are still forthcoming; some which, though they bear
> Ill names, can render no ill services,
> In recompense for what themselves required.

So meet extremes in this mysterious world,
And opposites thus melt into each other. (1520–30)

Oswald's speech, one of the richest in *The Borderers,* ties together many of its central motifs. Presenting the interplay of act and memory in his obsessive language of mastery, Oswald typically reverses cause and effect: Marmaduke's act will render him its servant—and Oswald's. The "fellowship" that Oswald declares indispensable is his name for the bondage into which he draws Marmaduke while pretending to free him, the adamantine chain that binds Oswald as well to his servant's "required" acknowledgment. The last lines of the speech evoke the unstable borders pervading even the title of the drama. The meeting of extremes and merging of opposites convey on one level the psychic interpenetration of protagonist and antagonist, of the integral man of feeling and his solitary mentor. The seducer presents his infiltration of Marmaduke's consciousness as a mystery, the gradual, inevitable marriage of "independent" intellects. But his image of melting hardly does justice to the intricate process he has brought about, one imbued with all the violence which Hazlitt and De Quincey sensed in the mingling of human and demonic in *Macbeth.*

Oswald's reference to fallen angels evokes moreover an intertextual dimension of border violation and repetition. Of the three texts that border most extensively on Wordsworth's, *Paradise Lost* supplies the fewest direct verbal echoes, but the Romantic poet's awareness of a prior Fall (and a particular account of it) behind his own dramatization of seduction and repetition finds various expressions. Once Oswald, with his "restless mind" and his compulsion to betray and destroy, has owned to a place among Satan's followers, his victim grows uncomfortably aware of his subsidiary reenactment of the Fall. He anticipates the comparison when first resisting the criminal proposals of Oswald, who brands him a "fallen" slave of the world: "Fallen should I be indeed— / Murder—perhaps asleep, blind, old, alone, / Betrayed, in darkness!" (900–902). But Marmaduke does betray Herbert, and when he encounters Idonea after the act (still unaware of her innocence and that of her father) he names her a second Eve: "Thou art a woman / To bring perdition on the universe" (1636–37). By the time they meet again, Marmaduke has discovered that he himself has fallen through "a plot, / A hideous plot, against the soul of man" (2112–13).

The borders between Wordsworth's text and its Shakespearean models are noticeably unstable throughout, and echoes of the murders in *Macbeth* and *Othello* resound quite audibly in *The Borderers'* murder scene. One might suspect that Wordsworth turns to Shakespeare at such a high point out of a beginning dramatist's insecurity. But the echoes underscore the complex repetition that informs Marmaduke's act, adding to it a self-conscious, textual dimension. Marmaduke blatantly echoes Lady Macbeth ("Had he not resembled / My father as he slept, I had don't") in his similar excuse for at first sparing Herbert: "The features of Idonea / Lurked in his face" (966–67). In the early version, the reference is heightened by Oswald's remark, a few lines earlier, that "in the torrent nearby there is water enough to wash all the blood in the universe" (*EV* II.2.257–58). One of Othello's last remarks to Desdemona before murdering her—

> If you bethink yourself of any crime
> Unreconciled as yet to heaven and grace
> Solicit for it straight (V.2.76–78)—

is evoked when Herbert, unnerved by Marmaduke's agitation, begins the same thought:

> Lost Man! if thou hast any close-pent guilt
> Pressing upon thy heart, and this the hour
> Of visitation—(1305–7).

As often occurs in mental theater, the echo engenders a second repetition within the text when Marmaduke later hastens Oswald's imminent avowal of the parallel murder: "Quick—to the point—if any untold crime / Doth haunt your memory" (1703–4).

The self-conscious aura surrounding the theme of repetition grows explicit in several of Marmaduke's more prescient remarks. Sensing Oswald's excessive interest in the murder, he asks at one point, "Wherefore this repetition" (*EV* III.5.43), and later wonders "doubtfully" as Oswald begins to reveal the plot, "You do but echo / My own wild words?" (1874–75). The protagonist's growing fear of the instability created between the borders of his consciousness and Oswald's might be read as a manifestation of Wordsworth's anxiety before the unstable borders between his text and its models. In each case a youth discovers that his mind is inhabited by echoes and shaped by precedents, and self-consciousness must be fundamentally redefined as including consciousness of the other.

Repetition helps determine the fates of Herbert and Idonea as well. The Baron Herbert is usually regarded as saintly in demeanor but creaturely in behavior, recalling Milton's Samson in his blindness and Lear in his abandonment on a heath.[23] Herbert's unlikely but important resemblance to Oswald has, however, gone unnoticed. Like Oswald, Herbert continually relives a traumatic scene, the fire in Palestine that blinded him, destroyed his wife and son, and led to his dispossession upon returning from the Crusades. The first repetition of his narrative to Idonea (who comments "as you oft have told me") should not be dismissed as mere exposition, for he apologetically, mechanically retells his story to Marmaduke a few hours later:

> When from the Holy Land I had returned
> Sightless, and from my Heritage was driven,
> A wretched Outcast—but this strain of thought
> Would lead me to talk fondly. (828–31)

The recurring scene has moreover left him so attached to his surviving child that, like Lear, he finds the prospect of sharing his daughter's love intolerable—

> For that another in his Child's affection
> Should hold a place, as if 'twere robbery
> He seemed to quarrel with the very thought (56–58)—

a weakness Oswald makes much of in grooming Marmaduke for Herbert's murder.

Herbert's very saintliness rests partly on a rejection of all human bonds (save one) that further allies him to Oswald. Although he is preserved by a shepherd-boy and a fellow wanderer when Idonea is an infant, he attributes such assistance not to human kindliness but to divine intervention—the shepherd-boy, for example, is "sent from heaven" (1366)—and later spurns the protection of both Marmaduke and Clifford. The events of the drama, however, do little to justify his faith in celestial care. He declares to his self-appointed guides, Oswald and Marmaduke, that "there's a Providence for them who walk / In helplessness, when innocence is with them" (791–92), but when the "Ordeal of the Waste" places him in precisely that situation he stumbles to his death on the rocks, groping toward a bell rung by the wind in an empty church. He rejects his last chance for preservation by waving off the peasant who discovers him, one easily enough discouraged, as he fears the repetition of an unjust imprisonment in his own past.

Idonea's career is more directly enmeshed in the pattern of repetition. Radically alienated through Oswald's devices, Marmaduke tricks Idonea into abjuring her love by cursing him as her father's yet unknown murderer, an act worthy in its guilefulness and perversity of Oswald himself. The early version most clearly presents the curse as a repetition of Marmaduke's equally misguided act, with Marmaduke now wearing the mask of enlightened mentor.[24] "Thou must be wise as I am," he begins; "thou must know / What human nature is, decoyed, betrayed" (*EV* V.3.82–83)—and goes on to vary Oswald's echo of Satan as he pronounces the curse irrevocable: "'Tis done, and done so too / that I have cased her heart in adamant" (*EV* V.3.101–2). He takes up the Satanic heritage in seeking to ease his "mighty burden" by entrapping another in his new sense of cynical isolation, and breaks with the same act what Oswald calls the "soft chain" of love (1841).

Wordsworth may have deleted these lines from the published version because he found the final repetition too morbid (anticipating reactions such as Swinburne's), or perhaps because it left Marmaduke too absolutely Oswald's follower. The curse itself, however, which stands in the later version, seriously darkens Marmaduke's fate, and provides further examples of textual repetition. Rejecting her father's command to "bless all mankind," Idonea first wills evil in cursing his destroyer:

may vengeance haunt the fiend
For this most cruel murder: let him live
And move in terror of the elements;
The thunder send him on his knees to prayer
In the open streets, and let him think he sees,
If e'er he entereth the house of God,
The roof, self-moved, unsettling o'er his head;
And let him, when he would lie down at night,
Point to his wife the blood-drops on his pillow! (2146–54)

Idonea's curse takes immediate effect, for it merely confirms the haunted, restless state that has already overwhelmed Marmaduke. It evokes as well the prior fates of some of his antecedents: the Macbeths, haunted waking and sleeping by the blood they have shed; Milton's Samson (himself plagued by "restless thoughts"); and Lear's terror of the elements. In uttering the curse, Idonea all but guarantees its effects, since Marmaduke's strongest hope for regeneration resides in the love he self-destructively leads her to deny. "I am accurst: / All nature curses me, and in my heart / *Thy* curse is fixed" (2174–76). The transformation of Idonea's love into self-tormenting hatred for the murderer is foreshadowed when her father, while literally misguided by Marmaduke, utters a blessing into the wind: "the benediction fell / Back on himself; but changed into a curse" (747–48). Here, as with the death of Herbert's guide dog, crude dramatic irony accompanies deeper ironies of the subtlest kind.

When Marmaduke speaks of the "hideous plot against the soul of man," he goes on to declare: "and yet I baffled it, / In *some* degree" (2114–15). Does the qualification express a desperate wish that abandoning a blind old man is less than killing him, or hidden resolve, or a moment's self-deception? However eager to embrace his dubious guilt, Marmaduke resists acknowledging Oswald's influence on his remorseless pursuit of remorse: an intolerable self-consciousness allied to Oswald's own, and fed by the very guilt and curses he so disarmingly revels in. Satisfied with Marmaduke's disintegration, Oswald dies "scornfully and exultingly," though cut down by Wallace without a trial, condemned through hearsay evidence (the principal informant is none other than the perjured female vagrant), and given no opportunity to speak for himself. His death seems calculated to show that *The Borderers* is not concerned with questions of judgment and unsanctioned individual action, but with influence, memory, repetition.

Oswald's last words are characteristically loaded with sinister implications:

If I pass beneath a rock
And shout, and, with the echo of my voice,
Bring down a heap of rubbish, and it crush me,
I die without dishonour. Famished, starved,
A Fool and Coward blended to my wish! (2282–86)

The emblem expresses Oswald's dying conviction that his plot has succeeded. Though he has fallen into the Borderers' hands, their captain's voice can now no more than echo his own; he considers his death an accident that should not diminish his conviction of mastery. The adjectives "famished, starved" gain an enormous resonance through their grammatical detachment. They evoke Herbert, with whose abandonment Oswald taunts Marmaduke at the end; Oswald's own youthful crime, compulsively relived even at death; and Marmaduke himself, whose nourishing human bonds are now snapped and whose life will be, like Oswald's, one of intolerable emptiness. The phrase "blended to my wish" cuts still more deeply than the epithets it follows. Oswald implies that his will to power is inextricably mingled with Marmaduke's consciousness, that the inner hell survives him.

Marmaduke's self-exile, with which the drama concludes, has been viewed as a redemptive pilgrimage, but his final speeches seem rather to justify Oswald's triumph and confirm Idonea's curse. Directly before his betrayer is seized and killed, Marmaduke pledges himself "to endure" through life, "to feed remorse, to welcome every sting / Of penitential anguish." He would share this destiny with Oswald:

> we may find
> In such a course fit links of sympathy,
> An incommunicable rivalship
> Maintained, for peaceful ends beyond our view. (2275–78)

Despite his attempt to ironically reverse the effects of Oswald's plot, Marmaduke's words betray his continued adherence to his mentor's vision. He can conceive of his future only in terms of mental agony, and though he would keep Oswald at a distance, they remain joined in a silent partnership, still doubles and still linked in a reflexive struggle. Oswald can triumph because Marmaduke has simply changed the purported goal of their fellowship, without so much as attempting to break the chain itself, the "links" of Oswald's perverse "sympathy." Marmaduke's final speech similarly implies Oswald's lasting posthumous influence:

> No more of that; in silence hear my doom:
> A hermitage has furnished fit relief

To some offenders; other penitents,
Less patient in their wretchedness, have fallen,
Like the old Roman, on their own sword's point.
They had their choice: a wanderer *must I* go,
The Spectre of that innocent Man, my guide.
No human ear shall ever hear me speak;
No human dwelling ever give me food,
Or sleep, or rest: but, over waste and wild,
In search of nothing, that this earth can give,
But expiation, will I wander on—
A Man by pain and thought compelled to live,
Yet loathing life—till anger is appeased
In Heaven, and Mercy gives me leave to die. (2307–21)

Marmaduke depicts his fate in terms of compulsion, haunted psychic restlessness, social estrangement, and unending self-exile. His character has become much like Oswald's in all but the hope for expiation (not redemption) and in the death wish that replaces (or simply reverses) the will to power. His vision desperately lacks any faith in the healing power of human sympathy, embracing instead a self-defeating cynicism that leads him to reject the Borderers' offer of lasting fellowship and unchanged loyalty just as he has rejected Idonea's love. Though (at least in the final version) Marmaduke escapes the fate of Satan, he does become a Cain, inheriting Oswald's (and Satan's) eternal torment and isolation, if not like them inflicting his pain on others. Oswald may overstate his final triumph, but his words are much more accurate than Marmaduke seems to realize.

In Marmaduke's rejection of stoic suicide one hears a last echo of Macbeth, who asks, "Why should I play the Roman fool and die / On my own sword?" (V.8.1–2). A few lines earlier Marmaduke evokes the conclusion of *Othello* as well, requesting that the Borderers properly "record" his story, as Othello dies framing the narrative of his tragedy. But unlike Othello or Macbeth, whose deaths release them from their shared restlessness ("neither poppy nor mandragora"; "Macbeth doth murder sleep") and restore a measure of tragic nobility to each, Marmaduke departs with his psychic torment unresolved and his fate obscure. Critical opinion divides at this point, some readers impressed by the hero's remorse and endurance, others by his anguish and isolation. Though Marmaduke's prospects are undeniably bleak, I would argue that the ending is left intentionally open, and reflects the unresolved conflicts underlying the composition of the drama. Because Wordsworth so self-consciously manipulates the theme of repetition, it is peculiarly difficult to measure the originality of *The Borderers*. To an extent the echoes and allusions heighten its thematic interplay, and yet they proliferate to such a degree as to threaten the text's integrity. As with Marmaduke, Wordsworth's ability to overcome rather than merely echo an antecedent comes into question; as with Oswald, his strength and weakness seem inextricably related.

Wordsworth's exploration of self-consciousness, repetition, and border violation is highly appropriate to a young Romantic's first attempt to write in one of the major genres exemplified by Shakespeare and Milton. In reaction to the pressure exerted by the poets he considered his greatest predecessors, Wordsworth created a dramatic fable of the insistence of tradition and its power to condition the living poet's imagination. Romantic mental theater invariably presents self-consciousness as violated, for the poet no less than for his characters. The poet's Other is constituted by the prior texts that resonate in his creative imagination. Wordsworth uncovers the same unsettling truth in a dramatic lyric composed three years later, the "Song for the Wandering Jew." Its speaker is a figure who, like Cain, came to exemplify self-consciousness for the Romantics, the tormented, restless state passed on by the villains to the failed heroes of their drama. The song concludes:

> Day and night my toils redouble,
> Never nearer to my goal;
> Night and day, I feel the trouble
> Of the Wanderer in my soul.

Double, toil, trouble: The song enacts its theme of redoubling, as its wandering protagonist rehearses the burden of a spell cast in *Macbeth*.

The absence of a definite conclusion to *The Borderers* also serves to more deeply engage the reader in its troubling uncertainties. For the same reason, Oswald's villainy, unlike that of Iago, emerges only gradually, and initially causes a conflict in the reader's sympathies. In the early version his duplicity remains hidden until his soliloquy at the beginning of the second act. The published version of the drama opens with the Borderers voicing their suspicions regarding

Oswald, but Marmaduke is given a counterbalancing defense that looks forward to the ideal poet of the "Preface" to *Lyrical Ballads:*

> Strong feelings to his heart
> Are natural: and from no one can be learnt
> More of man's thought and ways than his experience
> Has given him power to teach. (33–36)

During the first act the reader empathically struggles with a disquietude regarding Oswald's intentions that parallels Marmaduke's ambivalence throughout most of the drama, and the ending leaves the reader suspended regarding both Oswald's success and Marmaduke's tragedy. "Plumbing the abyss for judgement" like Marmaduke and like Oswald before him, the reader's mind in turn falls back on itself, in a position to behold the frightening chasm that inevitably marks self-consciousness in Romantic mental theater.

Wordsworth resumed his depiction of the problematic nature of self-consciousness in *The Prelude* and again in *The Excursion,* inserting into each lines originally spoken by Oswald. In his epics Wordsworth goes on to resolve the dilemma with which *The Borderers* concludes, and though his resolutions differ, each hinges on the outward movement of sympathy that Oswald and Marmaduke are unwilling (or unable) to effect. It is no coincidence that Wordsworth addresses self-consciousness in similar terms in these works, for all three embody the desire to revive the major genres, a project which, for the Romantic poet, intensifies his awareness of the creative challenge posed by his models, the great literary works of the past. The dramatization of his struggles with influence, echo, and repetition in *The Borderers* helped Wordsworth take up the problem of self-consciousness in his epics with greater clarity and imaginative strength.

In the tenth book of *The Prelude* Wordsworth recounts his attempts to think through the mental "revolution" catalyzed by his torn sympathies at the outbreak of the French Revolution. His inner conflict was, he says, greatly intensified when "become oppressors in their turn, / Frenchmen had changed a war of self-defence / For one of conquest" (*1805* X.791–93). (These lines, with their stress on borders and imperialism, help elucidate Wordsworth's remark that "the changes through which the French Revolution passed" partly inspired *The Borderers.*)[25] His reaction presses the Wordsworth of *The Prelude* toward an attempt to extricate himself from the complexities of history and society by retreating into psychic autonomy, Oswald's "independent intellect" (*1805* X.829).[26] But Wordsworth immediately distinguishes his former condition from Oswald's by stressing the persistence of his sympathetic feelings: "never once / Had I thought ill of human-kind, or been / Indifferent to its welfare" (*1805* X.830–32). His growing faith in the sympathetic mind, strengthened by the examples and affection of Dorothy, his sister, and Coleridge, his friend, ultimately leads him out of his crisis and to the realization that the love of nature must be subsumed in the love of mankind.

The Solitary who tells his story in the third book of *The Excursion* is, like Wordsworth in *The Prelude*, a disappointed sympathizer with the French Revolution. His psychic crisis begins, however, immediately before his involvement in the Revolution, when the deaths of his children, followed by that of his wife, leave him both desolated and isolated. He describes the birth of self-consciousness—"Then my soul / Turned inward"—in words taken from Oswald's description of the same event:

> By pain of heart—now checked—and now impelled—
> The intellectual power, through words and things,
> Went sounding on, a dim and perilous way. (III.699–701)

Wordsworth's description of "Despondency Corrected" in the fourth book manifests the change of faith informing such transitional lyrics as "Peele Castle" and the "Ode to Duty." The path to psychic wholeness now lies in "acquiescence in the Will supreme" (IV.20); but though Christian resignation has replaced human sympathy, its end is still human regeneration: "That spirit only can redeem mankind" (IV.317). The participation in the divine will homilized in *The Excursion*, like the "gathering thoughts / Of man and his concerns" (*1805* XIV.257–58) celebrated at the conclusion to *The Prelude*, exposes and heals the radical insufficiency of a detached self-consciousness.

The Borderers should not, however, be thought of primarily as a cathartic exercise of Wordsworth's early career. It is a substantial work in itself, one of his most demanding and complex texts, expressing some of the deepest concerns of English Romanticism. As an exploration of the dramatic emergence and problematic nature of self-consciousness, the poet's relation to his antecedents, the vitality of sympathy and the deathliness of isolation, it anticipates Byron's *Cain* and Shelley's *Cenci*, dramas, like *The Borderers*, of seduction and crime, restlessness and repetition. The younger Romantics were not, however, influenced directly by Wordsworth's drama, which remained long in manuscript. They arrived independently at what Wordsworth had created in *The Borderers:* the great dramatic myth of the Romantic age.

3

Manfred: "The Language of Another World"

Byron wrote eight dramatic works, more than any major poet since Dryden. His own remarks on the theater, however, have left him open to the widespread prejudice against the Romantics as dramatists. Although Byron worked in two distinct dramatic modes, one which he called "regular," inspired by Greek tragedy and by Alfieri, and one the "metaphysical" or "speculative" mode that he created, he tended to collapse them together when discussing his dramatic aims and practice.[1] The historical plays—*Marino Faliero*, *Sardanapalus*, and *The Two Foscari*—which Byron almost certainly wished (contrary to his protestations) to see produced and with which he meant to "reform the stage,"[2] are verbally rich but static and somewhat pedantic tragedies that rather justify his poor reputation as a playwright. His experimental dramas, however, are charged with psychological depth and visionary techniques, qualities that led Goethe to call *Manfred* "a wonderful phenomenon . . . the quintessence of the most astonishing talent born to be its own tormentor."[3]

When Byron coined the term "mental theatre," he seems to have been speaking more of the historical tragedies than of the visionary dramatic poems. "I want," he told Murray, "to make a *regular* English drama—no matter for the Stage or not—which is not my object—but a *mental theatre*."[4] Writing to Lady Byron a few weeks later, he grouped *Cain*—distinguished as "poetical enough"—with the histories, and flatly rejected the stage: "I am trying an experiment—which is to introduce into our language—the *regular* tragedy—without regard to the Stage—which will not admit of it—but merely to the *mental* theatre of the reader."[5] As the term "metaphysical" suggests, the visionary dramas are concerned with the mind not only in presentation but in subject as well, informed by a singleness of purpose that has drawn criticism on Byron as a dramatist: "states of mind intrigue him; events hardly at all."[6] The dichotomy here is only apparent; Byron is intrigued most by mental events, and he portrays psychological interaction most surely when, as in *Manfred* and *Cain*, he avoids the distractions of historical trappings and dramatic unities.

Manfred shares its subtitle, "A Dramatic Poem," with Milton's *Samson Agonistes*, and the two works are similar in structure: Each describes a series of rhetorical encounters between a tormented hero, who dominates the stage, and various antagonists, who are slightly developed. The encounters in *Manfred*, however, are not simply rhetorical. They represent Manfred's increasingly desperate attempts to find release from an intolerable, flawed self-consciousness, whether through oblivion or, in the more complex encounters, through a scene of recognition that could render him psychically whole. All of Manfred's acts and desires emanate from his sense of psychic disintegration, and the emerging account of his past, with its seemingly obscure crime, is the story of how and why his psychic torment came about.

Francis Jeffrey, one of the most sensible critics to have yet written on Byron, complained in a contemporary review of *Manfred* that "it has no action; no plot—and no characters; Manfred merely muses and suffers from the beginning to the end."[7] To the extent that the other *dramatis personae* exist mainly for the exposition of Manfred's fluctuating mental states, Jeffrey was correct in noting the absence of full-bodied characters, and the plot—hinging as it does on rather cryptic references to the past—has eluded many critics besides Jeffrey. Because the hero finds no single strong opponent, as in *The Borderers* or *Cain*, but rather a series of willfully antagonistic spirits and unintentionally antagonistic men, the psychic conflict underlying *Manfred* emerges only through a succession of gradually intensified dramatic encounters.

The poem opens with Manfred, in a scene indebted to Goethe's *Faust*, alone at midnight in a "Gothic Gallery":

> The lamp must be replenish'd, but even then
> It will not burn so long as I must watch.
> My slumbers—if I slumber—are not sleep,
> But a continuance of enduring thought,
> Which then I can resist not: in my heart

There is a vigil, and these eyes but close
To look within; and yet I live, and bear
The aspect and the form of breathing men.
But grief should be the instructor of the wise;
Sorrow is knowledge: they who know the most
Must mourn the deepest o'er the fatal truth,
The Tree of Knowledge is not that of Life.[8]

Manfred's first lines introduce several motifs central to Romantic mental theater: a restless, self-regarding consciousness, a deep estrangement from humankind, and a persistent awareness of the Fall. In *The Borderers* these were features associated with the villain, and only gradually transferred to the hero; in *Manfred* the hero's temptation and fall precede the drama, which portrays their painful consequences and his attempts to escape them.

Manfred may have inherited his disillusionment with philosophy, science, and the "wisdom of the world" from Faust, but his characterization of knowledge is his own: "in my mind there is / A power to make these subject to itself" (I.1.15–16). For Manfred, mastering an art is indeed an exercise in power and subjection. His attitude toward the occult arts (which he has long studied) is fundamentally the same, and he addresses his attendant spirits always in the language of mastery. Failing in the first scene with two invocations, he tries a third, successful spell which hints metaphorically at the paradoxical nature of his domination:

—Spirits of earth and air,
Ye shall not thus elude me: by a power,
Deeper than all yet urged, a tyrant-spell,
Which had its birthplace in a star condemn'd,
The burning wreck of a demolish'd world,
A wandering hell in the eternal space;
By the strong curse which is upon my soul,
The thought which is within me and around me,
I do compel ye to my will. (I.1.41–49)

Manfred grounds his claim to mastery in the same fate—imaged by his ill-omening star—that brought about his relentless self-torment. The melodramatic cast of his expression here, as elsewhere, reflects not an unthinking adoption of Gothic stage rant but Byron's adaptation of it to underscore Manfred's self-delusion. Here he assumes falsely—as the spirits he summons know well—that the source of his urge to mastery also guarantees his power.

The first six elemental spirits who appear flatter Manfred's sense of dominion with such servile remarks as "Thy will be my guide," but the Seventh Spirit, who acts as a sort of shop steward for the rest, undermines Manfred's claims with a series of rhetorical reversals. The Spirit asserts his rule over the star that rules Manfred, and reminds him that it became a "wandering Hell" or "curse" only in the hour of Manfred's fall; for the Spirit the star emblematizes at once Manfred's destiny and the psychic torment attendant upon it. In what should probably be taken as an aside, the Spirit then counters Manfred's vaunted rule and autonomy: "Forced by a power (which is not thine / And lent thee but to make thee mine)" (I.1.126–27). The strategy adopted by each of the spirits whom Manfred summons lies in first granting him an appearance of the power he thirsts for, then asserting a greater power, beguiling and outfacing him in turn as they attempt to enslave him.

Manfred, however, will not fall easily into such traps, for he has made as yet no Faustian compact and demands at this point nothing save "Oblivion, self oblivion" (I.1.144). He realizes that his show of intellectual and thaumaturgic mastery is at bottom a palliative for his inability to master his inner torment, and in his despair he desires a complete cessation of self-consciousness. The Spirit will never grant Manfred oblivion, however, for in order to prevail he must first, on the contrary, aggravate Manfred's suffering. The various spirits that Manfred deals with are often regarded as psychic projections: What they know and force him to confront is already within him.[9] But the supernatural beings in *Manfred*, like those in *Macbeth*, are at once externalizations of the protagonist's character and external antagonists that seek to deform it. In both works the demons seem motiveless, abstract embodiments of a craving for domination who encourage, only to thwart, a similar craving in their victim. But the Witches find a human counterpart in Macbeth's "fiend-like queen," who brings both motivation and consistency into his temptation (as Lucifer will to Cain's). And while *Macbeth* describes the hero's seduction, the struggles in *Manfred* merely heighten the perverse will to power that has effectively dehumanized the hero even before the action begins.

The first scene opens with Manfred seeking to escape his continual psychic torment; it ends with the Spirit intensifying it. Aware of his failure to obtain release, and vainly hoping for supernatural fellowship, Manfred asks the Spirit to appear in his own form; but these spirits are formless. So that the invocation will not have been entirely pointless, he then asks to see the Spirit in a form of his choice, which might at least produce some sublime effects. The Spirit instead cruelly appears as Astarte, Manfred's sister, lover, and the victim of his past crime. The spectacle overwhelms him, and the Spirit takes advantage of his fit with an incantation of his own:

> Though thy slumber may be deep,
> Yet thy spirit shall not sleep;
> There are shades which will not vanish,
> There are thoughts thou canst not banish;
> By a power to thee unknown,
> Thou canst never be alone. (I.1.202–7)

The spell threatens Manfred with what he most fears. His dominion, even over himself, is held in question by an alien power within his mind, which, far from relieving his aloneness, exists to threaten his autonomy. As Webster's Flamineo remarks, " 'Tis not so great a cunning as men think / To raise the devil . . . The greatest cunning were to lay him down." The spell also includes the first of several references to *Paradise Lost* that underscore the Satanic nature of Manfred's psychic torment: "I call upon thee! and compel / Thyself to be thy proper Hell!" (I.1.250–51). This aspect of the curse takes full effect only toward the end of the drama.

The next scene begins as Manfred acknowledges his weakness: "The spirits I have raised abandon me . . . The remedy I reck'd of tortured me" (I.2.1–3). Although the transition from lordly mage to dejected suicide might seem at first illogical or at least facile, both characters arise from Manfred's desire to utterly forget himself. Having found that magical art avails no more than human science to erase self-consciousness, Manfred now seeks oblivion through death. Twice he fails to hear the calls of a chamois hunter who worries to see him approach a dangerous cliff of the Jungfrau—a situation that would be ridiculous enough on a conventional stage. But in its imagined setting in the high Alps, Manfred's disregard is convincing in itself and at the same time a tacit comment on his state of mind.

Manfred, one critic has stressed, is as uniformly courteous to other men as he is overbearing toward spirits,[10] but this reflects not so much humanism as a patronizing and inhuman distance from his own kind. His near-solipsism (highlighted by the extremely narcissistic and rather poor soliloquy in this scene), engendered by unremitting introspection, along with his unnatural rejection of social relations, has left Manfred all but deaf to mortal voices. For all his claim to the "Promethean spark" (I.1.153), he has been aptly called a "Prometheus manqué."[11] He shares with the predecessor he invokes Titanic stature, isolation, and continual torment, but unlike Shelley's Prometheus—or for that matter Byron's—Manfred does and has done nothing for humankind. His stance throughout is one that Shelley's Prometheus must be trapped into, and must learn to give up. The Titan's isolation arises from his pain, while to a large degree Manfred's pain is born from his isolation.

Manfred is shocked out of his solipsistic despair when the hunter drags him from the cliff and leads him to his cottage. The human contact provided by the hunter has a calming and strengthening effect on Manfred, who still, however, suffers from the obsessive thoughts of Astarte inflamed by the Spirit the night before. When the hunter offers him wine he beholds, in the tradition of *Macbeth*, an image of his blood-guilt: "Away, away! there's blood upon the brim! / Will it then never, never sink in the earth?"(II.1.21–22). The reference is heightened by a later scene (II.3) in which the Destinies arrive on stage describing the mischief they have been at, echoing the Witches in *Macbeth* (I.3).[12] The presence of *Macbeth* can be felt often in *Manfred*. As a hero-villain haunted by his past, Manfred obviously resembles Macbeth; moreover, the succession of antagonists in *Manfred* owes something to Macbeth's complex temptation by both the Weird Sisters and Lady Macbeth, in contrast to the single tempter in *Othello*. The most significant parallel, however, resides in the interpenetration of two worlds, human and demonic, with the protagonist in each case compromised and entrapped through his violation of the borders between them. The demonic (if not hallucinatory) transubstantiation of wine into blood is in itself a complex image of border violation, and the implicit reference to *Macbeth* underscores Manfred's memory of a crime which, as the next scene reveals, depended on a violation of borders. That Byron should remember *Macbeth* even as Manfred cries out at the presence of the past signals as well a relation between protagonist and poet that becomes significant in the third act.

References to Astarte and hints of her questionable fate build steadily throughout the drama, attesting to Manfred's obsession and engendering a parallel curiosity in the mind of the reader. In his first soliloquy Manfred speaks of an "all-nameless hour" (I.1.24) that marked the beginning of his psychic torment, the "hour" equated by the malicious Spirit with the fall of Manfred's natal star from a virgin world to a hellish "wandering mass of shapeless flame" (I.1.117). The Spirit's apparition as a "beautiful female figure" that stuns and tortures Manfred defies interpretation until his outburst to the hunter supplies an identifying clue:

> I say 't is blood—my blood! the pure warm stream
> Which ran in the veins of my fathers, and in ours
> When we were in our youth, and had one heart,
> And loved each other as we should not love,
> And this was shed: but still it rises up,
> Colouring the clouds, that shut me out from heaven,
> Where thou art not—and I shall never be. (II.1.24–30)

Here the reader is given a strong intimation of the nature of Manfred's fatal hour, events he characterizes in terms that recall Oswald's lines on action and suffering in *The Borderers:*

> actions are our epochs: mine
> Have made my days and nights imperishable,
> Endless, and all alike. (II.1.52–54)

The motive of Manfred's actions remains obscure, however, until he confesses his past to the Witch of the Alps.

In outline, Manfred's encounter with the Witch resembles his struggle with the Seventh Spirit. He calls her up with his magical powers, which she immediately qualifies: "Son of Earth! / I know thee, and the powers which give thee power" (II.2.126–27)—taunting him with his mortality as does the Spirit, who calls him "Child of Clay." He asks again for oblivion, and is answered dubiously by the

Witch, who moreover demands he relinquish the pose of mastery and instead "swear obedience" to her will. Manfred's anger finds expression in his characteristic language of dominion and servitude:

> I will not swear—Obey! and whom? the spirits
> Whose presence I command, and be the slave
> Of those who served me—Never! (II.2.252–54)

As with the Seventh Spirit, Manfred's claims and defiance rest on an advantage completely unacknowledged by his antagonist. Though delusive, however, his self-image as indomitable master helps explain the fragmentary story of Astarte which he tells the Witch immediately before their brief struggle.

Recounting the experiences that have led to his desire for self-forgetfulness, Manfred begins with his isolation from other men: "though I wore the form / I had no sympathy with breathing flesh" (II.2.150–51). As he later tells the Abbot who comes investigating his traffic with spirits, Manfred fought against his misanthropy only briefly, and in the interests of domination:

> I have had those earthly visions
> And noble aspirations in my youth,
> To make my own the mind of other men,
> The enlightener of nations. (III.1.104–7)

But his youthful hopes (which further ally him to Oswald) for psychic empire and the status of an "enlightener"—or Lucifer—gave way to his disgust with his humanity as reflected in others. "For if the beings, of whom I was one,— / Hating to be so—cross'd me in my path," he tells the Witch, "I felt myself degraded back to them, / And was all clay again" (II.2.170–74).

Without sympathy, abstracted from humankind, unable to approach others even in the interests of dominion, and despising his own humanity, Manfred was designed for the isolated and self-estranged condition which, in Romantic mental theater, is usually imposed by a seducer on his naive victim. As Manfred's story continues, it becomes clear that he has been his own betrayer; but as in *The Borderers* or *The Cenci* or Byron's later *Cain*, the act of betrayal still requires a transforming encounter with another. This other for Manfred is his sister, Astarte.

The crime involving Astarte, mysterious enough as presented by Manfred, has been further obscured by a succession of commentators, who have interpreted it as everything from the human sacrifice allegedly used in black magic to a product of Gothic stage conventions.[13] In the context of Romantic mental theater, Manfred's crime can be understood as a variation on the struggle for recognition involved in the misguided quest for an autonomous selfhood. Manfred's description of Astarte as a glorified reflection of his self-image takes on a new and sinister aspect when one reads into his past the unspoken but obvious need to escape a crippling psychic isolation. Though he tells the Witch that there was no one "with whom I wore the chain of human ties," he goes on to describe the one figure with whom he approached a sympathetic relation:

> She was like me in lineaments—her eyes,
> Her hair, her features, all, to the very tone
> Even of her voice, they said were like to mine;
> But soften'd all, and temper'd into beauty;
> She had the same lone thoughts and wanderings,
> The quest of hidden knowledge, and a mind
> To comprehend the universe: nor these
> Alone, but with them gentler powers than mine,
> Pity, and smiles, and tears—which I had not;
> And tenderness—but that I had for her;
> Humility—and that I never had.
> Her faults were mine—her virtues were her own—
> I loved her, and destroy'd her! (II.2.199–211)

Manfred's approach to an erotic relation took an incestuous form because he sought not a sympathetic partner but a reflection, a double that could reassure him in his total and self-imposed isolation with a subservient and flattering image of his psyche.[14] As for the poet of Shelley's *Alastor,* Manfred's desire could find as its object only an idealized projection of his own subjectivity. And at the same time, his confounding of fraternal and erotic love—breaking a taboo that anthropologists from Frazer to Lévi-Strauss have considered fundamental to human society—constitutes another aspect of border violation. If one follows Lévi-Strauss's contention that prohibition of incest functions to bind family or clan groups into larger social unions, making the "transition from nature to culture" possible, Manfred's incest can be seen as regressively antisocial, another sign of his alienation from humankind.[15]

The relation destroyed Astarte evidently because she was too weak to withstand her brother's aggressive, literally consuming love. Manfred makes of her his shadow, and as a shadow she has no life; her fate brings out the tragic element in Hamlet's banter regarding Laertes: "his semblable is his mirror, and who else would trace him, his umbrage, nothing more."[16] However her blood was shed (the hints, though ambiguous, point to suicide), her destruction proceeded, as Manfred states, from his desire, which initiated a one-sided struggle for recognition. As he tells the hunter, more simply, his "embrace was fatal" (II.1.87). Here again Hegel's "Master and Servant" model for the early, unsuccessful emergence of self-consciousness is highly instructive. The first consciousness, in order to confirm his identity and escape from a solipsistic isolation, engages another consciousness in a life-and-death struggle. If the struggle ends in a master and servant relation (a relation we see Manfred belatedly and hopelessly trying to impose on his familiar spirits throughout the drama), the outcome is unhappy enough. But if the first consciousness ends by destroying the second, the struggle has been for nothing. "Death certainly shows that each staked his life and held it of no account . . . but that is not for those who survived this struggle."[17] The result would be instead to seal the survivor's isolation by rendering the necessarily reciprocal act of recognition impossible.

Oblique as such a reading of Manfred's history may seem at first, it accounts for the painfully flawed self-consciousness ("these eyes but close / To look within"), the despair, and the pathetically delusive pose of mastery that characterize Manfred at the outset of the drama. Manfred is not, like Macbeth, plagued simply by the memory of his crimes; he desires complete forgetfulness of self, a self that has proved radically insufficient to maintain the posture of autonomy—"The lion is alone, and so am I" (III.1.123)—which he assumes before men but abandons when seeking help from spirits. Both of the men he encounters sense his lack of psychic integration, which they express in terms of self-alienation. The hunter tells him his "mind and body are alike unfit / To trust each other" (II.1.23); the Abbot offers "To reconcile thyself with thy own soul" (III.1.99).

"Half dust, half deity, alike unfit / To sink or soar, with our mix'd essence": Manfred's emblem for the human condition expresses his own sense of a divided self. Seeking at once death and power, oblivion and autonomy, repelled by his humanity and disdainful of spirits, tormented by the past and yet compelled to relive it in each supernatural encounter, Manfred's "mix'd essence" (what Shelley's Cenci will call his "divided being") expresses his unbearably estranged self-consciousness. The inhuman reserve that marked his youth, and led him to a closed alliance with his sister, was transformed by their relation into a deep alienation from self no less than from society. Manfred's continuing search for autonomy resembles, in its inevitable failure, that of the equally self-enclosed "sceptical consciousness" described by Hegel later in the *Phenomenology:* "It is just in this process that this consciousness, instead of being self-identical, is in fact nothing but a purely casual, confused medley, the dizziness of a perpetually self-engendered disorder."[18] Since Manfred ultimately acknowledges no being—supernatural or otherwise—outside himself, his sense of identity remains fluctuating, untenable, and grows finally unbearable in its insecurity.

When the Witch leads Manfred on with the intimation of supernatural aid, he expresses two contrary desires: "To do this thy power / Must wake the dead, or lay me low with them" (II.2.245–46). Self-oblivion through extinction is one alternative; the other, more desperate, would be to somehow revive Astarte—the only human being whom Manfred has ever considered as a possible sympathetic partner—and attempt to relive the drama of recognition which once ended so tragically. It is the more desperate hope that presses him toward a final invocation of the most powerful spirit yet.

In the heterodox mythography of *Manfred,* Arimanes is the ruler of the spiritual realm, the "Prince of the Powers invisible," and a governor of human events as well, "Sovereign of Sovereigns." His attendants, the Destinies, are shocked by Manfred's nonchalant entrance into the Hall of their master—"Bow down and worship, slave!" (II.4.401)—but for once it is Manfred who reverses the hierarchy of power, reminding the spirits that Arimanes is himself subordinate to the "overruling Infinite." Interceding for him, however, one of the Destinies makes yet another reversal at Manfred's expense:

> He is mine,
> And thine, it may be;—be it so, or not,
> No other Spirit in this region hath
> A soul like his—or power upon his soul. (II.4.439–42)

Intrigued with the prospect of subjecting so unparalleled a mortal, Nemesis, Arimanes's deputy, asks Manfred what he wants. "Call up the dead . . . call up Astarte."

Whatever Manfred hoped to gain by once more confronting Astarte, her Phantom overwhelms him as did her image: "Oh God, that I should dread / To look upon the same—Astarte! No, / I cannot speak to her" (II.4.472–74). The scene grows extremely poignant as Manfred, faced by the Phantom's silent gaze, expresses his need for Astarte, and only Astarte, to answer or acknowledge him, while reliving his inability to recognize her in turn, continuing to see her only in terms of himself: "the grave hath not changed thee more / Than I am changed for thee"; "Thou love'dst me / Too much, as I loved thee"; "I feel but what thou art—and what I am"; "many things answer'd me— / Spirits and men—but thou wert silent all." The irony of Manfred's situation becomes especially painful as Astarte, responding at last, utters only his name, underscoring Manfred's lasting inability to see in her anything but his own reflected identity.

> [*Manfred.*]—Speak to me!
> Look on the fiends around—they feel for me:
> I fear them not, and feel for thee alone.
> Speak to me! though it be in wrath;—but say—
> I reck not what—but let me hear thee once—
> This once—once more!
> *Phantom of Astarte.* Manfred! (II.4.514–20)

Provoked again into speech, she makes a single pronouncement: "Manfred! Tomorrow ends thine earthly ills," leaving him doubtful whether his torment will end with his mortal life, and certain that even a repeated encounter with Astarte cannot yield him the psychic integrity he requires. In his final knowledge of despair, Manfred finds a strength he has so far lacked, and in the third act of the drama his defiant courage approaches sublimity. As the scene ends, Arimanes's Spirits announce the change:

> He mastereth himself, and makes
> His torture tributary to his will.
> Had he been one of us, he would have made
> An awful spirit. (II.4.529–32)

But even as he approaches the self-mastery he has up to now sought in vain, his ability to maintain it is thrown into question.

Many of Manfred's characteristics—his sleepless, tormented self-consciousness, his isolation, his pretense of autonomy, his thwarted urge to impose his will on others—are attributes as well of Milton's Satan. But in the first two acts, Manfred is not directly or explicitly related to Satan; his lineage could be traced instead through the traditional Gothic villain and through such related figures as Cain and the Wandering Jew.[19] When Manfred accepts the irreversibility of his fate and strengthens himself to meet it, however, he becomes less a conventional descendant than a literary avatar of Milton's devil. Toward the end of the drama Manfred inherits not only Satan's sublime defiance but its limitations as well, as Byron's echoes of *Paradise Lost* show.

Rejecting the Abbot's proposal to "reconcile [him] / With the true church, and through the church to heaven" (III.1.50–51), as he has earlier rejected mediation in the form of the hunter's prayers (II.1.89), Manfred proclaims his autonomy in words deeply indebted to *Paradise Lost:*

> Old man! there is no power in holy men,
> Nor charm in prayer, nor purifying form
> Of penitence, nor outward look, nor fast,
> Nor agony, nor, greater than all these,
> The innate tortures of that deep despair,
> Which is remorse without the fear of hell
> But all in all sufficient to itself
> Would make a hell of heaven,—can exorcise
> From out the unbounded spirit the quick sense
> Of its own sins, wrongs, sufferance, and revenge
> Upon itself; there is no future pang
> Can deal that justice on the self-condemn'd
> He deals on his own soul. (III.1.66–78)

Manfred's great claim is now his embodiment of the Satanic mind, which (in a Miltonic locus frequently invoked in Romantic mental theater) "is its own place, and in itself / Can make a Heav'n of Hell, a Hell of Heav'n" (*Paradise Lost* I.254–55).[20] It is equally clear that Byron—with his emphasis on tortures, despair, the mind's self-punishment—has weighed the immense cost of Satan's ultimately self-defeating autonomous stance: "Which way I fly is hell; myself am Hell" (IV.75). He is no uncritical adherent of a "Satanic school"; and yet his resort to the Satanic mind in the third act of *Manfred* is not part of a "critical parody" of Satan either.[21] Byron had great difficulties in resolving *Manfred;* he was forced to discard the first version of Act III when its weaknesses were pointed out to him by a few trusted readers.[22] His solution was to lean heavily on Milton's characterization of Satan, but Byron was clearly ambivalent about his reliance on a literary model at such a critical point in his first dramatic work.

This ambivalence finds graphic portrayal in the final confrontation between Manfred and the Seventh Spirit, who has returned—this time unbidden—in the form of an "infernal god" (III.4.323) to carry Manfred to Hell. The Spirit now appears as himself a type of Satan—"on his brows / The thunder-scars are graven; from his eye / Glares forth the immortality of hell" (III.4.336–38)—and as such he reflects not only (as one critic has subtly argued) the Satanic villain-heroes of Byron's early tales but Byron's latest version of this hero—Manfred—as well.[23] Manfred opposes the Spirit with a speech again heavily indebted to Milton's Satan:

—Back to thy hell!
Thou hast no power upon me, *that* I feel;
Thou never shalt possess me, *that* I know:
What I have done is done; I bear within
A torture which could nothing gain from thine.
The mind which is immortal makes itself
Requital for its good or evil thoughts,
Is its own origin of ill and end,
And its own place and time. (III.4.384–92)

Manfred concludes with a confrontation of doubles that must end in stalemate. When the Abbot, unable to exorcise the Spirit, demands his identity, the Spirit replies with a cunning phrase: "The genius of this mortal" (III.4.341). Byron draws here on a complex word to express a complex relation. "Genius" can signify both demon (as in "genie") and *daemon,* or attendant spirit. It can, of course, signify one's creative gifts—emphasizing in this sense the Spirit's alliance to the heroes of Byron's earlier career—but it also bears here a more threatening meaning, evoking the good and evil genii, "the two mutually opposed spirits by whom every person was supposed to be attended," thus implying the disintegration of Manfred's psyche.[24] Finally, in the Spirit's claim to be a usurping presence within Manfred's mind, one can sense Byron's own discomfort with the prominence of an antecedent text in his attempt to resolve his first dramatic poem.

One of Manfred's richest soliloquies, which occurs in a scene separating the two echoes of Milton's Satan, is a commentary on the irresistibility of the past in its incursions on the present. Alone in the tower in which he practiced magic, Manfred muses on his studies of divination and alchemy—"the language of another world"—and tries to gather his thoughts before the approaching death announced by Astarte. He finds himself instead reliving a night from his youthful travels when he visited the Coliseum in Rome. In the moonlight—a symbol here, as in Wordsworth's *Prelude,* of the transforming powers of the imagination—the "ruinous perfection" of the Coliseum was overlaid, without being obscured, by the spectacle of the theater as it once was. During this sublime moment, the combined powers of perception, memory, and imagination gave way to awe of the mighty dead:

> Leaving that beautiful which still was so,
> And making that which was not, till the place
> Became religion, and the heart ran o'er
> With silent worship of the great of old,—
> The dead, but sceptred sovereigns, who still rule
> Our spirits from their urns.—
> 'T was such a night!
> 'T is strange that I recall it at this time;
> But I have found our thoughts take wildest flight
> Even at the moment when they should array
> Themselves in pensive order. (III.4.296–305)

Manfred's exclamation on the mind's resistance to conscious control provides a key for understanding this passage—both in its dramatic context and as a manifestation of Byron's difficulties with concluding his dramatic poem. For Manfred, the past has been a sovereign force ever since the events that culminated in Astarte's death, and it is doubly appropriate that his vision of the past superimposed on the present recurs now as a memory intruding on his present efforts to steel himself for the coming ordeal. The image of the dead ruling over the spirits of the living intimates Manfred's deep awareness of his psychic disintegration, along with the corresponding fear of an ulterior force within his mind, a fear the Seventh Spirit will play on as Manfred's "genius" in their final confrontation.[25] Byron, in framing that confrontation, is himself haunted by the language of another world, the lines from *Paradise Lost* on which he relies so heavily in the last scenes of the drama.[26]

At the end of *Manfred* Byron resolves neither his hero's nor his own dilemma. Manfred escapes the Spirit's hell only through his claims to bear a greater hell within him. The Satanic division of his self-tormenting mind renders the "infernal god" superfluous, and Manfred's victory is only a function of his ultimate defeat. *Manfred* is a brilliant portrayal of the alienated self-consciousness, but its convoluted design allows for no solution of the problems it explores. From choosing an inhuman isolation, Manfred inevitably becomes his own seducer, self-betrayed into a crime that eternally resists his struggles to avoid its consequences: "[I] was my own destroyer, and will be / My own hereafter" (III.4.398–99). He dies embracing the private damnation emblematized by the star of his destiny, "a wandering hell in the eternal space."

The contention (shared by several critics) that *Manfred* was a cathartic work which led Byron to the more generous poetic stance of *Don Juan* is suggestive but overstated.[27] In *Manfred* Byron discovered the limitations of the autonomous, Satanic stance of his early poetry, and it is as a portrayal of limitations that the drama succeeds. But Byron's analysis of self-consciousness, as presented in *Manfred,* is sketchy and incomplete, largely because he chose not to separate villain and hero, seducer and seduced. And his appeal to Satanic autonomy at the conclusion falls very much short of forming an analytical and liberating critique. These are problems to which Byron returned with greater force and ingenuity in his next "metaphysical" drama, *Cain.* But I do not wish to leave *Manfred* without remarking that, perhaps because of the energy of desperation, the incompleteness of *Manfred* contributes to its strength. As Jeffrey remarked in 1818: "Its obscurity is a part of its grandeur; and the darkness that rests upon it, and the smoky distance in which it is lost, are all devices to increase its majesty, to stimulate our curiosity, and to impress us with deeper awe."[28]

4

Seduction and Repetition in *Cain*

Before the appearance of Lucifer, Byron's Cain is an uncompromising, proud figure, painfully conscious of his exile from a Paradise that remains visible in the distance, eerily lit up by the guardian cherubim and their flaming sword. Cain does not require a demon, as many readers have noted, to render him dissatisfied with what Byron called "the politics of Paradise."[1] At the outset of the drama, however, his dissatisfaction is undirected, and still far enough from despair to allow him a part, if a sometimes grudging one, in the original human community. As Cain withdraws from his family to brood on his apparently unwarranted exile, Lucifer appears. The difference between the emerging drama of *Cain* and the largely retrospective drama of *Manfred* grows clear already at this moment: Manfred summons his spirits, while Lucifer intrudes opportunely and unbidden into Cain's world.

Byron returned to both the form and the thematic concerns of his first dramatic poem in what he referred to as "a 'Manfred' sort of thing called 'Cain'."[2] The Seventh Spirit had cursed Manfred as—among other epithets—one of the "brotherhood of Cain" (I.1.249), a figure in Romantic iconography for the tormented, criminal self-consciousness characteristic of the protagonists of mental theater.[3] As *Manfred* began with a memory of the Fall and the lament that "the Tree of Knowledge is not that of Life," *Cain* opens with a scene evoking a Fall at once metaphoric and immediate, Adam wondering "O God! why didst thou plant the tree of knowledge?," and his eldest son, Cain, returning: "And wherefore plucked ye not the tree of life?" (I.32–33).[4] But *Manfred* was concerned primarily with the repercussions of a past fall; *Cain* begins with the dilemma of life in a postlapsarian world and moves toward a reenactment of the crime that brought about its Fall.

Byron took as his original from which to reimagine the first murder not the Bible but the account of the first sin in *Paradise Lost*, as though Milton's phrase "Sin and her shadow Death" (IX.12) posed a challenge which the later poet could not—particularly after his ambivalent appeal to Milton's Satan in the conclusion of *Manfred*—resist. Byron tried to discount his close familiarity with *Paradise Lost* in the preface to *Cain:* "Since I was twenty I have never read Milton"—a statement immediately qualified: "But I had read him so frequently before that this may make little difference." He was, in any case, obviously courting comparison with *Paradise Lost*, and, at least for a number of his contemporaries, the comparison was not unfavorable. Scott wrote that Byron had in *Cain* "certainly matched Milton on his own ground"; Shelley that "it contains finer poetry than has appeared in England since *Paradise Regained*"; Hunt that the physical description of Lucifer was "worthy of Milton."[5] Byron himself, addressing the charges of blasphemy which almost immediately met its publication, held that "If 'Cain' be 'blasphemous'—Paradise lost is blasphemous."[6]

Jeffrey's contemporary review, however, set the tone for much later criticism in declaring it "absurd" for Byron to "plead the authority of Milton" in defending *Cain* when its "*whole argument* is directed against the goodness or the power of the Deity, and against the reasonableness of religion in general . . . The Devil and his pupil have the field entirely to themselves—and are encountered with nothing but feeble obtestations and unreasoning horrors."[7] For Jeffrey, *Cain* would, if anything, stand opposed to Milton's justification of God's ways, and the drama has in fact been read more recently as a "refutation" of Milton, or even a "frontal assault" in what is colorfully termed the "Romantic war with *Paradise Lost*."[8] Jeffrey's view rests on a presupposition that, although it has remained influential, is far from obvious. Such readings must assume that Lucifer—Cain's seducer and a quite lineal descendant of Milton's Satan—expresses views reflecting, or at least approaching, Byron's own. And if this is the case, Lucifer's antagonistic role loses most of its point, while Byron's remarks distancing himself from Lucifer's views become at best disingenuous: "I really thought 'Cain' a speculative and hardy, but still a harmless production. As I said before I am really a great admirer of tangible religion; and am breeding one of my daughters a Catholic that she may have her hands full . . . I am afraid this sounds flippant, but I don't mean it to be so."[9] Although the letter (which goes on at some length) does sound flippant, there is no reason to believe that Byron, in 1821, was the nihilistic or proto-existentialist opponent of revealed religion dear to twentieth-century critics.[10] Byron was by no means an orthodox Christian, but granting this does not consign him to his own devil.

To minimize Byron's distance from Lucifer is both to oversimplify the relation of *Cain* to *Paradise Lost* and to reduce a dramatic portrayal of seduction, repetition, and crime to a static philosophical tract in blank verse. Seen as a "defender" of mankind, a light-bringer, Lucifer merely encourages and perhaps hastens Cain's Promethean defiance, making a number of anti-theistical harangues along the way. But viewed as a malevolent tempter, Lucifer transforms Cain from a disaffected exile from Paradise into a murderous, self-tormented exile from humanity.[11] Byron's initial "Thoughts for a Speech of Lucifer" point to a devil who is hardly benign: "Were *Death* an *evil*, would *I* let thee *live?* / Fool! Live as I live . . ."[12] The speaker could be one of the antagonistic spirits in *Manfred*, save that the urge behind the demon's antagonism begins to take shape as a desire to communicate torment to another: "Live as I live."

These first, broad strokes are hardly recognizable in the subtle characterization of Lucifer in *Cain*, but a careful reading of the drama reveals all of the malevolence of Byron's sketch. Though he reverses Iago's "I am not what I am" (I.1.65) in reassuring Cain that "I seem that which I am" (II.1.88), Lucifer belongs to the tradition of demonic seducers exemplified by Satan, Iago, and the Witches of *Macbeth.* Whether he lies like truth or tells truths—like the devils in Chaucer's *Summoner's Tale* or Marlowe's *Faustus*—with the effect of lies, his arguments should be judged more by their effect on his disciple than by their appeal to a post-Romantic sensibility. Lucifer's notions are no more adequate to Cain's actual situation than the pious bromides traded about by his repentant family at the outset of the drama. Or rather, as Byron put it, the devil's insinuations are designed to render Cain's situation unbearably inadequate in itself: "the object of the demon is to depress him still further in his own estimation than he was before—by showing him infinite things—& his own abasement—till he falls into the frame of mind—that leads to the

Catastrophe—from mere *internal* irritation—*not* premeditation or envy—of *Abel*—(which would have made him contemptible) but from rage and fury against the inadequacy of his state to his Conceptions."[13]

Lucifer's malevolence is advertised even in the epigraph from Genesis: "now the Serpent was more subtil than any beast of the field . . ." Although Byron, probably out of advance irritation with pious critics, makes a show in the preface of supporting with Scripture Lucifer's denial of having tempted Eve, Lucifer repeatedly incriminates himself in the drama, as when he passionately defends the serpent's acts ("Did *I* plant things prohibited . . .") on first meeting Cain (I.194–211), or when he later offers Cain advice on avoiding tempters like the Serpent, "Giv'n chiefly at my own expense" (II.2.204–13). The preface is complicated further by Byron's insistence that his "present subject has nothing to do with the *New Testament*, to which no reference can be made without anachronism," when in fact there are a number of unambiguous references to the "Son" who "will be a sacrifice" (I.166).[14] Both of these misleading remarks may well be related to Byron's uneasy reference to *Paradise Lost.* If true, each contention would help distance *Cain* from Milton's epic, one by rejecting the presence of Christ essential in *Paradise Lost,* the other by dissociating Byron's devil from Milton's. In fact, what Lucifer reveals of his past and his character fits remarkably well with those elements of the Miltonic Satan which most captivated—and disappointed—the Romantics.

Cain does not, however, rely on such unassimilated quotations of Satanic rhetoric as embarrass the conclusion of *Manfred.* Instead, Byron has reimagined Milton's devil and developed the temptation scenes from the epic along Romantic lines into a thoroughly dramatic argument. Byron's approach to *Paradise Lost* in *Cain* is part creative assimilation, part Romantic revision. And his most searching criticisms are directed primarily against the "Satan" in Lucifer, as Byron comes to terms with the figure that haunts his early work from *Childe Harold* to *Manfred.* When Cain, a few moments into the first scene, blames his father for losing his Edenic birthright, complaining, "What had *I* done in this?—I was unborn: / I sought not to be born" (I.67–68), Byron echoes Adam's doubts in *Paradise Lost:*

what if thy Son
Prove disobedient, and reprov'd, retort,

> Wherefore didst thou beget me? I sought it not.
> (IX. 759–61)

But his attitude toward Milton is neither the simple defiance of a Cain nor the naive assimilation of an Abel.[15]

In the preface Byron also explained his subtitle, "A Mystery," as being "in conformity with the ancient title annexed to dramas upon similar subjects, which were styled 'Mysteries or Moralities'." Byron did not know, as modern editors invariably point out, that "mystery" referred to the craft guilds (*métiers*) which performed the medieval pageants. But what he evidently thought the term did mean—the central dramatic presence of a mystery beyond human comprehension, the miracle of the related term "miracle play"—is entirely appropriate to the conception of *Cain*. Lucifer suggests at one point that Cain's fallen parents were doubly defrauded by the Tree of Knowledge: They ought in fairness to have been initiated into "the mystery of death" (I.460) as the culmination of the knowledge for which they paid so unreasonably high a price. The promise of a revelation through death will tantalize Cain throughout the drama, leading ultimately to its tragic conclusion. And the most powerful phase of Cain's temptation, the metaphysical journey with Lucifer in Act II, is fundamentally mysterious as well, breaking the illusion of clock time, disrupting the otherwise untrammeled "dramatic unities" of the framing acts, and rendering the work unstageable save through mental theater:

> With us acts are exempt from time, and we
> Can crowd eternity into an hour
> Or stretch an hour into eternity.
> We breathe not by a mortal measurement,
> But that's a myst'ry. (I.535–39)

These lines, which capture without mimicry the self-reflexiveness (note the pun on "acts") and colloquial ease of Shakespeare, express an appeal to the reader's imagination as the only appropriate stage for the drama of psychic influence and transformation.

Lucifer outlines his program for Cain in his first words, identifying himself as "Master of Spirits," and claiming to sympathize with mortality: "I know the thoughts / Of dust and feel for it and with you" (I.100–101). When Cain incredulously wonders, "You know my thoughts," Lucifer replies:

They are the thoughts of all
Worthy of thought. 'Tis your immortal part
Which speaks within you.

Lucifer's is the first mention Cain has heard of such a self—he immediately interposes "What immortal part?"—and his first intimation of the possibility of psychic division, of a "part" which can utter thoughts beyond the reach of his mortal (and social) self. Lucifer's ensuing temptation of Cain expands and elaborates on this first interchange. Enticing Cain, who has begun to feel a distance from his family, with the promise of supernatural fellowship, Lucifer gradually asserts instead a claim to mastery over his disciple, and his most effective methods will include suggesting thoughts which Cain believes his own, and undermining Cain's sense of self by implanting and nourishing a feeling of psychic division. As with Oswald's program for Marmaduke in *The Borderers*, the temptation leads inexorably toward murder, a crime designed by Lucifer to seal Cain's inner division and effective bondage.

The temptation is both intricate and subtle—as befits the tempter—and nearly every one of Lucifer's remarks, however casual or high-toned, contributes to its development. His role as seducer accounts for the wide discrepancies (which readings such as Jeffrey's must suppress) between Lucifer's first, guarded probings of Cain and his gradual (but never complete) self-revelation as he grows more certain of success. When Cain, initially amazed at the apparition of this new and awesome spirit, comments, "Thou look'st almost a god," Lucifer answers:

I am none,
And having failed to be one, would be nought
Save what I am. He conquered; let him reign! (I.127–30)

Lucifer dissembles his obsessive urge to dominion until he feels more confident of exerting it successfully in the present case. As Cain, who grows exhilarated at seeing his own alienation reflected in the spirit, begins to participate in Lucifer's vision of righteous rebellion against a tyrannous order, Lucifer reverses his position:

Where are
Thy God or Gods, there am I. All things are

Divided with me; life and death and time,
Eternity and heav'n and earth and that
Which is not heav'n nor earth, but peopled with
Those who once peopled or shall people both—
These are my realms! So that I do divide
His, and possess a kingdom which is not
His. (I.546–54)

What we learn of Lucifer in this speech is precisely what we would expect of a literary avatar of Milton's Satan. Lucifer is motivated by an ever present and never ending imperialistic drive, drawing into his "realms" all who will follow him. He has in fact been building toward this revelation from his initial suggestion that Cain's psyche was not integral but divided. Now he implies that in his feeling of alienation—the protest of his "spiritual part"—Cain can find the microcosm of a macrocosmic dichotomy. The unconventional and at times jarring line breaks, incidentally, such as the first stress caesurae in the speech quoted above, are intentional, underscoring the unruly, unstable division which Lucifer depicts.

Lucifer impresses upon Cain the relation of cosmic and psychic division with his most explicitly Satanic lines, which echo the same locus—"the mind is its own place"—that supports the uneasy conclusion of *Manfred.* Addressing himself to Cain's "immortal" self, Lucifer hints that the fruit of the Tree of Life might still be seized by fallen man:

By being
Yourselves in your resistance. Nothing can
Quench the mind if the mind will be itself
And centre of surrounding things; 'tis made
To sway. (I.212–16)

The mind forms itself, in Lucifer's divisive scheme, through a continuing state of opposition supported by an egocentric stance which he later calls "an independency of torture," and presents as the sole alternative to divine enslavement (I.385). Self-consciousness—"if the mind will be itself"—is the condition of freedom, but the freedom Lucifer presents is paradoxically characterized by compulsion: " 'Tis made to sway." Dwelling on the ambiguities in this last phrase helps elucidate a difficult and often misinterpreted passage. Its first suggestion is one of power: For Lucifer, the mind becomes the autonomous center of its world by exerting dominion over it. But the mind is "made" or compelled to seek power, for the painful state of isolation that such autonomy demands can be endured—as Lucifer's career illustrates—only in the continual exercise of psychic domination. As applied to his disciple, the phrase takes on still more unsettling connotations. Cain's mind will be forced to "sway," to subsist in a state of painful vacillation, torn by the conflict of "parts"—human and "immortal," social and privative—that arises as his psychic moorings in sympathetic bonds are cut loose under Lucifer's tutelage. And with Cain thoroughly weakened by such inner conflict, the tempter hopes to "sway" him altogether from human to demonic allegiance. Overingenious as such a reading may seem at first, all of these connotations are borne out by Cain's developing story.

In Act I Cain is led toward a new psychic condition modeled on that of his mentor and away from the human ties that sustain him. Initially Lucifer promises Cain spiritual sympathy, as in their first exchange and, slightly later, in Lucifer's set piece contrasting a tyrannical Creator with his fraternal creatures. Lucifer's God is, however, a projection of the character that lies beneath his sophisticated and enlightened mask. His depiction ironically exposes the isolation, the torment, the compulsion to hold sway over subservient reflections which he dissimulates before Cain:

> But let him
> Sit on his vast and solitary throne,
> Creating worlds, to make eternity
> Less burthensome to his immense existence
> And unparticipated solitude.
> Let him crowd orb on orb, he is alone
> Indefinite, indissoluble tyrant.
> Could he but crush himself, 'twere the best boon
> He ever granted. But let him reign on
> And multiply himself in misery. (I.147–56)

Recognizing Lucifer's theology as self-projection is not necessarily to deny its accuracy. In the first act of *Prometheus Unbound,* Shelley portrays Jupiter and Prometheus as mutually reflexive antagonists, linked in a struggle between creator and created in which each seeks mastery over the other and both suffer restless agony. It is conceivable that the God of *Cain* is the imperialistic tyrant "wretched in his restlessness" depicted by Lucifer, but Byron gives us no way of deciding such questions, since he establishes nothing if not Lucifer's unreliability. In contrast to his parents' unfallen experience, Cain's deity remains a hidden God. What must not be lost sight of, however, is that Lucifer's words, accurate or not, help shape Cain's tragedy.

Opposed to this tyrant are his enslaved creatures, who can resort, however, to Promethean sympathy:

> Spirits and men, at least we sympathise
> And, suffering in concert, make our pangs
> Innumerable, more endurable
> By the unbounded sympathy of all
> With all!

Cain is intrigued by the prospect of sympathetic bonds which do not tie him to his family's guilt-ridden orthodoxy, and moved by Lucifer's revolutionary pose. He confesses: "Never till / Now met I aught to sympathise with me" (I.190). Even Adah, his sister-wife, "understands not / The mind which overwhelms me," he explains; " 'Tis well. I rather would consort with spirits." His words attest to the swift effect of Lucifer's pernicious rhetoric. The germinal hint of a psyche riven by internal conflict begins to take root in Cain's now alienated notion of a mind that somehow "overwhelms" its subject.

Cain's confession falls still more dangerously into line with Lucifer's strategy as the first hint of distance from Adah, who up to now has used her gentle influence to keep Cain from open conflict with their parents and siblings. Though Cain begins to resemble Manfred in choosing to "consort with spirits" rather than with "dust," his incestuous relation with Adah actually reverses that of Manfred and Astarte. Cain and Adah are twins, "Born on the same day of the same womb" (I.331), and mirror one another by nature, whereas Manfred had imposed his self-reflection on Astarte in such a manner as to destroy her. Adah expresses the contrasting reciprocal nature of her love eloquently and simply: "Bear with me what we have borne, and love me. I / Love thee" (I.362–63).

Lucifer does not underestimate the power of the first siblings' love, and he strives to separate them as quickly as he dares. His first attempt to draw Cain away on a journey, forbidding Adah to join them, prompts her to ask, "Who / Art thou that steppest between heart and heart?" (I.348–49). Cain answers for him, "a god"; Adah immediately, with a sure intuition that never leaves her, equates the spirit with "the serpent." At this point Lucifer responds with one of his most ingenious ploys. He prophesies the incest taboo that will one day forbid the love of siblings, hoping to shock Adah's generous sensibility into at least momentary outrage against the Lawgiver. She responds instead with distrust of the spirit who could utter such a thought: "Go not / Forth with this spirit. He is not of ours" (I.375–76). Adah's use of the first-person plural is very much in character. Her conception of the deity is, like Lucifer's, a self-projection: Just as she could not imagine happiness apart from a human community—"those around us"—she defines God's happiness as "diffusing joy." "What else can joy be, but the spreading joy?" (I.467–81).

Lucifer belies his Promethean set piece on "the unbounded sympathy of all" with his next attempt to distance Cain from Adah by varying his theme of division. With masterful sophistry, Lucifer turns Cain's vague memory of hearing that the "seraphs love most," while the cherubim, closer to God, "know most" (I.421), into a proof that "the higher knowledge quenches love." Far from being compatible, love and knowledge are contraries that exclude one another, as the painful lesson of Cain's parents (more painful now for Cain than for them) made clear:

> Since the all-knowing cherubim love least,
> The seraph's love can be but ignorance.
> That they are not compatible, the doom
> Of thy fond parents, for their daring, proves.
> Choose betwixt love and knowledge, since there is
> No other choice. (I.425–30)

Again, Lucifer divides to conquer. By entrapping Cain in a rhetoric of false dichotomies, he establishes a psychic rift receptive to his influence. With Cain more firmly under his spell, Lucifer will deny more categorically his universal sympathies: "Mortal, / My brotherhood's with those who have no children" (II.2.274).[16]

As one of the first of his race, Cain manifests that combination of intellectual boldness and naivete that Milton's Raphael remarked in Adam. Both qualities play into Lucifer's hands, who finds in Cain a pliant and sometimes even eager disciple. After the tempter contrasts the tyrant god with his created servant, Cain attests to his skill: "Thou speakest to me of things which long have swum / In visions through my thought" (I.167). But Lucifer is not merely Cain's alter ego. He utters what for Cain has been unutterable and inconceivable; his dissatisfaction has inspired "visions" which have not formed into distinct thoughts. Lucifer does not simply confirm or encourage ideas which Cain has repressed; he in fact introduces his own ideas where Cain has felt only dim, formless desires and fears. Lucifer's method is as much Socratic as sophistical. Like Socrates, he poses as a midwife of unborn ideas when in fact the conceptions are his own, often expressed in the form of myths.[17]

Unlike Socrates, however, Lucifer argues for wholly self-serving ends. We have noted his tendency, allied to those of Manfred and Oswald, to dwell on yet another dichotomy, that of master and slave. Once more he abandons his pose of fraternal solidarity when he offers to teach Cain "true knowledge" only upon condition: "That / Thou dost fall down and worship me, thy Lord" (I.302–3). The "Master of Spirits" can never rest from recruiting new servants. But at this point the tempter's sway is not so firmly established as he could wish. Although Cain is far less sophisticated in his dealings with spirits than Manfred (who had learned much to his own cost), he shares Manfred's fierce pride: "I never / As yet have bowed unto my father's God . . . Why should I bow to thee?" (I.310–14). Lucifer saves face for the moment with a characteristic rhetorical ploy, drawing a false dichotomy from Cain's answer: "He who bows not to him has bowed to me" (I.317). In this case the Devil comes near to proleptically quoting Scripture for his purpose: "He that is not with me is against me" (Matthew 12:30). Thomas Arnold accordingly found this line a moral oasis in the desert of Byron's apostasy: "There is something to me almost awful in meeting suddenly, in the works of such a man, so great and solemn a truth."[18] But it is precisely such an either/or conception of "truth" that Byron attacks in his characterization of Lucifer. The theology of Byron's devil all too often resembles that of a Dr. Arnold sermonizing from the other side of the fence. His reasoning is antithetical but falls critically short of dialectic. He maintains the polarities of orthodox religion—the Heaven and Hell of *Paradise Lost*—and merely reverses their positive and negative charges. His dichotomized view of the cosmos leaves no middle ground for an unaligned humanity—skeptical or indifferent—standing on earth and bending to neither God nor the Adversary. Lucifer's pedagogical method similarly relies on blinding Cain to the possibility of mediation, and confronting him instead with one arbitrary set of contraries after another. Tired of merely debating, however, Lucifer now begins pressing Cain to accompany, or rather "follow" (I.322), him on an exploration of cosmic mysteries. The voyage is calculated to aggravate the psychic unrest, division, and disassociation that will reduce Cain to a more willing (though in many ways unknowing) follower of Lucifer.

The journey into space which constitutes the second act of the drama forms a second, more intense phase in the seduction of Cain. The act opens with an allusion to Eve's temptation in *Paradise Lost* (which also hinged on the separation of lovers): "I tread on air and sink not; yet I fear / To sink." Cain's words (heightened by an intentionally uncomfortable line break) recall Eve's dream foreshadowing her temptation: "Forthwith up to the clouds / With him I flew . . . suddenly / My guide was gone, and I, methought, sank down" (V.86–93). The allusion underscores both Lucifer's resemblance to Milton's devil and Cain's unwitting repetition of his mother's career. Both Eve and Cain are, of course, tempted with the promise of greater knowledge, and perhaps the "pleasing fear" that Lucifer inspires in Adah (I.408) owes something to Satan's reaction to Eve's beauty: "Not terrible, though terror be in Love, / And beauty, not approached by stronger hate" (IX.490–91).

Byron uses intertextuality in Act II for purposes of contrast as well. He inverts a particularly rich literary topos when Lucifer, after remarking on the earth's dwindling during their ascent, moralizes on Cain's comparison of its distant sparkling to the dim glow of "fireworms": "Thou hast seen worms and world, / Each bright and sparkling. What dost think of them?" (II.1.126–27). In the same manner Scipio learns to scorn empire when his grandfather Africanus shows him the smallness of the earth "*de excelso*" ("from high above") in the *Somnium Scipionis*; Dante smiles on "*l'aiuola*" (the "little threshing floor" of the earth) shown to him by Beatrice from the sphere of the fixed stars in the *Paradiso;* Troilus laughs at his mortal woes on "this little spot of erthe" seen from the same sphere in his soul's ascent at the end of *Troilus and Criseyde.*[19] But each of these celestial voyages provides its protagonist with a transcendent perspective from which the earth appears as a necessary place of trials preparing the virtuous for eternal life—in Cicero's no less than in the Christian visions—and enmeshed in a grand providential scheme. Lucifer, on the contrary, presents the earth in such a manner as to make mortality meaningless and immortality uncertain.

Cain's journey begins not in an ordered, coherent cosmos but in "The Abyss of Space." The Abyss both emblematizes and, by heightening his sense of metaphysical dislocation, helps to create the widening abyss within Cain's psyche. The second stage of the voyage takes place in "Hades," where Lucifer shows Cain "The phantasm of the world, of which thy world / Is but the wrack" (II.1.152). Manfred's crippling past was imaged by the "burning wreck of a demolish'd world" (I.1.45), a wandering hell in space that reflected his psychic torment. It is in this spirit that Lucifer takes Cain through space to Hades, confronting him with a past that will blight the present and render him a metaphysical exile. As a vision of what Lucifer claims is "the history / Of past and present and of future worlds" (II.1.23–24), the voyage contrasts with Adam's ascent of the "Hill / Of Paradise the highest" (XI.377–78), where Michael shows him in a vision the history of his race. Michael reveals the world's future in order to temper Adam's postlapsarian despair with hope; Lucifer shows Cain visions of a vastly greater past in order to augment his despair, presenting an earth that had fallen even before the Fall.

As with Lucifer's depiction of God, the question as to whether the spectacles Cain sees in Hades are illusions or actual fossils of a former world is left open. In the preface Byron is studiously ambiguous on this point: "The assertion of Lucifer that the pre-Adamite world was also peopled by rational beings much more intelligent than man and proportionately powerful to the mammoth, etc., etc., is, of course, a poetical fiction to help him to make out his case." Is the "fiction" solely attributable to Byron, or does he mean that the father of lies invents the myth to help develop his "case" within the drama? Although the text is as silent on this point as on the accuracy of Lucifer's inverted theology, it shows clearly that, however he has amassed the shadowy artifacts, he uses them not for enlightening but for "depressing" Cain. Lucifer's bitter speech on his gallery of "phantoms" is calculated to settle upon Cain the burden of a past which really has nothing to do with his own world:

> I show thee what thy predecessors are
> And what they were thou feelest, in degree
> Inferior as thy petty feelings and
> Thy pettier portion of th'immortal part
> Of high intelligence and earthly strength.
> What ye in common have with what they had
> Is life, and what ye shall have—death. The rest
> Of your poor attributes is such as suits
> Reptiles engendered out of the subsiding
> Slime of a mighty universe, crushed into
> A scarcely-yet shaped planet, peopled with
> Things whose enjoyment was to be in blindness—
> A Paradise of Ignorance, from which
> Knowledge was barred as poison. But behold
> What these superior beings are or were;
> Or if it irk thee, turn thee back and till
> The earth, thy task. (II.2.89–105)

One cannot easily reconcile the satirist of this passage with the self-proclaimed Promethean ally of mankind. Lucifer withholds any hint of the nature of death—"What these superior beings are or were"—and augments Cain's growing sense of psychic disintegration by now characterizing his immortal "part" as an insignificant "portion" of what his forerunners possessed.

Cain's response, the wish to remain in Hades, is in effect suicidal: "I am sick of all / That dust has shown me; let me dwell in shadows" (II.2.107–8). The drama opened with Cain's discontent, but it was still balanced with hope (if hope only of eventual resignation): "Abel, I'm sick at heart, but it will pass" (I.58). His malaise has now become a sickness unto death. Cain's reaction parallels that of Keats's Endymion, who also views the remnants of an antique world in the course of a supernatural journey:

> . . . mouldering scrolls,
> Writ in the tongue of heaven, by those souls

> Who first were on the earth; and sculptures rude
> In ponderous stone, developing the mood
> Of ancient Nox;—then skeletons of man,
> Of beast, behemoth, and leviathan,
> And elephant, and eagle, and huge jaw
> Of nameless monster. A cold leaden awe
> These secrets struck into him; and unless
> Dian had chaced away that heaviness,
> He might have died.[20]

One might be inclined to dismiss this parallel as incidental, since Endymion's journey is often read as inspired (like those described by Cicero and Dante) by the Platonic vision of the soul's ascent from sensual to ideal love, a contrary to Cain's voyage of abasement. But Keats's rich and confused romance is sometimes an adaptation, sometimes a critique of the Platonic myth of the maturing soul learning to despise the earth and earthly attachments. Byron and Keats are both suspicious of a teaching which, in the name of a mystical, ineffable transcendence, would alienate men and women from human sympathy, a doubt often expressed in *Endymion:*

> There never liv'd a mortal man, who bent
> His appetite beyond his natural sphere
> But starv'd and died.[21]

Many related passages in *Endymion* herald what might be termed Keats's anti-Platonism, his criticism of supernatural experiences which poison mortal life without replacing it, in such works as "La Belle Dame Sans Merci" and "Lamia."[22] Byron, who never tired of satirizing Platonic love in his letters and in *Don Juan*—

> Oh Plato! Plato! you have paved the way,
> With your confounded fantasies, to more
> Immoral conduct by the fancied sway
> Your system feigns o'er the controulless core
> Of human hearts, than all the long array
> Of poets and romancers:—you're a bore (I.116)—

attacks such a myth of transcendence more systematically (if more obliquely) in *Cain*, where Lucifer adopts a Socratic pose for Satanic ends. Lucifer's misguiding cynicism should not be mistaken for Byron's mature skepticism. Those who read *Cain* as the vehicle for a sympathetic Lucifer compare his bleak worldview to such poems as "Darkness" and "Prometheus,"[23] but both lyrics were written in 1817, when Byron was, with *Manfred*, still in the process of divesting the Satanic stance that marks the heroes of his earlier poetry. *Cain*, however, is contemporaneous with *Don Juan*, which (as W. H. Auden has phrased it) is "not a satire but a comedy," persuading its reader to accept human "contradictions with good humor as facts of life against which it is useless to rebel."[24] Adah alone in the drama intuits the need for a comic view of acceptance, but she is too weak or perhaps too unsophisticated to retain her hold on Cain, who falls victim instead to Lucifer's corrosive satire.

Cain grows disoriented by inhuman distance from the earth and dejected by phantoms of a superhuman past. The loss of his natural perspective is only the first penalty for his violation of metaphysical borders. Through consorting with the transgressing spirit Lucifer (who embodies border violation), he learns to confound the regions of Earth, Space, and Hades, and to superimpose the past upon the present. His literal dislocation is underscored by the disjunction between the naturalistic stage of Acts I and III and the fantastic, purely mental one of Act II. Cain strives with diminishing success to keep his world picture intact. When Lucifer expatiates on the greater earth of the past—"Oh what a beautiful world it *was*"—Cain replies, "And is" (II.2.124–25), and attempts, "agitated," to quiet the tempter's growing insinuations against Abel: "Here we are in thy world; speak not of mine" (II.2.357). His resistance yields altogether, however, to Lucifer's skillful embedding of his divisive conceptions through a final rhetorical onslaught.

Lucifer opens by resuming his attack on human love. When Cain defends the beauty of his earth, for all its newly apparent insignificance, by rhapsodizing on Adah, Lucifer returns to his Juvenalian mode to speak against "frail mortality" and "delusion" (II.2.245f.). When Cain asks suspiciously whether the spirit loves at all, he answers with a rhetorical question—"What does thy God love?"—and then with a statement both conditional and vague:

thou canst not see if *I* love
Or no, except some vast and gen'ral purpose,
To which particular things must melt like snows.
(II.2.313–15)

Adah, he continues, is one of the particulars that will age, lose its brightness, and die: "I pity thee who lovest what must perish." "And I thee," Cain replies, "who lov'st nothing."

Now Lucifer finally despairs of breaking—at least through words alone—the strength of Cain's love, and attempts instead to induce hatred. Shifting his tone from satire to sarcasm, he answers Cain with another leading question: "And thy brother— / Sits he not near thy heart?" Cain continues to bear his part well in the exchange until Lucifer once more exploits the naivete of one who cannot distinguish vague emotions from purposeful thoughts:

[Lucifer.] *His* sacrifices are acceptable.
Cain. So be they. Wherefore speak to me of this?
Lucifer. Because thou hast thought of this ere now.

Cain has again been led to encounter a rift within his psyche, graphically represented here by aposiopesis: "And if / I *have* thought, why recall a thought that—" (II.2.355–56).

Bent on widening that rift, Lucifer intensifies his myth of a cosmos divided between matched and continually warring antagonists, Jehovah and himself: "we reign / Together, but our dwellings are asunder." When Cain asks, "Are ye not as brethren," the devil archly replies, "Art thou not Abel's brother," and again confesses that "to reign" he would indeed go on "jarring and turning space to misery" (II.2.375f.). Finally Lucifer forestalls Cain's questions by declaring him too weak to comprehend the principle of the cosmos, or rather, in Lucifer's ultimate dichotomy, "the great double mys'tries, the *two principles*" (II.2.404). He has already stated, in language parodying the phrasing of Wordsworth's "Tintern Abbey," that evil "must still roll on the same, / A part of all things" (II.2.235–36).[25] Now he leaves Cain ignorant of where to locate good, where evil, but convinced that the two are opposed, fragmenting existence into parts, and engaged in eternal, omnipresent conflict.

When Cain tries to refute Lucifer's dualism (as Manfred had countered Arimanes, the Manichean evil principle, himself) by asserting the devil's subordination to God, Lucifer protests with a concluding set piece:

> No! by heav'n, which He
> Holds, and the abyss and the immensity
> Of worlds and life, which I hold with him—No!
> I have a victor, true, but no superior.
> Homage he has from all, but none from me.
> I battle it against him, as I battled
> In highest heav'n. Through all eternity
> And the unfathomable gulfs of Hades
> And the interminable realms of space
> And the infinity of endless ages,
> All, all, will I dispute. And world by world
> And star by star and universe by universe
> Shall tremble in the balance, till the great
> Conflict shall cease, if ever it shall cease,
> Which it ne'er shall, till he or I be quenched.
> And what can quench our immortality
> Or mutual and irrevocable hate? (II.2.426–42)

Lucifer's last speech captures his Satanic essence. He reveals his existence to be one of eternal, irrevocable hate, endless struggle impelled by a will to mastery and empire. Tormented by the restless consciousness of his defeat, and justifying his claim to power only through endlessly continued strife, he leaves Cain with words designed to nurture a parallel restlessness and conflict in the mind of his disciple:

> One good gift has the fatal apple giv'n—
> Your reason; let it not be over-swayed
> By tyrannous threats to force you into faith
> 'Gainst all external sense and inward feelings.
> Think and endure and form an inner world
> In your own bosom, where the outward fails.
> So shall you nearer be the spiritual
> Nature, and war triumphant with your own. (II.2.459–66)

From the drama's first moments Cain has sought some justification for his inherited Fall. Lucifer provides it in celebrating a "reason" that exists by opposing tyranny through building itself an enclosed autonomy. Cain is again urged to conceive of his self in terms of division, to form a private world opposed to the outward world he shares with Adah and with the rest of his family. This inner world, however, is to be modeled on Lucifer's picture of the cosmos: one of struggle between a "spiritual nature" and a weaker nature significantly referred to as Cain's "own." Isolated from others and divided within himself, Cain would in turn become a Satanic figure, trapped in an impossibly autonomous stance, torn within by a hateful siege of contraries.

Before leaving Lucifer altogether it may seem worthwhile to speculate on what would have become of Cain without him. I have noted throughout Cain's susceptibility to his mentor's suggestions, which were not in any case required to make Cain chafe at his lost birthright, refuse to kneel to Jehovah, or suspect some disorder lodged at the heart of things. And readers continue to view Cain as an incipient Lucifer, awaiting less a guide than a mere catalyst. Such interpretations will have a great deal of trouble accounting for the elaborateness, the deviousness, and the blatant contradictions informing Lucifer's teachings, all of which must seem rather gratuitous if Cain is not misled but merely encouraged. And the Cain who murders Abel should be contrasted with Cain as he originally appears. Pride, skepticism, and defiance are traits that throughout his career Byron would hardly condemn. Vacillation, spite, gullibility, and purposeless violence are not, however, much applauded in Byron's canon, and even the brooding and recklessness of his early heroes find little room in the later poems. Cain may show the makings of an intellectual hero, but he swiftly becomes an intellectual victim instead. What path he might have taken is, of course, an unanswerable question. One wonders in vain, for example, how Adah's naive, healthy ethic of sympathy might have affected Cain's intellectual development. Byron's Juan discovers that every Paradise is both preceded and succeeded by a fall: his romance with Dona Inez framed by his parents' and his lover's divorces, his idyll with Haidée set in motion by a shipwreck and disrupted by the vengeance of an enraged pirate—whose characterization satirizes not only the Regency bourgeois father but the wrathful corsairs of Byron's early tales as well. Juan, however, emerges from these lessons not in despair, but with a maturing sense of comic acceptance gradually approaching that of the narrator. But Cain's development is not, like Juan's, left unmolested; his original character is rapidly and thoroughly deformed by a cunning seducer for ends of his own.

The deformation of his character emerges in Act III, which begins with Cain once more among his family but no longer of them. Sensing his heightened discontent, Adah laments Cain's obsession with their disinheritance, and wonders why they cannot make another Paradise: "Where'er thou art, I feel not / The want of this so much regretted Eden" (III.39–40). A true daughter of the repentant Eve, Adah echoes her mother's reconciling words to Adam on their expulsion from Eden: "Thou to me / Art all things under Heav'n, all places thou" (XII.617–18). But it is not for Cain and Adah to approach through love, "by name to come call'd Charity," the "paradise within" vouchsafed their parents at the end of *Paradise Lost*, the contrary to the inner hell that Lucifer would bequeath to Adam's son. Cain has begun to lose his former character altogether, and his heartless condemnation of his parents—"They sinned, then let them die!"—is correctly interpreted by Adah as an intruding, alien conception:

> Thou hast not spoken well, nor is that thought
> Thy own, but of the spirit who was with thee. (III.77–78)

More than rancor, however, lies behind Cain's impatience to see death's entrance into his world—the drama's ultimate, tragic border violation. Lucifer had darkly hinted, in the course of their metaphysical voyage, that "It may be death leads to the highest knowledge" (II.2.164). The suggestion strikes deeply, for in "highest knowledge" Cain stakes his chance to mend the psychic chasm skillfully opened by his tempter. Channeled by the irritation with Abel which Lucifer has fanned, however, Cain's quest for the mystery of death leads instead to the irreversible widening of that rift through murder.

Like Wordsworth's Oswald, Lucifer draws recruits for his intellectual empire with rhetoric and binds them to him through an act of repetition. Lucifer's last speech makes clear that, even if we cannot identify his past precisely with that of Milton's Satan, the two devils share a history marked by the first Fall, a defeated act of rebellion against God that frustrates, haunts, and impels them toward aggressive conquest. Satan had, in *Paradise Lost*, brought about the repetition of his rebellion and Fall by leading Eve into committing the first mortal sin. In *Cain* as in *The Borderers* the Romantic seducer learns from his original that, while words can only guide the deformation of character, a deed can effect it in a fatal moment of self-betrayal. Cain's crime, like Marmaduke's, is designed to change its perpetrator into a weaker, subservient version of the tempter on whose crime it is modeled—a tempter whose own character is modeled (in *Cain* quite closely) on that of a prior figure. Cain's fate is ironic both in itself and as a textual phenomenon. Plagued by his parents' Fall, he finishes by reenacting it, both within the context of his own drama and on an intertextual level as well.

When Abel approaches, Cain grows troubled by the changes that now distinguish him more than ever from his brother. He tries to warn Abel off, explaining (more truly than he knows) that the "overpow'ring mysteries of space" and the "overwhelming" past worlds have rendered him "Unfit for mortal converse" (III.179–84). Like his mentor, he feels both isolated and interminably restless in his new consciousness of an alienated, fragmented self: "Nothing can calm me more" (III.204). The scene proceeds inexorably to the murder, which, plotted by Lucifer, seems to Cain the unforeseeable (or unimaginable) accident of a moment. The noncommittal dedication Cain first makes, "standing erect" over the sacrifice Abel has induced him to perform (III.245–79), has been justly praised for its proud humanism,[26] and its cool skepticism should be contrasted to Lucifer's defiant rant. But the speech is Cain's last heroic moment. Though he briefly recovers, in the clarity of ritual, his originally proud but generous character, the apparent favoritism of Jehovah's response to the sacrifices—which Cain had in fact discounted in his dedication—coupled with Abel's frustrating single-mindedness, launches him into an intensified fit of dislocation and rage. He fells Abel, and the complex nature of Romantic self-consciousness is dramatically portrayed in his shocked reaction to his brother's suddenly prostrate form:

> *(A long pause. Looking slowly round.)*
> Where am I? Alone! Where's Abel? Where
> Cain? Can it be that I am he?

Cain has been read as an allegory of the artist's "spiritual awakening" to a new "intensity of consciousness," much as *The Borderers* has been described as depicting the birth of "genuine consciousness of self."[27]

But Cain's new consciousness, like Marmaduke's, is that of a divided, disintegrated self, and its intensity is that of torment. The murderous act guarantees his psychic isolation—"Alone!"—and therefore renders Cain not autonomous but radically incomplete: "Where's Abel? Where / Cain?" Here again we can see the fundamental parallel between the English Romantic poet's conception of self-consciousness and that of Hegel in the *Phenomenology*. "Genuine" self-consciousness can never be autonomous, for it can neither emerge nor subsist in isolation. Cain's internalized struggle against "tyrannous threats" through his resort to Lucifer's "inner world" has led, as does the master-slave struggle in Hegel, to a consciousness only of the self's poverty in its unmet need for recognition. Far from attaining consciousness of self, Cain has merely inherited the pseudo-autonomy of his seducer, with the restless torment that informs the last exchange of the drama:

> [Cain]. Oh Abel!
> Adah. Peace be with him.
> Cain. But with *me!*

In Cain's reaction to his brother's murder we begin to understand the compulsive imperialism of his seducer, who continually battles against the consciousness of his own self-alienating crime.

Cain's surviving relatives return to the scene and react in a manner that objectifies the isolation he has purchased with Abel's murder. Eve—who incidentally evokes the literary precedent of Macbeth's murder of Duncan, echoed here as in *The Borderers* and *Manfred*, by remarking on Cain's "hands / Incarnadine" (III.398–99)—utters, like Wordsworth's Idonea after Herbert's murder, a curse that takes instant effect. She condemns Cain to the fate Lucifer has shaped him: exile from man and nature and continued inner torment, imaged by nightmares, pursuit, dread, and hallucinations (II.419–43). Adam realizes that the curse is superfluous, and remarks simply: "I curse him not; his spirit be his curse" (III.449). In his frightened reaction to Abel's corpse—"This is a vision, else I am become / The native of another and worse world"—Cain ironically reveals the double effect of his deed, for the introduction of death has rendered his world not less but more meaningless, and him an exile from it. It is his realization of self-betrayal, not the heralding of spiritual birth, that informs his hopeless words: "I am awake at last—a dreary dream / Has maddened me; but he shall ne'er awake" (III.378–89).

Shelley called *Cain* "apocalyptic," but was writing of its impact—"it is a revelation not before communicated to man"—and not of its argument.[28] For what distinguishes *Cain* most from Shelley's *Prometheus Unbound*, which opens along similar thematic, formal, and narrative lines, is its lack of a resolution which, in the context of mental theater, could only be apocalyptic. Blake, whose Romanticism was closer to Shelley's than to Byron's, emphasized precisely such a lack in *Cain* in his own brief essay in mental theater, "The Ghost of Abel: A Revelation in the Visions of Jehovah," addressed "To LORD BYRON in the Wilderness."

Blake's visionary scene criticizes Byron for failing to resolve the dramatic argument of *Cain* in his failure to meet the imaginative challenge posed by *Paradise Lost*. Byron had concluded *Manfred* by falling back on the defiant self-torment of Milton's Satan; having rejected Satan's stance, and exposed its untenability in *Cain*, Byron approaches and then draws back from the opposite pitfall of having Adah re-humanize Cain through a love that would evoke too strongly the reconciliation of Milton's Adam and Eve. Adah's pleas must fall on deaf ears if Cain is to avoid simply adopting his father's obedience in place of Lucifer's defiance. Blake's ironic criticism is that Byron has fallen victim to the penchant for false dichotomies manifested by his own character Lucifer. To demonstrate this, Blake picks up the drama at the moment of the reaction of Cain's family to Abel's death, and gives us the Miltonic resolution that Byron neither imitated nor moved beyond:

> Adam— Father of Mercies
> That appearest to my Spiritual Vision: Eve seest thou also.
> Eve—I see him plainly with my Minds Eye. I also see Abel living:
> Tho terribly afflicted as We also are. yet Jehovah sees him
> Alive & not Dead: were it not better to believe Vision
> With all our might & strength tho we are fallen & lost

> Adam—Eve thou hast spoken truly. let us kneel before his feet.[29]

Adam's "Spiritual Vision" here is not Blakean "four-fold" vision but akin rather to the redemptive vision inspired by Michael in *Paradise Lost,* and the act of contrition is Miltonic as well:

> What can we better do, than to the place
> Repairing where he jud'gd us, prostrate fall
> Before him reverent, and there confess. (X.1086–89)

Blake points up the limitations—"Tho terribly afflicted," "tho we are fallen & lost"—that made a Miltonic resolution, with a redeemed Cain, unpalatable to Byron, but Blake goes further and presents his alternative vision. The first, Miltonic resolution merely allows humankind to live in a world of dichotomies, and does not pretend to reconcile the apparent opposites themselves. Blake embodies the implicit, finally irrepressible contradictions in Abel and Satan, who refuse to remain hidden in the underworld. The Ghost of Abel rises up unable to forgive Cain—"My Soul in fumes of Blood / Cries for Vengeance"—and gives place to Satan, who emerges from Abel's grave as the divisive principle, and demands revenge on Jehovah through the "Human Blood" of Christ: "Thou shalt Thyself be Sacrificed to Me thy God on Calvary." The reflexive contraries of Cain and Abel, Jehovah and Satan, life and death are finally challenged and broken through by Jehovah, who speaks prophetically:

> Such is my Will. *Thunders*
> that thou thyself go to Eternal Death
> In Self Annihilation even till Satan Self-subdued Put off Satan.

"Self Annihilation" is the process by which even Satan can at last put off his eternal torment, but it is a concept foreign to Byron's *Cain.*

The mark branded on Cain's forehead is, like Eve's curse, an externalization of his psychic condition: "It burns / My brow, but naught to that which is within it" (III.300–301). Nevertheless, his fate is something of an open question; if we can entertain a measure of hope for Marmaduke at the end of *The Borderers,* even after he has effectively rejected Idonea, we can be less sure that Cain, still accompanied by Adah (who refuses to abandon him), will be unable to at length free himself from Lucifer's influence. Cain's fate (which, like Marmaduke's, is still debated among critics) is one of several unresolved dilemmas which Byron passes on to the reader. Is Lucifer, for all his ill intentions, essentially accurate as a *philosophe;* is history providential or cyclical; is Adah's intuitively generous view of the cosmos and human nature viable?

These are questions which the mature Byron will not answer for his reader. He delineates complex problems in *Cain* with intense dramatic clarity, but he recommends neither Milton's traditional nor Lucifer's antithetical solutions. It is enough, he feels, to explore and represent the intricate dilemmas of influence, self-consciousness, and metaphysical dislocation without pretending to solve them. Blake's criticism would not have troubled Byron; his reply would probably have been to ridicule the complexities and obscurities of Blake's system as he did those of Coleridge's:

> Explaining Metaphysics to the Nation—
> I wish he would explain his explanation.

Byron's surprise at his contemporaries' devout fulminations against *Cain* was not disingenuous; as he wrote Murray, *Cain* is "hardy and speculative" but nothing like an atheistical tract. If anything, the effect of *Cain* should be the reverse of propagandistic: In his "metaphysical" drama, Byron casts suspicion on metaphysical rhetoric. Lucifer's cant is finally no more acceptable—and no more benign—than that of a less shadowy imperialist like, say, Castlereagh. But the comparison of real and imagined evil leads to another remark of Byron's on the subject of his drama's corrupting influence: "*who* was ever altered by a poem?"[30] Unlike Blake and Shelley, Byron did not view poetry as a socially regenerative force, and did not feel called upon to supply the reader with the sort of redemptive system that Blake drew on in "The Ghost of Abel." The genial skepticism of *Don Juan* is Byron's human alternative to apocalyptic vision.

5

On the Borders of *Heaven and Earth*

The Deluge is read, in traditional Christian typology, as an antetype of the Apocalypse: The earth's first destruction by water foreshadows its ultimate purgation by burning, as the sacrament of baptism prefigures the spirit's baptism by fire.[1] Such associations underlie the image of the Deluge in most English poetry before the Romantic period; Donne, for example, brings all of them to bear in Holy Sonnet 5, "I am a little world made cunningly":

> Pour new seas in my eyes, that so I might
> Drown my world with my weeping earnestly,
> Or wash it if it must be drowned no more.
> But O, it must be burnt! Alas the fire
> Of lust and envy have burnt in heretofore,
> And made it fouler; let their flames retire,
> And burn me, O Lord, with a fiery zeal
> Of thee and of Thy house, which doth in eating heal.

Byron's mystery of the Flood is written against this tradition. Byron reads the Flood backwards rather than forwards; he presents it as a shadow of the Fall of Man and evokes apocalyptic connotations only to reject them. As in *Cain*, he portrays humankind suffering the remembrance of one Fall—

> the flaming sword
> Which chased the first-born out of Paradise
> Still flashes in the angelic hands (1050–52)—

even as a repetition of the Fall takes place. The God of *Heaven and Earth* is not the Judge of Revelation but the incomprehensible creator and destroyer of Job, which inspires the drama's sublime imagery as Genesis inspires its action.

The contemporary reception of *Heaven and Earth* leads one to question the twentieth-century tradition of dismissal and neglect. Hazlitt called it, in *The Spirit of the Age*, the "best" of Byron's dramas: While *Manfred* was too much a projection of Byron's personality, in his last mystery "the space between Heaven and Earth . . . seems to fill his Lordship's imagination; and the Deluge, which he has so finely described, may be said to have drowned all his own idle humours."[2] Goethe was deeply impressed with *Heaven and Earth*, and, according to Crabb Robinson, preferred it above any other of Byron's "serious poems."[3] And two contemporary reviewers, Francis Jeffrey and John Wilson, described the mystery in terms that attest to its power while suggesting a critical approach which does that power justice.

Wilson reviewed *Heaven and Earth* in *Blackwoods* in January 1823, a few months after its publication, and characterized it as "dark and massy, like a block of marble." The simile encapsulates Wilson's appreciation of Byron's ability to compress violently mingling contraries in dramatic form: "passion seen blending in vain union between the spirits of mortal and immortal, love shrieking on the wild shore of death, and all the thoughts that ever agitated human hearts dashed and distracted beneath the blackness and amidst the howling of commingled earth and heaven."[4] Jeffrey, writing a month later in the *Edinburgh Review*, found in Byron's mystery "more poetry and music . . . than in any of his dramatic writings since Manfred." Like Wilson, Jeffrey was impressed by the dialectical intensity of the drama's thematic movement. "It is truly, in every sense of the word, a meeting of 'Heaven and Earth': angels are seen ascending and descending, and the windows of the sky are opened to deluge the face of nature. We have an impassioned picture of the strong and devoted attachment inspired in the daughters of men by angel forms . . . There is a like conflict of the passions as of the elements—all wild, chaotic, uncontrollable, fatal—but there is a discordant harmony in all this—."[5]

The reactions of Wilson and Jeffrey, however impressionistic they sound to modern ears, capture as no later criticism has the principal thematic concern of Byron's last work of mental theater: the complex violation of spatial, metaphysical, and psychic borders. Border violation figures in Wordsworth's *Borderers* and in Byron's *Manfred* and *Cain* as the thematic accompaniment to a drama of seduction; in *Heaven and Earth* it becomes a dramatic subject in itself. The mystery portrays effects rather than causes, and withholds even the retrospective glimpses of past actions that underlie the characterization of Manfred. The past is equally omnipresent in *Heaven and Earth,* but as a collective past shared by all the characters, a succession of prior falls—Satan's, Eve's, Adam's, Cain's—that leads inexorably toward the latest and most cataclysmic of all.

Heaven and Earth is concerned not with action so much as with reaction—the reaction of mankind to the Fall, the reactions of its characters to their fallen predicament. Byron appropriately described it as a "lyrical drama . . . *choral* and mystical—and a sort of Oratorio on a sacred subject."[6] Perhaps inspired by *Prometheus Unbound,* Byron revives the chorus—a conventional device for commenting on dramatic action—with brilliant effect, and the central characters most often adopt the lyric voice, crying out at events which they cannot alter. But the drama does not founder, as later would Arnold's lyrical monodrama, *Empedocles,* in closed subjectivity. Byron brings dramatic intensity to the internal debate of Japhet, Noah's divinely chosen but unregenerate son, and to the clashes of his beliefs with those of the angels and their mortal lovers, the "offspring of Cain." The inexorable approach of the Deluge adds immediate relevance to the ideological conflict and underscores its dramatic progression with a steadily building suspense. In another respect, however, the "lyrical" aspect of the drama is less successful, as Byron varies the strong and eclectic blank-verse measure of *Cain* with a great deal of lyrical verse which, again, seems directly inspired by *Prometheus Unbound,* but which rarely captures the sureness or the beauty of Shelley's lyrical style.[7]

Heaven and Earth is also a departure in that Byron no longer grounds his poetic argument on allusions to Shakespeare and Milton, but draws instead on his own works of mental theater. The subject of *Heaven and Earth* can itself be found in germ in Manfred's apostrophe, on the eve of his death, to the setting sun:

> the idol
> Of early nature, and the vigorous race

> Of undiseased mankind, the giant sons
> Of the embrace of angels with a sex
> More beautiful than they, which did draw down
> The erring spirits who can ne'er return. (III.2.174–79)

Like Manfred, the angels and their mortal lovers in *Heaven and Earth* are doomed through engaging in forbidden sexual union, and like Cain, the mortals (who are, moreover, his direct descendants) fall through choosing to consort with spirits rather than with humankind. Interwoven with the story of the angels and their consorts is that of Japhet, who shares Manfred's haunted and brooding consciousness, and who struggles like Manfred against an irrevocable destiny, though Japhet is fated, paradoxically, not to be damned but to be saved.

Heaven and Earth opens, as does *Manfred*, with a midnight "invocation" of spirits as Anah and Aholibamah, Cain's granddaughters, call to their seraphic lovers. Anah's name underscores the family resemblance in her gentle, loving nature to that of Adah in *Cain*, while she inherits her desire to consort with a spiritual being rather than with "dust" (13) from Cain himself. Although Anah settles for sensual rather than intellectual companionship—"With me thou canst not sympathize, / Except in love" (52–53)—her dilemma is Cain's, the inner conflict aroused in a mortal by traffic with immortal spirits:

> Great is their love who love in sin and fear;
> And such, I feel, are waging in my heart,
> A war unworthy. (67–69)

She feels compelled to hide a love that, again like her forefather's relation with Lucifer, alienates her from God: "I love our God less since his angel loved me" (12). She does not resist, however, the attraction of the immortal for the mortal, the unfallen for the "Adamite" continually aware of the Fall:

> For sorrow is our element;
> Delight
> An Eden kept afar from sight,
> Though sometimes with our visions blent.

In union with the angel Anah finds forgetfulness, however transient, of her fallen condition, with an intensification of the Edenic feelings "blent"—one of many terms for interpenetration and mingling used by Byron throughout the work—with her dreams of a deathless world.

Aholibamah has been described, due to her pride and her open defiance of God's commands, as a "true descendant of Cain,"[8] though it would be more accurate to call her a child of Lucifer. Like Byron's devil (and like Milton's before him), she claims an immortal nature that renders her equal to strife with the omnipotent, and worthy of her angel's love:

> Change us he may, but not o'erwhelm; we are
>   Of as eternal essence, and must war
> With him if he will war with us: with *thee*
> I can share all things, even immortal sorrow. (120–23)

She adopts many of the Satanic gestures characteristic of Manfred and Lucifer, and the beginning of her invocation, following Anah's, is marked by the language of mastery and struggle and by a bitter post-lapsarian consciousness:

>   Wheresoe'er
> Thou rulest in the upper air—
> Or warring with the spirits who may dare
>   Dispute with him
>   Who made all empire, empire; or recalling
> Some wandering star, which shoots through the abyss
>   Whose tenants dying, while their world is falling
>   Share the dim destiny of clay in this. (82–89)

Anah desires only to escape the pain of mortality through melting in the embrace of an immortal. Aholibamah, however, imagines her lover as the embodiment of her own craving for power, and portrays him as a master of cosmic destinies, not a servant of God. The preposition in "warring *with* the spirits" is intentionally ambiguous, for although Anah believes the seraphs descend from heaven, Aholibamah (like the Brontë heroines she in some ways anticipates) prefers to envision her lover as a fallen angel. However the line is read, she depicts the war between God and Satan, like Byron's Lucifer, as a dispute between equally imperialistic antagonists. The "wandering star" that mirrors her fallen world draws two related emblems from Byron's earlier metaphysical dramas into a single, complex figure. It recalls the "wandering hell" that ruled Manfred's destiny and imaged his psychic anguish, as well as the "phantasm" of a greater, previously fallen earth with which Lucifer tormented Cain in their voyage through the "abyss" of space. Aholibamah inherits both the apparent strength of Manfred and Lucifer and the false autonomy that underlies their essential weakness.

After deftly characterizing the sisters through their invocations, Byron renders the angels (named, after the pseudepigraphical Book of Enoch, Samiasa and Azaziel) somewhat indistinct, giving them a shadowy, sublime aspect. Their metaphysical allegiance is nebulous as well. Although they do not (as Aholibamah would have it) follow Satan, the angels forsake God without hesitation when forced to choose between their earthly desires and His commands. The verse from Genesis which Byron takes as one of his epigraphs is suitably ambiguous: "And it came to pass . . . that the sons of God saw the daughters of men that they were fair; and they took them wives of all which they chose." The "Sons of God" can be read two ways. Milton considers them the "just" sons of Seth in Adam's vision of biblical history in *Paradise Lost* (XI.573–97), but draws elsewhere on the other traditional reading (adopted by Byron) in contrasting the Archangel Raphael's "unlibidinous" admiration for Eve's nakedness to the license of the later "Sons of God" who would be "Enamour'd at that sight" (V.445–50).

As much seduced as seducing, Byron's angels are not demonic tempters like Lucifer but fall instead at the same moment as their lovers. They sin by transgressing the borders between heaven and earth, immortal and mortal, and at the same time they objectify the supernatural cravings of Cain's fated descendants. Byron's second epigraph, "And woman wailing for her demon lover," belongs to Coleridge's "Kubla Khan," a poem that expresses the Romantic desire to weld contrary states together through an erotically charged vision of earthly paradise. But Coleridge's vision of a pleasure dome mingling nature and "device," hedonism and "ancestral voices prophesying war," proves untenable, like the mismatch of woman and demon, an image that evokes the related erotic encounters of mortal and immortal in poems such as Coleridge's *Christabel,* Shelley's *Alastor,* and

Keats's *Lamia*. Such matches prove invariably dangerous, figuring the power of a transient, supernatural vision to ravish the human heart of its attachment to the world "where," as Wordsworth says, "in the end / We find our happiness or not at all."[9] Anah and Aholibamah deny the earth before it is denied them; the angels readily abjure heaven; and both pairs find themselves living out an ungrounded, evanescent fantasy. The immortal no less than the mortal lovers suffer a failure of the imagination to make a home in its native sphere; in the last scene the seraphs are proscribed from Heaven even as the Deluge overwhelms the Earth.

As the Flood is both a repercussion and a repetition of the Fall of Man, so the fates of the women and the angels are presented as both effects and reflections of previous falls. Repetition does not here, as in *The Borderers* or *Cain*, accompany the successful grafting of a seducer's psychic condition onto the mind of his victim, but signifies instead the ineluctability of the Fall's resonance through successive generations and epochs. The innocence that Anah would recapture is simply not viable in the postlapsarian world, and the sisters find themselves living out instead the Fall they would repeal. Invoking her angel, Aholibamah boasts:

> And shall *I* shrink from thine eternity?
> No! though the serpent's sting should pierce me through
> And thou thyself wert like the serpent, coil
> Around me still! (125–28)

Craving the angels' "immortal essence," the sisters succumb to an urge similar to Eve's; and just as their grandfather's crime was presented in *Cain* as a version of Eve's, their own inheritance of Cain's legacy is stressed throughout the mystery:

> Too much of the forefather whom thou vauntest
> Has come down in that haughty blood which springs
> From him who shed the first, and that a brother's! (663–65)

The fall of Azaziel and Samiasa constitutes a complex act of repetition as well. Beguiled by woman, the angels have "shared man's sin" (619), repeating Adam's fall in following a voice more subtle than the serpent's: "The snake but vanquish'd dust; but she will draw / A second host from heaven, to break heaven's law" (858–59). As erring angels, Azaziel and Samiasa repeat Lucifer's fall and that of the first heavenly host as well, a parallel which the archangel Raphael will make explicit near the drama's close.

The first scene ends as Anah describes the angels' approach with a passage that exemplifies Byron's reading of the Flood not as a purgation but as another fall.

> On Ararat's late secret crest
> A mild and many-colour'd bow,
> The remnant of the flashing path,
> Now shines! and now, behold! it hath
> Return'd to night, as rippling foam,
> Which the leviathan hath lash'd
> From his unfathomable home
> When sporting on the face of the calm deep,
> Subsides soon after he again hath dash'd
> Down, down, to where the ocean's fountains sleep.

As the passage begins, Anah's reference to the hidden summit of Ararat seems to herald man's ultimate salvation—although the sisters have yet to hear of the approaching deluge. The accompanying image of the rainbow would then evoke the covenant that God will soon make with man, an antetype of the union of heaven and earth that follows the Apocalypse. Read only so far, the passage places Byron, as a poet of the Deluge, well within the typological tradition exemplified by Donne. But as the rainbow track of the departing angels—a wonderfully audacious celestial equivalent of a snail's prismatic trail in the dew—subsides, its evanescence causes Anah to picture a sounding whale, an image resonant with several layers of dramatic irony. The association of the angels with the leviathan, a traditional emblem for Satan, prefigures their fall and the danger they present to the transgressing sisters. As a central figure in Job for God's awful and inscrutable power, the leviathan augurs as well the near destruction of mankind; finally it heralds the form of their destruction in the flood later depicted by Japhet as

> When ocean is earth's grave, and, unopposed
> By rock or shallow, the leviathan,
> Lord of the shoreless sea and watery world,
> Shall wonder at his boundlessness of realm. (239–42)

What begins as an intimation of the marriage of heaven and earth ends by foreshadowing the earth's engulfment through heaven's wrath.

Japhet, whose story begins in the second scene, is a complex, though not deep, character. His passionate nature allies him to Anah and Aholibamah, and Noah condemns his desires for Anah—the "daughter of a fated race" (253)—as "forbidden yearnings" (259). He resembles Anah more particularly through his own likeness to Adah in *Cain:* Just as she begs her beloved to "go not / Forth with this spirit" (I.372–73), he asks Anah, "why walk'st thou with this spirit" (596). And like Cain's enduring (but not saving) love for Adah, Japhet's love for Anah leads him to "pity" his friend Irad, who "lovest not" (186), as Cain pities Lucifer, "who lov'st nothing" (II.543). But another side of his character stems from Byron's tragic protagonists, Manfred and the "abased" Cain. Like them he is restless; although his "nights inexorable" to sleep (218) initially reflect only erotic disappointment, he grows increasingly torn within by the conflict of his mortal sympathies with loyalty to his father's intolerant creed.

As Noah's son, Japhet tries at times to justify God's ways, but though singled out for salvation, he can neither unquestioningly accept the divine will nor wholly reject his divine mandate. Noah himself is something of a comic character, as was the henpecked patriarch of the medieval mysteries, though Byron's Noah more resembles the sententious stage Puritan of Jonson's comedies. Not that Noah is a hypocrite, but his tendency to wallow in sanctification reaches Jonsonian dimensions, most memorably when he reproaches the dignified, laconic angels:[10]

I am
But man, and was not made to judge mankind,
Far less the sons of God; but as our God
Has deign'd to commune with me, and reveal
His judgments, I reply, that the descent
Of seraphs from their everlasting seat
Unto a perishable and perishing,
Even on the very *eve* of *perishing,* world,
Cannot be good. (746–54)

Although Japhet has been placed among the elect, he feels no trace of the confidence of justification; only the burden of surviving the natural and social worlds in which he feels at home. Like Cain, he finds himself trapped by a crudely dichotomized system that allows for no creative resolution, though the principal spokesman for a divided cosmos is in this case not a devil but a saint. The terror of Byron's mystery—felt by his contemporaries if not by his editors—arises from the absence of a middle ground on which to stand. Japhet struggles vainly to reconcile his father and the seed of Cain; the angels must choose between submission and exile; Raphael sadly can provide only ultimatums, despite his wish to mediate between God and his noble, beautiful apostates. In many respects Japhet's dilemma is a study in the limits of Calvinism. Goethe's perception that in *Cain* "we see . . . how the inadequate dogmas of the church work upon a free mind like Byron's and how by such a piece he struggles to get rid of a doctrine which has been forced upon him" applies equally well to *Heaven and Earth.*[11]

The last scene opens with Japhet at his most Manfred-like. He has departed from Irad to muse alone at the cavern beneath the Caucasus, whose mouth

> opens from the infernal world
> To let the inner spirits of the earth
> Forth when they walk its surface. (201–3)

The description resonates with literary and thematic associations. It recalls the "deep romantic of chasm" of "Kubla Khan," and is clearly allied to the chasms and abysses that throughout mental theater figure psychic disintegration. Its location evokes the Prometheus myth—an association that becomes explicit later in the scene—and the cave not only conjoins earth and hell but "opens to the heart of Ararat" (249)—the locus of heaven's future covenant with man—as well. The spot accordingly marks the convergence of the drama's various worlds and worldviews, represented by Japhet, the demonic "spirits of the earth," the erring angels and the "Cainite" women, God's terrestrial representative, Noah, and his heavenly messenger, Raphael. The struggle within Japhet between earthly passions and the divine ethic will give place by the end to the catastrophic mingling of Heaven and Earth in the Deluge.

Japhet's soliloquy begins as he struggles to understand why an earth "so varied and so terrible in beauty" (268) should be sacrificed to God's anger. His expression of natural piety leads to a loving elegy for his doomed race:

> And man—Oh men! my fellow beings! Who
> Shall weep above your universal grave,
> Save I? (279–81)

Japhet's expression contrasts vividly with Shelley's millennial vision of a redeemed, unified humanity in the fourth act of *Prometheus Unbound:* "Man, oh, not men! a chain of linked thought." For Byron, human strife cannot be transcended through a higher, collective consciousness; the pathos of Japhet's fallen, falling world lies instead in Byron's individualization of suffering—not man, but men will perish. Here his father's proto-Calvinism breaks down for Japhet. Far from glorying in self-righteousness, he protests his common humanity—"what am I better than ye are / That I must live beyond ye" (282–83)—and his fundamental kinship with a race "So young, so mark'd out for destruction" (313).

Like Manfred before him, Japhet is mocked in his deep musings by a chorus of infernal spirits, led by a Mephistophelian spokesman, an "unknown, terrible, and indistinct / Yet awful Thing of Shadows" (327–28) that personifies the abyss, recalling both Milton's Death and Manfred's "dusk and awful" accuser. The Satanic spirits celebrate the approaching extermination of their replacement and enemy,

> The abhorred race
> Which could not keep in Eden their high place
> But listen'd to the voice
> Of knowledge without power. (341–44)

This last phrase touches on a dilemma felt variously by many of the English Romantics. Wordsworth writes in *The Prelude* of "knowledge not purchased by the loss of power"; Coleridge, in the *Logic*, "For that alone is truly knowledge . . . which reappears as power."[12] The protagonists of Byron's metaphysical dramas are betrayed by knowledge that saps, rather than augments, their power: "The Tree of Knowledge is not that of Life." Manfred and Cain both founder in a delusive, empty self-knowledge, discovering not an empowering, authentic truth, but the crippling consciousness of guilt and the mocking presence of a misleading, alien voice that disrupts rather than guarantees psychic integrity. The power they give up in order to "purchase" such empty knowledge is the power defined by De Quincey, in contrast to merely discursive knowledge, as the "exercise and expansion" of the "latent capacity of sympathy."[13] For Japhet, knowledge of God's will and design proves similarly empty; his consciousness of election only heightens his sense of impotence, and his prevision of the Flood torments him in his powerlessness to avert its consequences. The mocking voices of the demons that interrupt his soliloquy—voices that Japhet alone hears—embody the conflict between his sympathies and his inherited ideology.

Japhet struggles with his demons, identifying the "restless wretchedness" (388) that underlies their Satanic irony. They counter with one of Lucifer's stratagems in *Cain*, belittling Japhet and his race by comparing them to the "glorious giants, who / Yet walk the world in pride, / The Sons of Heaven by many a mortal bride" (396–99), and endowing them, as the "giant patriarchs" (422), with temporal priority as well. Celebrating the coming holocaust, they herald an anti-Millenium which inverts Isaiah's vision of the peaceable kingdom:[14]

even the brutes, in their despair,
Shall cease to prey on man and on each other,
And the striped tiger shall lie down to die
Beside the lamb, as though he were his brother;
Till all things shall be as they were,
Silent and uncreated, save the sky. (422–47)

Japhet opposes their satiric vision with his own intimations of an Apocalypse in which God will "abolish hell" and restore "Eden in an endless paradise / Where man no more can fall as once he fell" (468–69), the final reconciliation of earth and heaven. But the demons have the last word, deriding Japhet's Apocalypse as one indefinitely deferred, a mere vision with no effect on the world as it is lived:

The same old tears, old crimes, and oldest ill,
Shall be amongst your race in different forms;
But the same moral storms
Shall oversweep the future, as the waves
In a few hours the glorious giants' graves. (479–83)

The demonic voices portray the future as a succession of falls repeating man's "oldest ill," or original sin, and the Flood as an antetype not of the fiery Apocalypse but of the "moral storms" that will continue to assail mankind.

The demons vanish and give place to "shapes both of earth and air" (576), the two angels and the "children of Cain." Motivated by sexual jealousy as well as orthodox dismay, Japhet warns that "unions like to these / Between a mortal and an immortal, cannot be happy" (635–37), but Aholibamah dismisses his love and religion together:

> —But the enthusiast dreams
> The worst of dreams, the fantasies engender'd
> By hapless love and heated vigils. (713–15)

Aholibamah reproaches Japhet ironically (but not wholly inaccurately) with the imaginative failure shared by herself and Anah, the tendency to palliate mortal despair with erotic delusions (though the sisters would not characterize their own misdirected desire as such). Noah then enters the scene with sterner condemnations: "Has not God made a barrier between earth / And heaven?" (741–42). His proclamation of metaphysical borders, emphasized by the line break, is undermined, however, by the approaching Flood itself. Heaven and Earth are soon to mingle not in a millenial consummation but in a catastrophic rain of terror: "the fountains of the great deep shall be broken / And heaven set wide her windows" (490–91). The absence in *Heaven and Earth* of mediation, of a middle ground, finds graphic portrayal as the heavens open and the sea rises. The boundaries so stoutly maintained by Noah and so cruelly felt by his son grow meaningless as the border area itself yields to God's wrath. Manfred leaped into his abyss, Cain was enticed into Lucifer's; in *Heaven and Earth* the abyss wells up as the "fountains of the great deep" engulf the entire earth.

The angels are given a final chance to recant and obey by Milton's "affable angel," Raphael, whose appearance further broadens the variegated metaphysical spectrum of the final scene. As the storm clouds gather above, the language grows crowded with references to prior falls. First Raphael evokes the interdependency of Earth's creation and Lucifer's fall as codified in *Paradise Lost:*

why
Cannot this earth be made, or be destroy'd,
Without involving ever some vast void
In the immortal ranks? (827–30)

Even from Raphael's perspective, heaven and earth seem less conjoined in a divine plan than confounded in an encompassing Fall. Like Michael greeting Satan in the *Vision of Judgment* with "high, immortal, proud regret" (32), Raphael recalls his infernal opposite with a measure of longing:

I loved him—beautiful he was: oh heaven!
Save *his* who made, what beauty and what power
Was ever like to Satan's! Would the hour
In which he fell could ever be forgiven!
The wish is impious. (846–50)

But beauty and power are again crushed by heaven's inalterable law. The angels embrace their lovers' fate in terms that evoke their ancestor, Cain: "we have chosen, and will endure" (983).

Anah, "the last and loveliest of Cain's race" (652), embraces at the end a Promethean view of Satan, identifying her own dilemma with his fall:

The first who taught us knowledge hath been hurl'd
From his once angelic throne
Into some unknown world. (933–35)

The ensuing fall of man is evoked by Raphael's image of the cherubic sword "Which chased the first-born out of Paradise" (1051), and by Japhet's final lament, as impious and as impotent as Raphael's wistful lines on Satan:

Renew not Adam's fall:
Mankind were then but twain,
But they are numerous now as are the waves
And the tremendous rain,
Whose drops shall be less thick than would their graves,
Were graves permitted to the seed of Cain. (972–77)

Compassion, however, is not an Old Testament virtue. At last a pathetic "chorus of Mortals," fleeing the rising waters, dismally bewails that "The heavens and earth are mingling" (1060).

One should not read too much bitterness, however, into the final tableau. Byron does not, as a younger Byron might have, dismiss Genesis with Voltairean satire. Instead, he leads the reader into Japhet's dilemma: Neither the Cainites' escapism nor God's final solution seems acceptable. One of the last speeches is given to a nameless, doomed mortal, who echoes Job's heroic incomprehension:

> Time—space—eternity—life—death—
> The vast known and the immeasurable unknown.
> He made and can unmake;
> And shall *I*, for a little gasp of breath,
> Blaspheme and groan? (1163–67)

Heaven and Earth ends, as does *Cain*, with questions rather than with answers. It is no accident that Byron left this work fragmentary. The text we have is subtitled "Part I," but Byron seems hardly to have toyed with a sequel; Medwin reports him as saying that he had "talked of writing a second part of it; but it was only as Coleridge promised a second part to 'Cristabel'."[15] One remembers as well that an epigraph to *Heaven and Earth* comes from another unfinished work by Coleridge, and that the "poet of great and deserved celebrity" who induced him to publish "Kubla Khan" in its fragmentary form was Byron himself. Like Coleridge, he found in the fragment a device for remaining in uncertainties, mysteries, doubts, without reaching after a conclusion, and for plunging the reader into a similar dilemma, teasing us (again to paraphrase Keats) out of habitual patterns of thought.[16]

Heaven and Earth is the last of Byron's works that can be called mental theater. The two dramatic works that followed—*Werner* (1822) and the sketch *The Deformed Transformed* (publ. 1824)—bring thematic elements from the metaphysical dramas into forms more suited to conventional nineteenth-century stagecraft, but in neither does Byron return to his themes with any depth. Based on a youthful play that he wrote while associated with the Drury Lane, *Werner* clearly aspires to the contemporary stage, and is in fact his only drama to have succeeded in the theater.[17] Its subtitle, "The Inheritance," underscores the plot's indebtedness to Gothic conventions, although it touches at the same time on the presence of a theme developed in *Heaven and Earth*—the inheritance of an ancestral fall. The transference of crime and fall from Werner to his son, however, is a matter of simple imitation, involving neither the elaborate pattern of seduction and repetition developed in *Cain* nor the pervasive postlapsarian dilemma of *Heaven and Earth. The Deformed Transformed* similarly fails to bear out the promise of its *Faust*-like plot, the encounter of Arnold, a dejected hunchback, with a Mephistophelian tempter who takes on the name "Caesar" promising a Satanic psychic imperialism that the action fails to develop. Although the plot might have taken an interesting turn had Byron lived to complete the drama,[18] the extant scenes recall in their sentimentality, bluster, and melodrama less *Cain* than *Otho the Great*.

The anticlimax of Byron's dramatic career should not blind us, however, any more than should his static historical plays, to the importance of his three works of mental theater. The portrayals of psychic agony in *Manfred* and psychic agon in *Cain*, with the brief but intense drama of parallel and intertwining ideological struggles in *Heaven and Earth*, establish Byron as an innovative and profound master of the dramatic poem. Read on their own terms as addressed not to a deserted stage but to the reader's mind, Byron's three works of mental theater constitute a major Romantic achievement, rivaled in their genre only by Shelley's dramatic poems of 1819.

6

"Self-Anatomy" and Self-Consciousness in *The Cenci*

It is hard to imagine two verse dramas written during the same year by the same poet differing more widely than *Prometheus Unbound* and *The Cenci.* In his "Lyrical Drama," Shelley takes the genre of mental theater to its most rarefied extremes. Disciplined blank verse alternates with a growing profusion of lyric, choric, and hymnic measures; the spare Aeschylean conflict of Zeus and Prometheus yields to a mosaic of dramatic forms embracing pastoral, masque, pageant, and romance. Not only setting scenes in cosmic space, as did Byron in *Cain,* Shelley so divorces dramaturgy from stagecraft that such features as the dialogue of the Earth and Moon, the formless anti-character Demogorgon, and the celestial processions challenge even visualization, breaking the reader's customary sensory associations with drama. In *The Cenci,* "studiously composed in a different style,"[1] Shelley aims—though not entirely without ambivalence—for the contemporary stage. He adopts the "familiar language of men," abandoning "mere poetry" in description and imagery, and draws inspiration for the central character from the performances, "in the zenith of her glory," of the brilliant Irish actress Eliza O'Neil.[2]

The two works, nevertheless, address one problem: the growth and the potentially tragic limitations of self-consciousness. In both, self-awareness emerges through the same dramatically constituted process that Wordsworth and Byron portrayed in their works of mental theater. And in both Shelley exposes the dangers inherent in discovering the self, envisioning the transcendence of egoism in the figure of Prometheus and drawing the tragic limits of self-consciousness in the more human lineaments of Beatrice Cenci. Although *The Cenci* does not, as a play intended for the stage, strictly belong to the genre I call mental theater, it resembles *Prometheus Unbound* both in its thematic development and, up to the point at which tragedy and revelation part company, in the reflexive struggle of protagonist and antagonist. As inverse developments of the same thematic pattern and dramatic situation, the two works complement and illuminate one another. Both works, moreover, are informed by prior texts that Wordsworth and Byron also took as dramatic models: *Macbeth* and *Paradise Lost*.[3]

Shelley had broached a creative interpretation of these texts as early as 1810 in *The Wandering Jew*, his first essay in a major genre and his first attempt to grapple with the problem of self-consciousness.[4] The poem is an extended narrative interspersed with such dramatic elements as long soliloquies and dialogues introduced by speech headings. Shelley's Wandering Jew embodies—as throughout the Romantic tradition—the pangs of interminable self-consciousness. Living under the alias "Paulo" in an Italy derived from the Romance settings of Radcliffe and Lewis, the Wandering Jew has endured "sixteen hundred years of woe," the "self-inflicted torturing pangs / Of conscience" (634–35). The exuberantly Gothic plot (rescue from a sinister convent, obsessive and frustrated love, pacts with the devil) is negligible; remarkable, however, is Shelley's disingenuous advertisement in his epigraphs of the sources from which both the central character and the plot's rather mechanical resolution are borrowed. The epigraph to Canto I includes the Miltonic locus that bears on every villain of mental theater and, eventually, on every protagonist:

> Me Miserable! which way shall I fly
> Infinite wrath, and infinite despair?
> Which way I fly is Hell, my self am Hell. (IV.71–73)[5]

Paulo inevitably takes up this burden in recounting his tormented history: "Vain from myself the attempt to fly, / Sole cause of my own misery" (703–4)—an explicitly psychic burden, "the tortures of the mind" (727). The fourth canto (which begins with a long, apparently irrelevant, paean to the power of human sympathy that looks forward to *Prometheus Unbound*) recounts the misguided love of Paulo's friend Victorio for Rosa, Paulo's beloved. Victorio falls under the influence of a "weird female" (1218), a temptress whose antecedents, the Witches of *Macbeth*, are the subjects of the canto's epigraph:

> —What are ye
> So withered and so wild in your attire,

That look not like th' inhabitants of earth,
And yet are on't?

Both Victorio and Paulo are destroyed through the witch's subterfuge, and the poem ends as Paulo, anticipating Byron's Manfred, descends toward a hell that objectifies rather than augments his inner torment.

In *The Wandering Jew* Shelley had precociously sketched the outlines and discovered the sources for his verse dramas of 1819. During the intervening years, he returned to the problem of a tormented, Satanic consciousness in one poem after another. The Wandering Jew reappears in *Mab* as Ahasuerus, suffering a "Hell . . . within [his] brain"; as the haunted youth of *Alastor* and as Prince Athanase, tormented by "unresting multitudes" of thoughts, the figure becomes a type of the Romantic poet, and a projection of Shelley's self-image. Rosalind, in "Rosalind and Helen," endures "Remorse where sin was none; a hell," and the mad inmate of *Julian and Maddalo* bewails "the full Hell / Within" him. It was in his dramatic poetry, however, that Shelly portrayed not simply the burden but the entire course of self-consciousness: its emergence, its mechanisms, and its tragic limitations.

Shelley writes in his preface that he was attracted to the story of the Cenci family not for its lurid, Jacobean tone but as the focus of a "light to make apparent some of the most dark and secret caverns of the human heart." His phrase strikingly recalls Wordsworth's remark that the plot of *The Borderers* provided "lights penetrating somewhat into the depths of our nature";[6] and as with *The Borderers*, if theatrical considerations affected the composition of *The Cenci*, they were strictly subordinated to the analysis of psychological development, power, and influence. Orsino, the "equivocating" priest who aims at both Beatrice and her father's considerable wealth, describes the Cenci as connoisseurs of consciousness: " 'tis a trick of this same family / To analyse their own and other minds." His perception is anything but disinterested, for through playing on their fondness for wild analysis he hopes to control Beatrice, destroy Cenci, and have his will with both. He reasons that the mind, turning upon itself, discovers perilous depths:

Such self-anatomy shall teach the will
Dangerous secrets: for it tempts our powers,

> Knowing what must be thought, and may be done,
> Into the depth of darkest purposes:
> So Cenci fell into the pit. (II.2.110–14)

By making the mind object of its own subjectivity, self-anatomy introduces a division that easily grows pernicious. "Darkest purposes" arise with the force of compulsion, triggering a psychic mechanism that is strangely independent of "our" powers. Self-knowledge proves empty as the will learns seductive "secrets"—deep, hidden impulses—that undermine its integrity.

Cenci's fall through the seductions of introspection begins a series of interlocking tragedies of self-consciousness. Much like Wordsworth's Oswald, Cenci initially presents himself as one beyond good and evil, liberated from the conventional notions and social feelings that condition and limit others: "I have no remorse and little fear, / Which are, I think, the checks of other men" (I.1.84–85). An autocrat in his household and a Borgia-like tyrant in public, he swells with the intoxication of power until he becomes—in his own eyes—a god figure. But as George Bernard Shaw noted long ago, Cenci is more demon than god, "really a personification of the Almighty Fiend of 'Queen Mab,' the God whose attributes convicted the average evangelical Briton in Shelley's eyes of being a devil worshiper."[7] Those around Cenci consider him a "fiend"; Cenci himself boasts a will comparable to and independent of God's: "He does his will, I mine" (IV.1.139). Like Byron's Lucifer, he arrives at the extreme stance of autonomy, styling himself a kind of Manicheistic rival principle. As in Lucifer's case, however, the stance proves untenable, and Cenci's delusive quest for unconditioned autonomy predicates his tragedy and that of his daughter.

The contradictions underlying Cenci's illusory autonomy emerge clearly in the first act. The events that begin the drama seem at first designed to confirm Cenci's imagined independence, while the setting manifests his power over those around him. Cenci has assembled his most considerable relatives, associates, and enemies (the last category all but embraces the first two) at a banquet, in order to joyfully announce that, by "ways inscrutable," God has accomplished the wish of his heart in the sudden deaths of two of his sons. Cenci finds nothing unusual in the bizarre conjunction of two unlikely accidents for he considers Providence an extension of his will. Nor is he thwarted by any, or all, of the assembled guests. When Beatrice begs them to remove and protect her young brother, her stepmother, and herself, no one dares do more than grumble in asides. Cenci's power seems absolute, and indeed godlike.

Beatrice's act of defiance, however—despite its role in capping the triumph Cenci has staged—unmans him. Left alone with her, he confesses to an attack of disorienting faintness: "My brain is swimming round" (I.3.164). Beatrice represents for him both his greatest desire and his greatest fear—"Fair and yet terrible" (I.3.166), he calls her. For in *The Cenci,* as in Hegel's paradigmatic study of self-consciousness in the *Phenomenology,* psychic independence cannot emerge in isolation, but asserts itself only through a dramatic struggle. Cenci's pursuit of an autonomous identity, however, is undermined by the very social detachment on which his delusions of unconditioned power rest. His peers either shun or humor him, and his servants—including his unofficial legate to the Pope—are negligible cravens; he appears to others as an inhuman tyrant or a faceless demon. Beatrice alone demonstrates the strength to defy Cenci, and in her defiance lies the potential for an authentic dialogue. But that same defiance withdraws from Cenci the confirmation of autonomy—Hegel's "acknowledgment"—that her unique ability to face him seems to promise.

Cenci first expresses his awareness of Beatrice's unique capacity for "recognition" through a sexual metaphor. He tells Camillo, his pocket cardinal, that though a sensualist in his youth, he learned to value torment as the greater pleasure, living to feel "the soul within [his] power" (I.1.115). Now that sensual pleasures are altogether behind him, power manifested as sadism consoles him for his sexual impotence:

> True, I was happier than I am, while yet
> Manhood remained to act the thing I thought;
> While lust was sweeter than revenge; and now
> Invention palls:—Ay, we must all grow old—
> And but that there yet remains a deed to act
> Whose horror might make sharp an appetite
> Duller than mine—I'd do,—I know not what. (I.1.96–102)

Cenci has planned an act that will combine both pleasures, sensual and sadistic: his intended rape of Beatrice. Just as Beatrice alone can engage Cenci as a psychic antagonist, only the prospect of raping her can now sexually arouse him. As so often in literature (and out of it), a power relation lies behind a sexual proposition. To rape Beatrice is to dominate her—Cenci will approach her bedroom with "imperious step" (I.1.143)—and his arousal proceeds from the hope of bending her to his will. He has her "barred from all society" (I.1.46), not from a perverse combination of sexual jealousy and paternal tyranny, but from a still more perverse desire to impose on her an isolation modeled after his own, preparing her for the act he expects will confirm his identity. The significance of incest that remains obscure in *Manfred* becomes explicit in *The Cenci*. As an act of psychic domination it exemplifies the unbalanced process of recognition that Hegel expresses as a "master and servant" relation, terms that Cenci himself adopts in describing his designs on Beatrice.

The prospect of the rape both allures and daunts Cenci, for he rightly sees in it a desperate stratagem from which he cannot later retreat. Self-anatomy has revealed threatening depths within the mind, a chaos Cenci would bridge through beholding his identity reflected in a vanquished Beatrice. But the danger of his attempt necessarily heightens his awareness of the inner abyss, and his vulnerability to self-doubt. As the moment draws near, Cenci's ambivalence takes the form of a soliloquy remarkable for its complex evocation of antecedent texts:

> Come darkness! Yet, what is the day to me?
> And wherefore should I wish for night, who do
> A deed which shall confound both night and day?
> 'Tis she shall grope through a bewildering mist
> Of horror: if there be a sun in heaven
> She shall not dare to look upon its beams;
> Nor feel its warmth. Let her then wish for night;
> The act I think shall soon extinguish all
> For me: I bear a darker deadlier gloom
> Than the earth's shade, or interlunar air,
> Or constellations quenched in murkiest cloud,
> In which I walk secure and unbeheld
> Towards my purpose.—Would that it were done!
> (II.1.181–93)

Cenci shares his literary genealogy with Shelley's Wandering Jew. He echoes two related passages from Book IX of *Paradise Lost,* both of which underscore the Satanic elements of Cenci's character and of his design on Beatrice. Satan is evoked when he too is on the verge of betraying an innocent, Eve, into an act designed to inflict on her a condition as unbearable as his own. Cenci's ironically self-condemning vaunt that he bears a "deadlier gloom" through light or shade parallels Satan's bitter realization after contemplating the Earth's beauty, that he bears his torment within him—"and in Heaven much worse would be my state" (IX.123), restated in the narrative remark (directly preceding Eve's temptation) on "the hot Hell that always in him burns / Though in mid Heav'n" (IX.467–68). Cenci presents his inseparable "gloom" as a disguise facilitating the rape, but his agitated phrasing, the wish to "extinguish" some indeterminate "all"—light, his torment, consciousness itself?—and Shelley's allusion to Satan underscore the element of motivation, or rather compulsion, in Cenci's cloak of visible darkness.

The allusion to Macbeth's words preceding *his* crime (one that seals the disintegration of his own character rather than beginning that of his victim's) similarly helps define Cenci's project: "Stars, hide your fires, / Let not light see my black and deep desires" (I.4.50–51). Hazlitt emblematized the Romantic conception of Macbeth's psyche as "a war of opposite natures which of them shall destroy the other";[8] Satan's mind is the field for a hateful "siege / Of contraries." Cenci is likewise impelled toward his act of violation by a tormenting restlessness, an inner struggle that both demands and tragically deforms self-consciousness. The passage ends by underscoring the desperation of Cenci's project, once more alluding to Macbeth's: "If it were done, when 'tis done, then 'twere well / It were done quickly" (I.7.1–2).

Cenci's speech also highlights the mechanisms of his proposed assault on Beatrice's mind through assaulting her body. To "confound" night and day is Cenci's figure for the complex violation of borders entailed in the rape: the primal border between the paternal and sexual relations; the border between erotic love and hateful violence; the border, finally, between one identity, one consciousness, and another. (One should note that, as so often in mental theater, the theme of border violation appears in a passage that complicates the borders between the present text and antecedent texts as well.) The rape would weaken Beatrice through destroying whatever constants—the incest taboo, the limits of even Cenci's tyranny, the physical integrity represented by her chastity—remain to her, the resulting shock helping sexual penetration to facilitate psychic interpenetration. Cenci's strategy depends on his establishing Beatrice in a subordinate psychic relation, which he can manipulate in such a way as to impose his self-image onto her and receive it back from her. He anticipates its success by projecting, in this speech, his wish for night onto a Beatrice already transformed by the deed, transposing as well his encompassing gloom into the "bewildering mist" that will surround her.

Cenci's desire to introduce his psychic condition into Beatrice's mind becomes an explicit aspect of the campaign leading up to the rape. He places her in an artificial isolation—first within the Cenci Palace, then more melodramatically in the remote family castle of Petralla—intended to reflect his own, radical social detachment; and, through calculated suggestions of the imminent rape, he attempts to impress upon her his own mixed feelings of repulsion and desire. So Cenci describes her disgust and terror in terms of his own ambivalence:

> Then it was I whose inarticulate words
> Fell from my lips, and who with tottering steps
> Fled from your presence, as you now from mine.
> (II.1.112–14)

"I . . . your . . . you . . . mine": Cenci mingles two contrasting rhetorical patterns, chiasmus (the first-person surrounding the second-person terms) and synchesis (in the parallel nominative and possessive forms), graphically portraying the inextricable, specular relation in which he hopes to entrap Beatrice.

If Hegel's model for the approach to self-consciousness helps expose the motives behind Cenci's project, it underscores as well its predetermined failure. Having instituted, as Cenci tries to institute, a master-slave relation, the ascendant consciousness finds itself trapped in a cycle of dependence; far from achieving autonomy, the master guarantees his own servitude in his need to be continually (and yet never satisfactorily) acknowledged. Cenci falls victim to this new dilemma after the rape, and once brought face to face with the contradictions behind his autonomous stance, he disintegrates as a stage character. At the outset, Cenci treats his popular image—the inhuman "fiend"—with complacent sarcasm: "But I do hope that you . . . Will think me flesh and blood as well as you" (I.3.7–11). After the rape, he can no longer consider himself human:

> I do not feel as if I were a man,
> But like a fiend appointed to chastise
> The offences of some unremembered world. (IV.1.160–62)

Unremembered: a world forgotten by its God, in which Cenci can rage omnipotent as its Prince of the Air; or a world lost to Cenci's memory, his acts of cruelty motivated by causes he has forgotten, "appointed" by a compulsion beyond his control? Cenci now inherits the full burden of his model, Milton's Satan. Beatrice, invoking the Miltonic locus running through Shelley's poetry from *The Wandering Jew* on, speaks of "the Hell within him" (IV.2.33), and while Cenci claims to sleep soundly, she characterizes his sleep as a restless "hell of angry dreams" (IV.4.8), an intuition borne out by the reports of the assassins she hires to murder him (IV.3.18–20).

In manner Cenci becomes a caricature of the Gothic stage villain, and yet it would be uncritical to dismiss lines like these as stock rant:

> Might I not drag her by the golden hair?
> Stamp on her? Keep her sleepless till her brain
> Be overworn? Tame her with chains and famine? (IV.1.6–8)

Behind the accents of convention lie images of Cenci's frustrated design. Cenci seeks to master Beatrice, to engender in her his own restless torment, to starve her sympathies through isolation in order to chain her the more securely to himself alone. But his power over Beatrice's environment does not extend to her mind, and Cenci has ironically bound himself to repeat the act of rape interminably, continually seeking and failing to attain dominion:

> Less would suffice. Yet so to leave undone
> What I most seek! No, 'tis her stubborn will

> Which by its own consent shall stoop as low
> As that which drags it down.

Ensnared in his own plot, Cenci undergoes an eternal recurrence of repetition and frustration, doomed to enact again and again the original scene of thwarted seduction—seduction exposed as rape. Once more we hear him steel himself for Beatrice's bedchamber, now her cell:

> There shall be lamentation heard in Heaven
> As o'er an angel fallen; and upon Earth
> All good shall droop and sicken, and ill things
> Shall with a spirit of unnatural life
> Stir and be quickened . . . even as I am now. (IV.1.185–89)

The repetition is informed by further repetitions. The second rape will reenact the fall of humankind and the degeneration of Earth, which was itself a reeanactment of the angels' fall from heaven. Cenci's motive is allusively characterized as a profoundly alien, profoundly unoriginal compulsion. And in describing himself as "quickened" with "unnatural life," Cenci reveals a new plot for inflicting his torment on the daughter he now wishes to impregnate.

Cenci's fresh urge to repeat the crime follows directly on an anguished and revealing expression of frustration, his bitter curse on Beatrice, provoked by her recalcitrance and condemning her as:

> This particle of my divided being;
> Or rather, this my bane and my disease,
> Whose sight infects and poisons me; this devil
> Which sprung from me as from a hell. (IV.1.117–20)

Once more Cenci projects onto Beatrice the psychic condition he wishes her to internalize. He depicts her, in terms of his deformed self-image, as a fiend, and tacitly acknowledges his own fragmented identity or "divided being." His simile, once more, draws a parallel between his psychic disintegration and Satan's, whose rebellion entailed for Milton a simultaneous inner division, literally represented in *Paradise Lost* as the birth of his daughter Sin from his cleft brain. (The birth of error itself, of course, parodies the birth of wisdom, or Athena, from the head of Zeus.) Thwarted even in the act of seeking domination, Cenci consoles himself by envisioning for Beatrice her own literalization of psychic division, a sign that her fate will be a repetition of his. If he cannot impose his condition directly onto Beatrice's mind, he can—he hopes—instill an incestuous child into her body:

> May it be
> A hideous likeness of herself, that as
> From a distorting mirror, she may see
> Her image mixed with what she most abhors. (IV.1.145–48)

Cenci's curses are sometimes read as pale imitations of Lear's on his daughters,[9] when in fact (whatever Shelley owed in this case to precedent) they exert a very different thematic function. As Lear's daughters effectively disown him, he sees himself as childless, and wishes barrenness on them in turn. Cenci, on the contrary, beholds in Beatrice an aspect of himself—but not the subordinate reflection he wished to form. Rather, Beatrice becomes for Cenci an emblem, a living reminder of his incompleteness, and he wishes on her a birth that will similarly undermine her self-identity with a distorting, tormenting image: a reflection not of the independent self but of the self parodically, hideously mingled with the other.

In mental theater such curses usually serve merely to confirm a punishment that their object has already brought upon himself, as in Eve's curse on Cain, or Idonea's on Marmaduke, or the Seventh Spirit's on Manfred. Cenci's curse likewise entails a fate that Beatrice herself pursues, but in this case a profound dramatic irony marks its fulfillment. Beatrice comes to adopt a role much like her father's, one that culminates in an act unmistakably resembling his most outrageous crime. Like the rape, that act will take place in a bedchamber; it will, like the rape, proceed from a desperate bid for autonomy; like it, the act will complete and seal the psychic degeneration of its perpetrator. Finally, the act—Beatrice's murder of Cenci—will be informed by repetition: While Cenci's crime is structured after Satan's violation of Eve's innocence, Beatrice's crime replays the murder of Duncan in *Macbeth*.

The figure of Beatrice poses a dilemma for any reading, or reader, of *The Cenci*. She begins as her father's sole opponent, and ends by undertaking a career of transgression similar to his in its effects on herself and on those around her. And yet Cenci initiates his own destruction, while Beatrice is betrayed into hers; one thinks of Jung's image (in a quite different context) for Lucia Joyce and *her* father: "two people going to the bottom of a river, one falling and the other diving."[10] Beatrice falls through her own tragic error, a point made by Shelley in the preface and elaborated since by a number of comentators.[11] The subtlety and artfulness of Cenci's designs, however, should not be minimized. Although Beatrice cannot be exculpated, her "pernicious mistake" grows out of the events that precede, and all but determine, her act.

Cenci's projection onto Beatrice of his own characteristics is not entirely a matter of self-deception.[12] Beatrice inherits from her father certain traits—daring, social iconoclasm, the tendency to "anatomize" (I.2.84) others' minds—that Cenci attempts to aggravate even before her violation. Weakened by years of torment, and isolated by her brothers' sudden deaths and her imprisonment, Beatrice is nearly overwhelmed by the very suggestion of the rape. Her stepmother, Lucretia, finds her "Wrapped in some fixed and fearful meditation, / As if one thought were over strong" for her (II.1.30–31), and senses her "firm mind" unaccountably "subdued" (II.1.50). Cenci hints at the approaching rape not simply to harass Beatrice but to inspire in her a fixed obsession as well. He initiates a "fearful meditation" designed to turn her analytic mind inward, undermining her will through a process of self-anatomy that grows increasingly dangerous.

The rape is meant to hasten the collapse of Beatrice's will and place her in a divisive and tormenting mental crisis; it succeeds on both counts. When she appears on the stage shortly after her violation, she complains of an impaired, darkened vision:

> —My brain is hurt;
> My eyes are full of blood; just wipe them for me . . .
> I see but indistinctly . . . (III.1.1–3)

Visual imagery serves here, as in *The Borderers*, to convey the deterioration of the protagonist's self-view and vision of the world. Beatrice's "eyes . . . full of blood" is a metonymic figure associating the loss of her hymen with the radical obscuring of her vision, as though Cenci had indeed raped her psychically as well as physically.[13] Her darkened eyesight becomes a "clinging, black, contaminating mist" surrounding her (I.1.17), a sign that Cenci's desired transference—" 'tis she shall grope through a bewildering mist"—has begun to come about. Cenci's act is so inconceivable that Beatrice cannot explicitly recall it. Yet in the very disjunction it causes between memory and will lies the germ of a psychic wound that continues to warp her vision: " 'Tis gone; and yet its burden remains here / O'er these dull eyes" (III.1.30–33).

Beatrice's deflowering forms a literal analogue to the multiplicity of border violations brought about by the rape. The deed which Cenci promised would "confound both night and day" destroys for Beatrice the boundaries of reason and unreason ("I am mad beyond all doubt"), life and death ("No, I am dead"), self and other ("I thought I was that wretched Beatrice"), good and evil, the imaginable and the unimaginable:

> Horrible things have been in this wide world,
> Prodigious mixtures, and confusions strange
> Of good and ill; and worse have been conceived
> Than ever there was found a heart to do.
> But never fancy imaged such a deed
> As . . . (III.1.51–56)

The ellipsis is Beatrice's. Her inability to either image or obliterate the deed, to remember or forget it ("What memory shall be mine?"), confirms a rift in her psyche, one that can widen to reveal a void like that behind Cenci's mask, the "pit" into which he falls. Up to this point Beatrice has remained entirely a victim of the process set in motion by her father; *Prometheus Unbound*, the visionary analogue to the "sad reality" of *The Cenci*, will show that such a condition as Beatrice's is, although irreversible, not irremediable.[14] Beatrice, however, soon crosses a threshold from suffering to acting out her tragedy.

Beatrice's transition from Cenci's victim to his double takes place through a process that captures the essence of mental theater. Protagonist and antagonist become struggling opposites within a single mind, and tragically merge as Beatrice's consciousness becomes the self-estranged image of her father's. Striving to recall the rape, to bring her past once more under control, she finds that torment can be so intense as to obliterate its cause:

> Like Parricide . . .
> Misery has killed its father: yet its father
> Never like mine . . . O, God! What thing am I?
> (III.1.37–39)

Beatrice searches for her father's crime and encounters the germ of her own. In describing a process within her mind that Freud would call repression, she invents a simile—parricide—that immediately generates a second process. The notion of murdering Cenci, and retaliating for the rape, enables her to recall it—memory had obliterated an event with much less justification than her own for contemplating her father's murder. The decision to assassinate Cenci has been made before she can even utter it, and she has at that moment become alien to herself, a "thing," and a reflection of her father even as a memory reflects its object. As Cenci has calculated, day and night, earth and hell, fair and foul are confounded in Beatrice's mind; she desires now only to find "refuge from the consciousness / Of what is yet unexpiated" (III.1.150–51). She believes herself "poisoned" in the "inmost spirit of life" (III.1.23)—a notion that Shelley takes pains to dismiss in the preface—and can imagine expiation only by revenge, the "naked idol," in Shelley's phrase, "of a semi-barbarous age."[15] From this moment she is, by her own confession, "transformed" (III.1.109); more than the crime she suffered, the revenge she undertakes subjects her to Cenci's restless torment: "neither life nor death can give me rest" (III.1.140). Recruiting Orsino for the vendetta, she declares her wrong "such / As asks atonement" (III.1.214–15), ironically choosing a term for revenge that subverts her intended meaning, revealing instead the at-onement with Cenci inherent in her adoption of his methods.

A curious analogue to the generation of revenge in Beatrice's psyche marks one of Orsino's soliloquies. Having chosen the priesthood for its considerable financial advantages, Orsino can neither put off nor satisfy his desire for Beatrice. Wish engenders fantasy:

> and thus unprofitably
> I clasp the phantom of unfelt delights

> Till weak imagination half possesses
> The self-created shadow. (II.2.140–43)

Orsino is himself an adept in the dangerous mysteries of self-analysis. "Unprofitably" is simply the verbal reflex of an acquisitive nature, worth remarking as an instance of Shelley's frequent revelation of character through diction. But Shelley further endows his characters with the tendency to expose their own deeper motives, as in Orsino's remarks on the dynamics of frustrated desire. Unable to possess (lust again shares a vocabulary with capital accumulation) Beatrice, he reaches toward a phantom or shadow—a metaphor—of Beatrice instead, and in its poverty the imagination is more than half willing to suspend disbelief. "Self-created" is double-edged: In one sense, the phantom of Beatrice is created onanistically by Orsino himself, and the term mocks his inability to actually seize the other he desires; and yet, from another angle, the shadow or metaphor seems to create itself, desire and imagination functioning outside Orsino's control.

Substitute rejection for desire, the memory for the fantasy of a sexual act, and Orsino's self-critique can be applied to Beatrice. She cannot remember the act, cannot possess or control it: "I, who can feign no image in my mind / Of that which has transformed me" (III.1.108–9). Nor can she escape it:

> What is this indistinguishable mist
> Of thoughts, which rise, like shadow after shadow,
> Darkening each other? (III.1.170–72)

Still enveloped by the "bewildering mist" envisioned and engendered by her father, Beatrice fails in her efforts to image the act, while "shadows"—reflections or, again, metaphors—rise self-created. The metaphor that finally emerges as the vehicle for expressing rape is murder:

> Mighty death!
> Thou double visaged shadow! Only judge!
> Rightfullest arbiter! (III.1.177–79)

As a metaphor, murder looks two ways: It enables Beatrice to grasp and (she thinks) to reverse the effects of the rape, and it will render the rape, for Beatrice, a mere antetype of the murder that atones for it:

> something which shall make
> The thing that I have suffered but a shadow
> In the dread lightning which avenges it. (III.1.87–89)

But Beatrice's attempt to undo the rape through reducing it to a metaphor, like Orsino's comparable fantasy, is merely wishful; her crime will in fact be a different sort of shadow altogether, a repetition of the violation she has undergone.

The scene of Beatrice's transformation proceeds to the only extended descriptive passage in the play, one illustrating Shelley's statement that "in a dramatic composition the imagery and the passion should interpenetrate one another."[16] Beatrice describes the spot where Orsino's promised assassins can most easily ambush her father:

> the road
> Crosses a deep ravine; 'tis rough and narrow,
> And winds with short turns down the precipice;
> And in its depth there is a mighty rock,
> Which has, from unimaginable years,
> Sustained itself with terror and with toil
> Over a gulph, and with the agony
> With which it clings seems slowly coming down;
> Even as a wretched soul hour after hour,
> Clings to the mass of life; yet clinging, leans;
> And leaning, makes more dark the dread abyss
> In which it fears to fall. (III.1.244–55)

Description becomes self-portraiture. The "abyss" that Beatrice describes appears throughout mental theater: One recalls Marmaduke "plumbing the abyss for judgement," or Cain's alienating voyage through the "Abyss of Space."[17] In each case the protagonist, guided, or rather impelled, by his seducer, abandons a familiar moral landscape and attempts the transition to a new, independent consciousness of self, but discovers instead that there is no crossing an abyss, and no retreat from it. Beatrice's comment on the murder, "The act seals all" (IV.3.7), becomes highly ironic when her full dilemma has been perceived. The crime, once accomplished, sets the mark of eternal self-alienation forever on Beatrice's brow.

It is remarkable that in *The Borderers* and *Cain*, as well as in *The Cenci*, not only must the protagonist cross an abyss, but the first intimation of the crime is expressed by ellipsis. Cain, responding to Lucifer's leading questions regarding Abel, protests, "why recall a thought that—"; Marmaduke, searching for judgment, strikes "something" which turns the "mind / Back on herself, I think, again—." In all three cases, the inner abyss first discovers itself as a gap in the thought process: The mind draws back from the unthinkable, and yet the unthinkable asserts itself independently of conscious control, becoming the unutterable instead. As Macbeth describes his own murderous "thought": "function / Is smothered in surmise, and nothing is / But what is not" (I.3.140–42). The protagonist's encounter with a mental process that resists the conscious will yields a first, frightening glimpse of a psychic rift, and with it the possibility of radical self-estrangement. In this way a criminal self-consciousness arises even before the crime has been perpetrated.

One could go on to ask whether the abyss already inhabits the mind, waiting to be exposed, or whether it emerges only with the protagonist's seduction. The Romantics are often credited with the popularization, if not the discovery, of the unconscious,[18] and a psychoanalytical reading would find no end of promising material in the case of Beatrice C.[19] A deconstructive reading would go further and argue that the protagonist of mental theater encounters at such junctures an "aporia" that throws the notion of a discrete thinking subject—let alone a subject in mastery of its thought—into question.[20] The Romantics themselves view psychic activity in more consistently dynamic terms, approaching neither the psychoanalytic attempt to map the mind nor the deconstructive imperative for finding it unchartable. In mental theater the mind forms itself through its dynamic relations with the social and material world, moving with an active and outward or an inward and reactive bias. Self-anatomy—as we find in the cases of Beatrice, Cain, Manfred, and Marmaduke—entails a centripetal motion, one continually skirting a dizzying inner abyss while steadily enclosing by revolving about itself. The centrifugal movement of sympathy—a naive stage of which is represented by Adah in *Cain*, and which Asia will exemplify at a more complex level in *Prometheus Unbound*—leaves the problem of the inner abyss behind. As the mind, become self-conscious, directs itself again outward, reaffirming social relations and bonds, forging a more human world, "spreading joy," as Adah puts it, self-expression through activity outmodes the quest for self-definition.

Beatrice, however, "violently thwarted from her nature," as Shelley remarks of her historical model,[21] founders in the abyss as Cenci did before her. The deformation of her character first grows manifest in her adoption of Cenci's self-exemption from social morality. Cenci glosses over his crimes by proclaiming himself a "scourge" of God (IV.1.63), and so Beatrice calls Cenci's assassin a "weapon in the hand of God" (IV.3.54), and the murder "the angel of His wrath" (V.3.114). Cenci boasts himself free of "fear" and "remorse," and so Beatrice urges Lucretia to "put off . . . Forbearance and respect, remorse and fear / And all the fit restraints of daily life" (III.1.208–10), the "checks" (Cenci's term) that make social existence, participation in the "mass of life," possible. Once more, an intertextual allusion lies behind the intratextual echo, relating Beatrice not only to her parent but to his literary forebear as well: "farewell Hope, and with Hope farewell Fear, / Farewell Remorse: all Good to me is lost" (*Paradise Lost*, IV.108–9).

Shelley relates the crime to Macbeth's murder of Duncan as well, through a second doubly allusive phrase. Lucretia cries "Would it were done" as the assassins return to Cenci's bedchamber, having recoiled from their first attempt. In repeating the close of Cenci's most densely allusive speech, Lucretia ties Beatrice's crime to his as his was tied to Macbeth's; another association with *Macbeth* is made earlier in the same scene as the assassin Marzio voices his moral qualms:

> I knew it was the ghost
> Of my dead father speaking through his lips,
> And could not kill him. (IV.3.20–22)

The same locus in *Macbeth* ("Had he not resembled / My father as he slept, I had done't") resounds at such a moment in *The Borderers* as well, suggesting a special thematic relevance (beyond the obvious contextual one) to mental theater.[22] To murder one's father is, in a sense, to murder one's origin, to kill figuratively the history of one's self. Marzio gives voice to the paradoxical element that Beatrice fails to perceive in her undertaking. In attempting to restore her self-image through killing Cenci, she loses her self-identity: As in the case of Oedipus, parricide leads not to freedom but to compulsion, loss, blindness.

Beatrice, in adopting Cenci's evil as her good, degenerates markedly from the noble heroine of the first two acts (although Lucretia and Bernardo, the younger brother, persist to the end in seeing her as their guardian angel). Not that Beatrice becomes as patently monstrous as her father; while he slips easily into the worn lineaments of the ranting Gothic tyrant, she remains invested with the dark splendor of the Jacobean villainess-heroine, resembling especially Lady Macbeth in the murder scene (IV.3) and Vittoria Corombona, the White Devil, during the trial (V.3). Arraigned by a papal court that effectively as well as nominally upholds the play's father figures, she pretends to a Promethean role, having "endured what never any / Guilty or innocent endured before" (V.2.139–40). But she finds the Promethean guise no more durable than did Byron's self-tormented protagonists; her last speech to her judge, in fact, could be spoken by Manfred: "My pangs are of the mind, and of the heart, / And of the soul; aye, of the inmost soul" (V.3.65–6). Like Manfred, she claims only a pyrrhic victory, for her "poisoned" inmost soul is no longer her own; she counters her tormentors at the end with an inner torment greater than any they can inflict, but no less agonizing for that.

And yet, what reader fails to sympathize with Beatrice: a victim of rape and torture, a rebel against paternal tyranny connived at by church and state, incarnating the rare union of "energy and gentleness" admired by Shelley in the historical Beatrice's portrait?[23] One's difficulty in coming to terms with Beatrice reflects no flaw in characterization or dramatic structure. Rather, the impossibility of either condemning or refraining to condemn Beatrice's actions is integral to Shelley's strategy for implicating the reader in the process of self-anatomy. "It is in the restless and anatomizing casuistry with which men seek the justification of Beatrice, yet feel that she has done what needs justification . . . that the dramatic character of what she did and suffered, consists."[24] Shelley's thoughts of Covent Garden should not prevent us from seeing here the central aim of mental theater. He states in the same paragraph of the preface that the "moral purpose" of drama consists in "teaching the human heart, through its sympathies and antipathies, the knowledge of itself." Through undergoing a struggle of sympathy and antipathy in relation to Beatrice, the reader is engaged in a siege of contraries that parallels the struggle within Beatrice's mind. The reader is at once caught up in Beatrice's dilemma and caught in a similar dilemma of her or his own, one that discovers new intensities of response and self-analysis.

Shelley suggests the intensity of such a divided response in the trial scene. The assassin Marzio has revealed (after considerable judicial torture) Beatrice's guiding role in the murder. Beatrice, whose composure in this scene is both admirable and chilling, demands that he approach her, look directly into her eyes, and again declare her guilt. He reacts with the painful sense of dislocation once felt by Cenci himself in confronting Beatrice: "Spare me! My brain swims round . . . I cannot speak" (V.2.88). Marzio's role as reader-spectator within the play is underscored by the judge's response, which unexpectedly evokes Shelley's preface:

> Drag him away to torments; let them be
> Subtle and long drawn out, to tear the folds
> Of the heart's inmost cell. (V.2.160–62)

The judge calls for a forced version of Shelley's dramatic investigation of the "dark and secret caverns of the heart"; torture becomes a crude counterpart to the instructive casuistry that seizes the engaged reader.

Beatrice's assumption of her father's inner restlessness finds analogues not only in the implication of the reader, but within the drama, in the fates of several subordinate characters, as well, building repetition on repetition. Here is another example of Orsino's brilliant but costly self-analysis:

> Some unbeheld divinity doth ever,
> When dread events are near, stir up men's minds
> To black suggestions; and he prospers best,
> Not who becomes the instrument of ill,
> But who can flatter the dark spirit, that makes
> Its empire and its prey of other hearts
> Till it become his slave. (II.2.155–61)

Orsino would entrap Cenci using his own methods. Both seek to exert power in the form of psychic imperialism, preying on the minds of those around them, and both reveal their ultimate intentions through a shared vocabulary of domination, empire, and enslavement. More particular to Orsino is his reference to an alien force visiting—if not inhabiting—the mind, related to the estranged self-conception implicit in his soliloquy on desire and imagination. Yet despite his tacit denial of an integral, self-governing consciousness, Orsino flatters himself with the prospect of mastering the master, and confiscating its harvest of mental slaves.

Hoping to eliminate her father and obtain Beatrice's person along with her inheritance, Orsino preys upon Giacomo, her brother, much as Cenci preys upon Beatrice. Through artful suggestions Orsino plants the germ of parricide—superfluously, as it turns out—in Giacomo's mind:

> O, had I never
> Found in thy smooth and ready countenance
> The mirror of my darkest thoughts; hadst thou
> Never with hints and questions made me look
> Upon the monster of my thought, until
> It grew familiar to desire . . . (V.1.19–24)

Giacomo falls through a mental process closely allied in its dynamics to his sister's psychic disintegration. He too encounters a distorting mirror, a perverse reflection that shapes, or rather misshapes, his mind. Under Orsino's tutelage, his consciousness is violated and disintegrated by a monstrous birth that parallels the genesis of parricide in Beatrice's psyche. The analogue brings out a common antecedent in Othello's words to his seducer, Iago:

> thou echo'st me,
> As if there were some monster in thy thought
> Too hideous to be shown. (III.3.106–8)

Once more repetition within the text underscores and is underscored by the echo of a prior text.[25] Like his sister, Giacomo arrives at an unbridgeable, unavoidable "gulph" (V.1.52), and his fate, eternal pursuit by the "hounds / Of conscience" (V.1.8–9), forms a melodramatic counterpart to hers.

Orsino's inevitable degeneration similarly reflects that of Beatrice. His "plot of mingled good and ill" ends in tragedy for him no less than for his intended tools, subverted by the "unbeheld divinity" that thrives on self-anatomy: "there arose a Power / Which graspt and snapped the threads of my device" (V.1.81–82). His self-estrangement becomes objectified when he is forced to assume a "vile disguise" and a "new name." He cannot, however, elude his fate, one he shares with Milton's Satan and Shelley's Wandering Jew:

> Have I not the power to fly
> My own reproaches? Shall I be the slave
> Of . . . what? A word?
> . . . where shall I
> Find the disguise to hide me from myself,
> As now I skulk from every other eye? (V.1.97–105)

So pervasive and inexorable is the chain of repetition that it draws in even Bernardo, Beatrice's pathetic younger brother, who comments at the end (evoking Macbeth): "I shall never sleep again" (V.3.6).

When more forced confessions have sealed Beatrice's condemnation, she gives way entirely to despair. Betrayed from without and from within, she takes refuge in a silence uncomfortably reminiscent of Iago's final obstinacy: "thus let it be / And so an end of all. Now do your will; / No other pains shall force another word" (V.3.87–89). No longer can she deny her lasting bondage, through the replicate act, to her father's will. Directly after the murder, she could remark with unconscious irony that "the spirit which doth reign within these limbs / Seems strangely undisturbed" (IV.3.63–64). Now the ruling spirit reveals itself, in Beatrice's dejected and remorseless state, as the resistless and ubiquitous image of her father:

> If all things then should be . . . my father's spirit,
> His eye, his voice, his touch surrounding me;
> The atmosphere and breath of my dead life! (V.4.60–62)

At the end Cenci grows as omnipotent in his daughter's eyes as he was in his own. All existence seems to her finally a struggle of "the oppressor and the oppressed" (V.3.75), a vast extension of the relation Cenci imposed on his children, as Giacomo states: "We / Are now no more, as once, parent and child, / But . . . the oppressor to the oppressed" (III.1.282–84).

Beatrice's last moments on stage, however, recapture the earlier portrayal of her courage and integrity. As she and Lucretia are ordered to proceed to their execution, she pauses for a final gesture:

> Here, Mother, tie
> My girdle for me, and bind up this hair
> In any simple knot; aye, that does well.
> And yours I see is coming down. How often
> Have we done this for one another; now
> We shall not do it any more. My Lord,
> We are quite ready. Well, 'tis very well.

Repetition becomes, in this final vision of Beatrice, something benign and enduring. Her image is caught and held in a haunting ritual that evokes the strongest aspects of her character: gentleness, courage, female and familial solidarity, eloquence.

Such a conclusion can only intensify the "restless and anatomizing casuistry" inspired in the reader by all that has gone before. It should come as no surprise that Shelley undertook his own reading of Milton in a similar spirit: "The character of Satan engenders in the mind a pernicious casuistry which leads us to weigh his faults against his wrongs, and to excuse the former because the latter exceed all measure."[26] Shelley praised Milton for this "bold neglect of a direct moral purpose,"[27] considering indirection Milton's best strategy as a poet working within a tradition that enshrined the dichotomies between good and evil, god and devil. But Shelley himself felt called upon to transcend such dichotomies, to have "Satan," as Blake suggested in his emendation of *Cain,* "self-subdued Put off Satan." *The Cenci* portrays a sad reality; in a "drama of the highest order," however, as Shelley wrote in retrospect, "there is little food for censure or hatred; it teaches rather self-knowledge and self-respect." Such a drama would move beyond the tragic self-anatomy engendered by myths like those of Beatrice and Satan, and lead the awakened reader onward toward greater imaginative power and a wider extension of sympathy. The highest drama had been attained in Athens: "mirrors in which the spectator beholds himself, under a thin disguise of circumstance, stript of all but that ideal perfection and energy which every one feels to be the internal type of all that he loves, admires, and would become."[28] Working from a Greek model—while still reworking his English models—Shelley created "a more poetical character than Satan . . . the type of the highest perfection of moral and intellectual nature, impelled by the purest and the truest motives to the best and noblest ends."[29] Shelley's reader, seeking to transcend the divided response to sublime, Satanic energy, could find a redemptive mirror in *Prometheus Unbound.*

7

Prometheus Unbound: Consciousness and the Spirit of the Age

We first encounter Shelley's Prometheus as yet another figure of tormented self-consciousness: sleepless, defiant, his Titanic heroism resting on continual struggle with a mighty opposite, Jupiter. In framing their conflict, Shelley draws—as he had in *The Wandering Jew*—on *Macbeth* and *Paradise Lost*, his principal models for the drama of psychic struggle. These texts hover in the form of extended epigraphs over the early narrative, guiding its thematic movement but patently resisting assimilation. In *Prometheus Unbound*, however, Shelley critically transforms his antecedents, exposing the limitations and contradictions inherent in a self-consciousness that originates in an act of transgression, and maintains itself through hateful struggle in a crudely dichotomized world. In the tragedy of Beatrice Cenci, he would resume only to intensify the critique of an egoistic, criminal self-consciousness; but in *Prometheus Unbound*, Shelley moves beyond critique and beyond tragedy. As a "more poetical character" than Milton's tempter, Prometheus puts off the Satanic aspects of his nature, but the drama does not end with his regeneration.[1] The protagonist's role itself grows outmoded as Shelley takes mental theater past the dilemma of self-consciousness.

The drama's opening tableau—Prometheus bound to the rocks, lamenting his "sleep-unsheltered" agony, and staring at the heavens "eyeless with hate"—immediately suggests Milton's Samson rather than his Satan. And the formal influence of *Samson Agonistes* on Shelley's lyrical drama should not be minimized. Shelley cites Milton's dramatic poem as a precedent for the "blank lyrical measure" he developed in *Queen Mab*, and Milton's was the only important precedent as well both for fusing Greek and English dramatic conventions and for the dramatic portrayal of consciousness at the expense of stage action.[2] It would be unwise, however, to extend the parallel too far.

Samson's "restless thoughts" (I.19) may resemble Prometheus's mental agony, but so—and in a much more profound manner—do those of Milton's Satan. The relation of Shelley's Titan to Milton's devil, discussed by Shelley himself in the preface and advertised in the text by numerous textual echoes, has received a good deal of critical attention. Too often, however, Shelley's very subtle reworking has been distorted into the schematic portrayal of a redeemed Satan confronting an unmasked version of Milton's "tyrannical" God.[3] Shelley's critical revision of the Satanic mind in *Prometheus Unbound* involves much more than a simple reversal, and viewing it as such loses much of the irony and complexity of the drama's first act. Though endowed with Satan's "courage, and majesty, and firm and patient opposition to omnipotent force," Prometheus is burdened initially with Satan's limitations as well; and Shelley's characterization of Jupiter owes no less to Milton's Satan than to his God.[4]

Prometheus and Jupiter resemble one another—and their common antecedent—through a shared psychic restlessness, an agony that at once feeds and subsists on their seemingly endless war of wills. Prometheus unconsciously reveals his bond to Jupiter in the drama's opening speech, in which the contradictions implicit in his moral autonomy consistently undermine his Titanic pose:

> Monarch of Gods and Daemons, and all Spirits
> But One, who throng those bright and rolling Worlds
> Which Thou and I alone of living things
> Behold with sleepless eyes! regard this Earth
> Made multitudinous with thy slaves, whom thou
> Requitest for knee-worship, prayer and praise,
> And toil, and hecatombs of broken hearts,
> With fear and self contempt and barren hope;
> Whilst me, who am thy foe, eyeless in hate,
> Hast thou made reign and triumph, to thy scorn,
> O'er mine own misery and thy vain revenge.—
> Three thousand years of sleep-unsheltered hours
> And moments—aye divided by keen pangs
> Till they seemed years, torture and solitude,
> Scorn and despair,—these are mine empire;—
> More glorious far than that which thou surveyest
> From thine unenvied throne, O Mighty God![5]

The opposition that Prometheus asserts between Jupiter and himself rests on a fundamental identification. He presents himself and his opponent as the two sole "sleepless" rulers of the universe—Jupiter the Monarch of all but Prometheus, Prometheus reigning over an "empire" of torment. The phrase "Thou and I alone of living things" is particularly telling: Both assert their rule at the cost of isolation, yet they are alone together, for each validates his claim to mastery through its effect on the other. Prometheus bound emblematizes Jupiter's power, while the god's "unenvied" throne provides the standard against which Prometheus measures his psychic empire. Although he blames Jupiter for creating a world of slaves, Prometheus subjects himself to a will to power modeled after Jupiter's own. His original, benevolent vision has given way to a siege of contraries; despite his "sleepless eyes," he remains "eyeless," prevented by his investment in continual struggle from envisioning its transcendence.

At the drama's outset Prometheus clearly belongs among the tragic protagonists of mental theater. Like Marmaduke, or Cain, or Beatrice, he has purchased his intensified self-consciousness with a tortured isolation. And like their seducers—Oswald, Lucifer, Cenci—his claims to psychic autonomy rest precariously on an unresolvable struggle for mastery. Prometheus, however, gradually learns to perceive the contradictions behind his stance, and his progressive self-discovery forms the dramatic core of the first act. The second thoughts that prod him to "recall" his ancient curse on Jupiter begin, rather than constitute, a process of self-analysis that extends throughout the act, complicated by Jupiter's efforts to subvert it and resolved only through Asia's parallel mental traveling in Act II.[6]

Prometheus's doubts begin when he hears the vindictiveness in his tone even as he condemns Jupiter's "vain revenge." Though as yet blind to the ironies of his own position, the Titan knows that Jupiter's assertion of an untenable autonomy will lead finally to inner collapse. He solaces his torment by prophesying Jupiter's inevitable downfall, the fatal "Hour" which

> Shall drag thee, cruel King, to kiss the blood
> From these pale feet, which then might trample thee
> If they disdained not such a prostrate slave.
> Disdain? Ah no! I pity thee.—What Ruin
> Will hunt thee undefended through wide Heaven!

How will thy soul, cloven to its depth with terror,
Gape like a Hell within! I speak in grief,
Not exultation, for I hate no more,
As then, ere misery made me wise.—The Curse
Once breathed on thee I would recall.

Prometheus begins by inventing a scene that would confirm his claim to ascendancy over Jupiter, and his accents grow as tyrannical as those we would expect of the god himself. His troubled repetition—"Disdain?"—opens the self-examination interrupted almost immediately by a literary echo evoking the Satanic "Hell within" that Jupiter holds at bay only through his constant exertion of dominion. Prometheus is far as yet from recognizing his own Satanic taints. But his desire to recall the curse—at this point merely to remember it—announces his growing discomfort with a stance far too reminiscent of Jupiter's, as he begins critically to review its history. The use of "recall" for remember does, of course, foreshadow Prometheus's eventual desire to revoke the curse. But at this point he is as much concerned with his forgotten words' continuing "power"—"let them not lose it now!"—as with the possibility that they contain "aught evil wish"; until he learns what he in fact had said, he will not be certain whether he means to take it back or not. The transition from a violence comparable to that of Jupiter (who later threatens to "trample" Demogorgon) to disdain to condescending pity hardly describes, let alone completes, the Titan's regeneration.

The repetition of Prometheus's curse functions on several dramatic levels, and each represents a dimension of the unfolding central conflict. The curse strengthens the parallel between Prometheus and Jupiter, and further emphasizes their common Satanic ancestry. Like the curses uttered in the mental theater of Byron and Wordsworth—*The Borderers, Cain, Manfred*—its utterance marks its fulfillment; like Cenci's curse on Beatrice, it returns ironically on the speaker as well.[7] The *repetition* of the curse is unique, however, and marks a critical stage in Prometheus's education: Through hearing it rehearsed by another, he begins to recognize the Jupiter in himself. Most readers share the Titan's own conviction that his inability to remember the curse reflects his sudden freedom from "what is hate." But he has in fact repressed a critical moment in his psychic history, which he cannot acknowledge without abandoning his pretense to moral eminence.

His forgetfulness underscores the self-deception that has allowed him to engage for so long in a pernicious struggle for untenable power.

No living creature will risk Jupiter's wrath by quoting Prometheus's forgotten curse, and Earth herself—the Titan's mother—will do no more than translate it into the "language of the dead," a tongue that unfortunately Prometheus can no more understand than Jupiter. Earth then suggests the stratagem of raising the spectral double—the "ghost" that awaits each living creature in the otherworld—of Prometheus, or one of his brother Titans, or whomever else he chooses, for the "vacant shades" cannot feel Jupiter's tortures. When Prometheus demurs at hearing "evil" from "aught resembling" him, his apparent remorse is complicated by his obstinacy, a continued unwillingness to acknowledge the evil of his own past action. He summons up instead the Phantasm of Jupiter; but in confronting Jupiter's shade he both discovers and rejects an image of himself.[8]

That the Phantasm shadows both Jupiter and Prometheus, bringing out their hidden likeness, emerges partly through allusions within the curse that link each to Milton's Satan. Prometheus notes the Phantasm's "looks of proud defiance, and calm hate" (I.259) with a sudden discomfort ("yet speak—O speak!") because the "gestures proud and cold" could be either Jupiter's or his own. The first words of the curse—"Fiend, I defy thee! with a calm fixed mind"—assimilate the reflected aspect of Jupiter to the repeated words of Prometheus, and underscore the relation of both to Milton's Satan, with his pride, his defiance, his "fixt mind," and his eternal struggle with an undefeatable opponent. The following lines of the curse—

> All that thou canst inflict I bid thee do
> Foul Tyrant both of Gods and Humankind,
> One being only shalt thou not subdue—

are inspired by Satan:

> yet not for these
> Nor what the Potent Victor in his rage
> Can else inflict, do I repent or change,
> Though chang'd in outward luster; that fixt mind . . .
> (I.94–97)

The curse next brings out the Satanic element of Jupiter's career: "Heap on thy soul by virtue of this Curse / Ill deeds, then be thou damned, beholding good" (I.292–93), recapitulating Milton's gloss on Satan's freedom to work ill: "That with reiterated crimes he might / Heap on himself damnation, while he sought / Evil to others" (IV.212–16). Prometheus would visit an "infinity" of "envenomed agony" on his tormentor, "a crown of pain," and yet to do so he must "imprecate" a parallel "sleepless agony" upon himself; Jupiter's "self-torturing solitude" (295) finds an emblem in the spectacle of an isolated, tormented Prometheus. Fiend and Tyrant, God and Titan, begin to blur together as complementary terms in a struggle that paradoxically sustains twin antagonists, each committed to the other's downfall yet invested in the other's recognition.

The lesson is not lost on Prometheus, who delivers himself from his own imprecation by annulling the curse and abjuring evil to others. The syntax of his retraction is appropriately reflexive—"It doth repent me . . . I wish no living thing to suffer pain" (I.304–5). When Earth mistakes his self-overcoming for capitulation—"Your refuge, your defense lies fallen and vanquished" (I.311)—two Echoes take up the refrain, underscoring the play of opposed doubles that the uncomprehending Earth desires to reinstate. Jupiter shares this desire, and at once dispatches his herald Mercury to the scene, ostensibly to threaten the Titan with harsher punishment, but in fact to reindoctrinate him. Mercury's threats constitute an intricate temptation, designed to lure Prometheus back into the bond of rivalry with an inimical double.

As the medium between Prometheus and Jupiter, Mercury absorbs something of their psychic restlessness. The Titan's form "pursues" him "night and day," and "Heaven seems Hell" (I.358–59) after Mercury visits him. The last phrase evokes, along with Prometheus's earlier remark on Jupiter's betrayal—"Evil minds / Change good to their own nature" (I.380–81)—Satan's desperate moment of self-anatomy in Eden: "all good to me becomes / Bane, and in Heav'n much worse would be my state" (IX.122–23). Mercury endeavors to neutralize Prometheus's own developing self-criticism with just such a Satanic despair, and to reenlist him in the struggle for parity with Jupiter. He first proposes a simple reversal, still based on mutual reflection, of the Titan's former urge to master the world's ruler: "Let the will kneel within thy haughty heart," he advises, for such submission will in turn "tame" the God (I.378–79). Prometheus rejects the pose of servility out of hand, and yet his high-mindedness brings him dangerously close to resuming the attitude of his enemy:

> Pity the self-despising slaves of Heaven,
> Not me, within whose mind sits peace serene
> As light in the sun, throned . . . How vain is talk!
> (I.429–31)

As in *The Cenci,* Shelley uses ellipsis here to convey a moment of psychic recoil. Though still unable to see through Jupiter's master-slave dichotomy, Prometheus balks at his own image of a moral throne, and uneasily breaks off the threatening and far from vain talk by means of which Mercury has skillfully led him back toward his initial error.[9]

Mercury next brings on a chorus of Furies, "Phantasms so foul" that they momentarily shake the Titan's sense of identity: "Methinks I grow like what I contemplate / And laugh and stare in loathsome sympathy" (I.450–51). The Furies take up Mercury's endeavor to restore the perverse equilibrium that, after three thousand years of contemplating Jupiter with sleepless eyes, Prometheus has begun to unsettle. Their relation exerts an imprisoning and introspective force—the opposite of the inclusive sympathy exemplified by Asia—that binds master and slave in mental struggle; Prometheus has felt its power when hearing his curse repeated in the unintelligible tongue of the dead:

> Obscurely through my brain like shadows dim
> Sweep awful thoughts, rapid and thick.—I feel
> Faint, like one mingled in entwining love,
> Yet 'tis not pleasure. (I.146–49)

His reaction to the Furies' torments brings him again dangerously close to "loathsome sympathy" with their master.[10] When they threaten to infiltrate his brain as "dread thought," his heart as "foul desire," literalizing Jupiter's psychic imperialism, the Titan responds:

> Yet I am king over myself, and rule
> The torturing and conflicting throngs within
> As Jove rules you when Hell grows mutinous. (I.492–94)

Again, resistance to Jupiter's threats contains within itself the greater danger. But the Furies, capitalizing on their successful opening, go still further toward engaging the Titan in a renewed struggle for mastery. In fact they go too far, and inadvertently awaken in him a saving revulsion at his implication in Jupiter's reign.

A second chorus of Furies enters the scene, and each recounts the evil act it has been called from. The scene recalls the entry of the Witches in *Macbeth* (I.3), though (as with Byron's imitation of the same scene in *Manfred*) their evil exemplifies political repression rather than the Witches' banality. The formal allusion helps define the Furies' program as Prometheus's seduction, an attempt to ensnare him in an equivocation that lies like truth. Along with the choric comment that summarizes their presentation—"Man and beast, and foul and fair, / Like a tempest in the air" (I.785–86)—the allusive entry frames Prometheus's temptation with references to the seduction of Macbeth.[11] Once assembled, the Furies present their victim with two pageants, first juxtaposing Christ's Passion with the debasement of Christianity into priestcraft and persecution, then portraying the degeneration of the French Revolution into the Terror. Each is designed to convince him that Promethean endeavor functions ultimately as part of Jupiter's repressive cosmic machine.

The French Revolution established a "legioned band of linked brothers"—a prototype of the human "chain of linked thought" celebrated later in Act IV—only to yield again to the previous status quo, a social version of the master-slave relation of Prometheus and Jupiter: "The struggling World, which slaves and tyrants win" (I.577). The lesson of this history is despair; Promethean love for humanity cannot fail to become, the Furies imply, the foundation for renewed tyranny. At one level, *Prometheus Unbound* can be read as Shelley's critical response to the failure of the French Revolution, which he had analyzed in the preface to *Laon and Cythna;* Wordsworth would similarly describe *The Borderers* as inspired by his own analysis of "the changes through which the French Revolution passed."[12]

Christ, nailed to his cross and gazing through "tortured orbs" (I.600), presents yet another counterpart to the bound Titan, one who necessarily becomes, in the Furies' poisonous logic, the tyrannous, Jupiter-like God of Christendom, perpetuating Heaven's reign of terror.[13] The implication is, again, ominous: As Christ, though a type of Prometheus, could not fail to become Jehovah, so the Titan, even in winning his struggle with Jupiter, would in turn become the oppressive God; and in fact the Furies, in the context of Shelley's critique of mental fight and simplistic dichotomies, are not far from the truth. The Furies then disperse, leaving one to explicate a final, encompassing "emblem":

> those who do endure
> Deep wrongs for man, and scorn, and chains, but heap
> Thousandfold torment on themselves and him. (I.594–96)

With a cruel irony, the Fury turns the force of Prometheus's curse ("Heap on thy soul . . . ill deeds") back on its author. He is thoroughly and inescapably, the Fury suggests, Jupiter's double. Like Satan, he will remain locked in unending struggle with his heavenly adversary, and like Satan's evil, his good merely adds chiaroscuro to the divine design.

The Fury, however, pursues an advantage too far; already repentant for the curse he once uttered, Prometheus can interpret the Furies' pageant as a painful but enlightening phase in his education. For a moment, his growing despair becomes compassion for the slaves of Heaven who remain ignorant of their implication in Jupiter's oppressive system: "Thy words are like a cloud of winged snakes / And yet, I pity those they torture not" (I.632–33). Like the "spring of love" that frees Coleridge's Ancient Mariner from his psychic burden, Prometheus's turn from introspective anguish to self-distancing sympathy disarms the Furies' temptation of its crippling force. But the movement is still only tentative. The Ancient Mariner merely internalizes his burden; self-condemned to a Cain-like wandering and to continual repetition of his tale, he can never fully act on his own message of sympathetic love. Prometheus stands to be caught in a similarly frozen existence, repentant but unredeemed. Though the Furies vanish, his remains a "woe-illumined mind." "Peace is in the grave" (I.638–39); as yet, only his endurance has been renewed.

Earth now summons a group of spirits from "the dim caves of human thought" who, forming the masque to the Furies' anti-masque, enter recounting triumphs of human kindness. But their eulogies contain an element of warning as well. The Fourth Spirit flies from the lips of a poet too like the haunted figure of *Alastor:* "Nor seeks nor finds he mortal blisses / But feeds on the aerial kisses / Of shapes that haunt thought's wildernesses" (I.740–42). The Sixth Spirit, speaking of the power of Desolation over "gentlest" minds, glosses her sister's description with an emblem of those who "Dream visions of aerial joy, and call the monster, Love, / And wake, and find the shadow Pain, as he whom now we greet" (I.778–79). Love, as Prometheus must now learn, can too easily become its own shadow; the outward movement of sympathy can turn inward, becoming merely ideal and inherently narcissistic. *Alastor* portrays, in the words of Shelley's preface, the tragic consequences of an "attempt to exist without human sympathy"; the poet perishes in a doomed, because egoistical, "search after its communities, when the vacancy of [his] spirit suddenly makes itself felt."[14] The Titan's perception of this very danger prompts him to a movement more crucial than both the first, from hatred to repentance, and the second, from despair to compassion. Prometheus seeks now to end his three millennia of isolation by renewing a sympathetic relation that would replace and counteract the enclosing struggle for power with Jupiter.

The first act opened with Prometheus calling on the world's "Monarch." At its end, he calls to a very different figure:

> Asia! who when my being overflowed
> Wert like a golden chalice to bright wine
> Which else had sunk into the thirsty dust. (I.809–11)

Shelley's Wandering Jew, Coleridge's Ancient Mariner, Milton's Satan can all be seen as flawed antetypes of Prometheus, who alone moves forward from the tormented self-consciousness born of an ideologically liberating yet psychically imprisoning crime. Of course, Prometheus's crime differs radically in nature: Unlike Lucifer's pursuit of mastery, or Paulo's moment of spite and disbelief, or the Mariner's *acte gratuite*, the Titan's theft of fire proceeds from compassion. In terms of its effects—an intensified self-awareness, social isolation, implication in a struggle for mastery—the theft resembles the crimes depicted elsewhere in mental theater; but in motivation, Prometheus's violation of the border between Heaven and Earth is a liberating act, destructive of the universal master-slave order exerted by Jupiter at the expense of humankind. Yet even a liberating crime, as Shelley demonstrates in *The Cenci*, can lead to isolation and self-division, no less than the deluded, misguided acts of Wordsworth's Marmaduke or Byron's Cain. Asia, and what Asia represents, makes the transition beyond a tormented self-consciousness possible; through her, Prometheus can renew the outward, overflowing movement that exemplifies the liberating principle of a new, revolutionary age.

With its elaborate portrayal of bondage and mastery, and its critique of a psychic identity precariously founded on relentless conflict, each antagonist projecting his self-image onto the other, the first act of *Prometheus Unbound* presents us with yet another version of the struggle for recognition that provides the dramatic argument of *The Borderers*, *Cain*, and *The Cenci*, and determines the career of Manfred as well. It is the struggle that makes the intensified self-awareness known as "Romantic" self-consciousness at once possible and problematic, created and inherently undermined by a single stroke. To go forward from the dilemma with which the other works of mental theater unhappily close, Shelley passes beyond the limitations of self-consciousness in *Prometheus Unbound*, but not through a simple change of heart in Prometheus, nor through the fiat of the deus ex machina which necessitarian readers have sometimes made of Demogorgon.[15] Instead, consciousness as represented by Prometheus is radically transformed; an open relation with others, in place of closed struggle with the other, redefines the Promethean mind. Where psychic borders were violated by the imperialistic incursions of the master-slave conflict, they become instead extended through the agency of imaginative sympathy, to a degree that finally tends to obliterate the enclosures of the egotistical self altogether.

In turning to imaginative sympathy as the ground for a social, rather than obsessively self-regarding, consciousness, Shelley could draw on a philosophical and literary tradition leading from Hume to Hazlitt, from Rousseau to the first generation of English Romantics.[16] The single work that best illuminates the role of sympathy in *Prometheus Unbound*, however, is Adam Smith's *Theory of Moral Sentiments* (1759), which has been called "the most popular ethical work of its time."[17] For Smith, sympathy is not a passion (or emotion) in itself but rather the principle informing "our fellow feeling with any passion whatsoever"; it makes moral life possible through enabling us to enter into the experience of others, "conceiving what we ourselves should feel in the like situation."[18] So for Shelley, "the great secret of morals is love, or a going out of our own nature and an identification of ourselves" with others.[19]

An extension of the conception of sympathy developed by Smith lies, of course, behind Shelley's theory of poetry. "A man, to be greatly good, must imagine intensely and comprehensively; he must put himself in the place of another and of many others; the pains and pleasures of his species must become his own. The great instrument of moral good is the imagination; and poetry administers to the effect by acting on the cause. Poetry enlarges the circumference of the imagination."[20] That the sympathetic imagination should play so central a role in *Prometheus Unbound* is all but inevitable given Shelley's vision of dramatic works, and particularly Athenian tragedies, as "mirrors" that strengthen and extend the sympathetic imagination. "The imagination is enlarged by a sympathy with pains and passions so mighty that they distend in their conception the capacity of that by which they are conceived."[21] In reimagining Aeschylus's lost drama, then, Shelley sought to unite the portrayal of sympathy with the vehicle most powerful to disseminate it. The conception of *Prometheus Unbound* is literally sublime, in the Longinian sense of "ec-static": a drama of the mind's capacity to transcend its limitations, designed to extend the same capacity in its readers.

Sympathy does more than enable us to imagine others, however; it also enables us to imagine ourselves. Not only, Smith argues, do we "either approve or disapprove of the conduct of another man according as we feel that, when we bring the case home to ourselves, we either can or cannot entirely sympathize" with his motives and sentiments; but "in the same manner, we either approve or disapprove of our own conduct according as we feel that, when we place ourselves in the situation of another man and view it, as it were, with his eyes and from his station, we either can or cannot entirely enter into and sympathize with the sentiments and motives which influenced it." We rely on the sympathetic imagination as much for grasping our own actions as for comprehending those of others. But for Smith sympathy plays a still more crucial role in psychic life. In a passage that anticipates nineteenth-century theories—among them Hegel's—of the socially constituted self, Smith claims that "character" cannot exist apart from a social context: "Were it possible that a human creature could grow up to manhood in some solitary place without any communication with his own species, he could no more think of his own character, or the propriety or demerit of his own sentiments and conduct, than of the beauty or deformity of his own face . . . Bring him to society, and he is immediately provided with the mirror which he wanted before."[22] Shelley's indebtedness to Smith and to the theorists influenced by him is manifest throughout his ethical writings in such statements as: "Man is in his wildest state a social being; a certain degree of civilisation and refinement ever produced the want of [i.e., need for] sympathies still more intimate and more complete."[23]

Working from Smith's and later theories of a self socially constituted through sympathetic projection and introjection, Shelley could understand the emergence of self-consciousness through the master-slave struggle—a scenario found, as we have seen, not only in Hegel but throughout Romantic mental theater—as a deformation or parody of the manner through which all self-awareness comes about. In parodic fashion, the master-slave conflict heightens by exaggerating the development of self-awareness, but it can intensify consciousness only by alienating the self from its social environment. Such estrangement makes further development through sympathetic projection impossible, and imposes in its place an exclusive and dessicating bond to the other. As the experience of Marmaduke or Cain shows, such conflict promises a shortcut to a strong, individuated selfhood but proves instead a blind alley. Reviewing the history of his conflict with Jupiter, hearing and revoking his curse, Prometheus retraces the path that has brought him a paradoxically alienated self-consciousness, but until he calls upon Asia, he cannot entirely break free from his isolation. Yet his very discovery of the encompassing abyss that he has half created, half allowed Jupiter to impose—

> I would fain
> Be what it is my destiny to be,
> The saviour and the strength of suffering man,
> Or sink into the original gulph of things . . .
> There is no agony and no solace left (I.815–19)—

brings home to him the need to once more "overflow" into Asia. Shelley writes in his "Essay on Love," in a phrase that complements his analysis of the *Alastor* poet, that "when we find within our own thoughts the chasm of an insufficient void" we turn toward that "beyond ourselves" and begin to love.[24] Prometheus finds in Asia precisely that for lack of which the *Alastor* poet perishes.

Love, or sympathy, not only renders the false relation of master and slave outmoded, but reverses its delimiting, corrosive effects as well, establishing a genuine union of self and other in place of the master's attempt to obliterate the otherness of the servant, and the servant's to subvert and overturn the master's dominion. Hegel writes in an early theological essay on "Love" that, in contrast to the "cleavage" between self and other demanded by the self's "immature" (or egocentric) quest for unity, love finally "completely destroys objectivity and thereby annuls and transcends reflection, deprives man's opposite of all foreign character . . . In love the separate does still remain, but as something united and no longer as something separate."[25] This last phrase could have been written to describe the union of Prometheus and Asia.

Promethean love finds its contrary in Jupiter's sexual domination over Thetis, another version of the master and slave relation in which sexual penetration becomes indistinguishable from psychic violation, much as with Cenci's rape of Beatrice. Jupiter remembers his conquest as:

> When thou didst cry, "Insufferable might!
> God! spare me! I sustain not the quick flames,
> The penetrating presence." (III.1.37–39)

Similar in tone to the deflowering scenes so pervasive in *The Pearl* and elsewhere in nineteenth-century pornography, Jupiter's account parodies the conventional sexual hierarchy of masterful male over helpless, conquered woman. The love of Prometheus and Asia breaks the conventions that Jupiter's account embodies. Not only is neither partner dominant, but their love, a unifying, sympathetic force continually challenging boundaries, is by definition non-exclusive. From the outset a third party, Asia's sister Panthea, joins in their union in the very act of reuniting them.

Panthea, who with Ione, a third sister, has witnessed Prometheus's suffering and education in Act I, enters Asia's vale as his emissary, wearing the "shadow" of his soul, pregnant with a dream he has inspired. Asia asks, "Lift up thine eyes / And let me read thy dream" (II.1.55–56), and Panthea's narrative begins with Prometheus making the same request: "more fair than aught but her / Whose shadow thou art—lift thine eyes on me!" (II.1.69–70). The term that described the confined, specular relation of Prometheus and Jupiter—with its emblem in Jupiter's "shade"—here finds a redeemed counterpart in Panthea as the "shadow" both of Prometheus and Asia, mediating their love through hers. Similarly, the mutual commingling with Prometheus that occurs in her dream corrects the one-sided penetration characterizing Jupiter's rape of Thetis:

> an atmosphere
> Which wrapt me in its all-dissolving power
> As the warm ether of the morning sun
> Wraps ere it drinks some cloud of wandering dew.
> I saw not—heard not—moved not—only felt
> His presence flow and mingle through my blood
> Till it became his life and his grew mine
> And I was thus absorbed—(II.1.75–82)

The antithesis and the intentional difficulty of the syntax ("Till it became his life and his grew mine") disarm the conceit—the sun's absorption of dew—of its potential imbalance; the sun becomes "ether," the dew a "cloud," and together they form a single "atmosphere." Their mingling becomes a comprehensive force that, widening continually, begins at once to form new bonds on several levels. Within the dream, Panthea and Prometheus interpenetrate one another; as Panthea lies, in sleep, next to Ione, the sisters are momentarily conjoined by the same force: "Thou hast discovered some inchantment old," Ione tells her upon waking, "Whose spells have stolen my spirit as I slept / And mingled it with thine" (II.1.101–2). And as Panthea relates the dream, Asia and Prometheus are brought together as well. Asia asks, yet again, "oh lift / Thine eyes that I may read his written soul," and Panthea replies, "what canst thou see / But thine own fairest shadow imaged there?"—meaning not only Asia's actual reflection in her pupils but her own image "written" in Panthea's responsive soul as well. Within Asia's reflection, however, beyond the "inmost depth" of Panthea's eyes hovers "a shade—a shape": the image of Prometheus incorporated through the previous night's ecstatic union.

The characterization of Asia has inspired a by now notoriously large number of allegorizations, but only the most obvious interpretations, those advanced within Shelley's text, are essential for understanding the drama's argument. Panthea embodies the universality that her name implies, as she addresses Asia:

nor is it I alone,
Thy sister, thy companion, thine own chosen one,
But the whole world which seeks thy sympathy. (II.5.32–34)

And Asia's response supports Panthea's recognition of sympathy as her defining quality: "common as light is love / And its familiar voice wearies not ever." The rest of the second act describes the sisters' journey from Asia's vale to Demogorgon's cave, bringing us to the threshold of Jupiter's downfall, and of the rise of universal sympathy. Asia's education parallels that of Prometheus in Act I: It also relies on a review of Prometheus's history, and entails a progressive self-discovery. It takes place through her interview with Demogorgon, who is imagined along inverted Miltonic lines. His encompassing "gloom divine" (II.2.22) reverses Satan's "darkness visible," and his oxymoronic figure—"neither limb / Nor form—nor outline; yet we feel it is / A living spirit" (II.4.5–7)—is a benign composite of Milton's Death and his "Anarch," Chaos.

Demogorgon's dramatic role lies in his very distance from the drama's central conflict; he encourages its collapse and that of the false contraries of Jupiter's order by remaining outside of them. To understand Demogorgon it is less useful to guess at what he represents—a line of inquiry rather inauspiciously founded by Jupiter in Act III—than to notice what he refuses to stand for. He consistently and flatly rejects the dichotomies that Asia, like Prometheus, must learn to leave behind. The approach to his cave evokes one image after another built on the confluence of conventionally opposed elements: a "wide plain of billowy mist," "stream-illumined caves," "sky-cleaving mountains," "icy spires of sunlike radiance." His attendant spirits lead the sisters down,

Through the cloudy strife
Of Death and of Life;
Through the veil and the bar
Of things which seem and are. (II.3.57–60)

The thematic imagery of border violation that usually in mental theater (including *The Cenci*) characterizes psychic incursions here evokes instead the artificiality and insufficiency of conventional oppositions. A part of Shelley's Romantic heritage, the assault on arbitrary boundaries affects many aspects of *Prometheus Unbound,* from its professed genre, "lyrical drama," through the most apparently casual, atmospheric imagery.

The thematic opposition of master and slave, equally pervasive throughout mental theater, is similarly broken down as the drama progresses. Demogorgon's formlessness enables Shelley to introduce a force mightier than Jupiter without replacing him by yet another ruler: "a mighty Darkness / Filling the seat of power" without assuming its vesture, prerogatives, or abuses.[26] When Asia stands before him, he draws her into a dialogue that resembles, but differs crucially from, the Socratic interviews of Lucifer and Cain, or Oswald and Marmaduke.[27] Oswald resembles the Socrates ironically portrayed by Kierkegaard in *The Concept of Irony* as a "vacuum pump," depleting his disciples of received notions together with social and familial ties, cutting the "umbilical cord of substantiality." Limited (in Kierkegaard's early thought) to a "purely negative dialectic," Socrates functions as indeed a seducer of youth, enchanting his charges only to abandon them to a lonely, dessicated enlightenment. Lucifer begins with the same method, but—like Kierkegaard's Plato—once having "called" his disciple "away from actuality," he goes on to impose a myth designed to advance his purposes where he has first created a psychic void.[28]

Demogorgon, however, reverses this process, using his dialectic to break down a distorting myth of Asia's making and lead her toward an "imageless" truth. Free of any metaphor or myth of Demogorgon's own, his truth demands instead that Asia achieve a deeper self-knowledge. His repetitive and noncommittal answers to her opening questions about the nature of the world and the origin of evil elicit from her a history of Prometheus and Jupiter that reveals conceptual limitations similar to those of Prometheus himself in Act I. Asia demands that Demogorgon name the world's evil principle—"a world pining in pain / Asks but his name; curses shall drag him down" (II.4.29–30). Like the unregenerate Prometheus, Asia would simply invert the world order without fundamentally altering it, assaulting Jupiter, the "Sceptred Curse" (IV.338), with his own methods. Demogorgon's refusal to say more than that "He reigns" plunges her into a self-justifying myth that, through its manifest contradictions, confronts her with the limitations of her present ideology.

Saturn's golden age was, in Asia's account, a benevolent tyranny that deprived earth's inhabitants only of "self-empire and the majesty of love" (II.4.42), terms that reveal her conceptual adherence to Jupiter's imperial ethic. Prometheus then helped Jupiter assume his reign, "Omnipotent but friendless" (II.4.47), with the provision that man be free; he failed to see, as Asia yet fails to understand, that a second empire could only perpetuate tyranny, that omnipotence is friendless not by choice but by definition. The full measure of Prometheus's continuing implication in Jupiter's system is revealed in his very efforts to alleviate its oppressive effects. His gifts to man are highly ambiguous: Like the race of Cain before the Flood, under his tutelage man built cities; "tortured to his will / Iron and gold, the slaves and signs of power," using "tamed fire"; aspired through science to "the thrones of Earth and Heaven"; and learned to "rule" the seas. Each of Prometheus's attempts to improve the human condition tends to replicate God's imperialism on earth. Asia's myth concludes with a question that suggests its eventual answer:

—but who rains down
Evil, the immedicable plague, which while
Man looks on his creation like a God
And sees that it is glorious, drives him on,
The wreck of his own will, the scorn of Earth,
The outcast, the abandoned, the alone?—
Not Jove: whole yet his frown shook heaven, aye when
His adversary from adamantine chains
Cursed him, he trembled like a slave. Declare
Who is his master? Is he too a slave? (II.4.100–109)

So long as man apes Jupiter's ruling perspective, he courts his Cain-like existence; so long as he remains enslaved to his own will, he cannot oppose God's tyranny. Prometheus's curse could expose the master as a slave, but it could not alter the master-slave relation itself. By adopting Jupiter's principle of hatred, the Titan, no less than his enemy, gives the Satanic "adamantine chains" their imprisoning force. Asia's reiterated questions, still couched in Jupiter's master-slave dichotomy, manifest both her continued entrapment in the god's conceptual scheme and her developing suspicion—fed by Demogorgon's refusal to accept her terms—that her terms are inadequate.

Demogorgon's deliberately evasive response—"All spirits are enslaved who serve things evil"—draws Asia toward the realization, implicit in her questions, that slavery consists as much in inner limitation as in outer constraint; that removing the constraint alone, without exposing the dynamic that supports it, would lead only to yet another dynasty. Asia, somewhat recalcitrantly, asks once more, "Who is the master of the slave," and Demogorgon answers:

> —If the Abysm
> Could vomit forth its secrets:—but a voice
> Is wanting, the deep truth is imageless;
> For what would it avail to bid thee gaze
> On the revolving world? what to bid speak
> Fate, Time, Occasion, Chance and Change? To these
> All things are subject but eternal Love. (II.4.114–20)

While it would be foolish to explicate what Shelley insists is ineffable, one can discover a great deal in the very constraints that Demogorgon's words impose on interpretation. Demogorgon's truth is, like Demogorgon himself, "imageless" because it exists in process, unfolding with the history of the revolving world.[29] The "Abysm" he speaks of—like the "grey, void Abysm" (II.3.72) that marks his dwelling—relates to the chasms and abysses confronted by the protagonists of mental theater. But here Shelley indicates a way through the abyss, or perhaps more accurately an imaginative stance equal to it. When encountering an inner void the tragic heroes of Romantic drama build an isolating and untenable outwork of autonomy against it—witness Manfred or Cain; the villains construct in its shadow an equally untenable identity out of endless psychic struggle. Both responses rest on an inward psychic movement, producing an intensified but tormented self-consciousness. Demogorgon gestures, with his identification of Love as freedom, toward the dynamic outward movement of sympathy. An activity, not a principle, love (or sympathy) expresses an inner freedom, continually challenging the barriers between self and other, self and world. It encourages the growth of political freedom at the same time by enabling individuals to participate in what Shelley will celebrate in Act IV as the ultimate classless society of interrelated minds. Demogorgon cannot impose such an ethic on Asia, but his statements prompt its emergence from within her:

> So much I asked before, and my heart gave
> The response that thou hast given; and of such truths
> Each to itself must be the oracle. (II.4.121–23)

Asia's awakening elaborates and clarifies the lessons learned by Prometheus in Act I. But even more important, it frees her to resume the sympathetic union with him that for both will activate what they have learned, as knowledge becomes power. The drama now takes up the unfolding of the possibilities they represent, and turns to the unseating of Jupiter and the dismantling of "Heaven's kingless throne" (II.4.149).

Jupiter's brief moment of smug triumph preceding Demogorgon's entry in Act III demonstrates why, unlike Prometheus, he cannot survive the end of their struggle. He has hoped to replace Prometheus with a more malleable substitute, the "fatal child" sired on Thetis. His son, the "terror of the Earth" (III.1.19), will be Jupiter's new double, a "mightier" reflection (through filial resemblance) and yet bound to serve him (through filial duty). The scene evokes God's proclamation of His own Son's debut in *Paradise Lost,* and parodies Their rather narcissistic (given Their consubstantiality) mutual adoration. When Jupiter, expecting to greet his son, is confronted instead by a power that refuses to assume power—"The tyranny of heaven none may retain, / Or reassume, or hold succeeding thee" (III.1.57–58)—he desperately gropes for a new order within which conflict, and the identity he has predicated upon it, can be resumed. Unable to "trample" Demogorgon into submission, he begs for a renewal of his struggle with Prometheus, offering to exchange positions—"Oh, / That thou wouldst make mine enemy my judge . . . is he not / The monarch of the world?" (III.1.64–69)—so long as their power relation might continue. When this too fails (the entire confrontation scene is as intentionally, comically undramatic as that at the end of Mozart's *Magic Flute*), Jupiter stubbornly attempts to engage Demogorgon in endless struggle: "We two will sink in the wide waves of ruin . . . twisted in inextricable fight . . . the conqueror and the conquered." He discovers, however, only in dissolution that such oppositions have ended. "Conquest is dragged captive through the deep" (IV.556) as the warring principles descend to dwell together in the abysss.

One of Jupiter's overconfident phrases has been used both to identify Prometheus with the collective spirit of mankind and to prove that the two are distinct:[30] "The soul of man, like unextinguished fire, / Yet burns toward heaven with fierce reproach and doubt" (III.1.5–6). The reader's uncertainty at this point is not accidental, but anticipates the modification of Prometheus's role announced in the following scene. The love of Prometheus and Asia exemplifies the ecstatic outpouring that begins to unify a world thirsting for sympathy. As barriers between individuals yield to the power of the sympathetic imagination, the distinction between Prometheus and the humanity he champions begins to blur. Individual heroic endeavor—Titanism—becomes outmoded as the great leveling progresses and the "Spirits of the human mind" take up the "work . . . called the Promethean" (IV.158). To lament or deprecate the deliberately anticlimactic unbinding scene or the hero's withdrawal into quiet retirement is to miss the point entirely.[31] Humankind, having stilled the "mingled voice / Of slavery and command" (III.2.30–31), would scarcely do well to create a cult of personality around a Titanic chairman. Precisely this danger underlies Hercules' well-meaning but reactionary offer to "Minister, like a slave" to Promethean wisdom (II.3.4); like the other Olympians in this act, Hercules is slow to comprehend the new human order. But Prometheus, having subdued his epic defiance in Act I, willingly assumes his new unheroic role, and retires with Asia to a cave where they will contemplate "all that man becomes" (III.3.58). One of the deeper lessons Shelley learned from *Paradise Lost* was that in human history lies an argument not less but more heroic than war in heaven.

The Cavern to which Prometheus, Asia, and her sisters retire, formerly an "oracular" site (III.3.128), recalls the "mighty portal" of Demogorgon, "Whence the oracular vapour is hurled up" as from a "chasm" (II.3.4),[32] and which leads through the "grey, void Abysm"—apparently the "Abyss" awaiting Jupiter—to Demogorgon's own cave. These associations suggest that Prometheus and Asia, Jupiter and Demogorgon share at the end a related fate, a twilight of the gods that leaves the human world free of heavenly tyranny, whether oppressive or benevolent. The dialogue of Apollo and Ocean, in the scene following Jupiter's descent, is filled with a related elegiac sadness. Apollo (like Hercules) fails to understand the events he has witnessed, and describes Demogorgon as a "conqueror," and Ocean withdraws to calm the "unpastured sea" as tragedy yields to pastoral. For Jupiter, the descent from Heaven can only lead to Hell, one, like Manfred's, of his own making; for Prometheus and his consorts, it accompanies a willing retirement into a world of sensuous forms animated by "echoes of the human world" (III.3.44); Demogorgon merely resumes his eternally self-subduing existence. The stage is cleared for the celebration of the new human society that begins with the Spirit of the Hour's choric speech at the end of Act III.

Asia's lesson—that the opposition of master and slave must give way within the mind before historical servitude can end—is borne out in the experience of humankind. Shelley stresses the interrelation of psychic and political conflict by punning on the terms subject and object, a dichotomy that must collapse before the struggle for mastery can be resolved:

none with eager fear
Gazed on another's eye of cold command
Until the subject of a tyrant's will
Became, worse fate, the abject of his own. (III.4.137–40)

Like Prometheus and Asia, men and women resist their enslavement first by subduing the tyranny within, reversing the historical process by which tyranny encourages inner bondage. Describing their liberation, the Spirit of the Hour contrasts unredeemed man, harrowed by "self-mistrust," "self-love or self-contempt," and spiritually "self-consumed," with the selflessness of the new age (III.4.134–52). Self-liberation becomes the foundation for a new social order: "Thrones, altars, judgement-seats and prisons" (164) are cast down, and humankind emerges "sceptreless, free, uncircumscribed" (194). "Uncircumscribed" refers equally to political freedom and the relaxation of psychic borders. Shelley had written a year before in his fragment "The Coliseum" that the "internal nature of each being is surrounded by a circle . . . which constitutes the misfortune of the condition of life."[33] In *Prometheus Unbound*, the advent of universal sympathy infinitely distends this constraining circle, freeing the "Spirits of the mind of man" to issue from the prison of selfhood and mingle in the masque-like pageant of Act IV. Each human being is psychically "unbound" so that a new social order based not on contract but on fellow feeling can emerge.

The self-maintaining dichotomy of master and servant—"Man, who wert once a despot and a slave,— / A dupe and a deceiver" (IV.549–50)—yields to an "equal, unclassed, tribeless and nationless" (III.4.195) humanity. A new, authentic relation through sympathy emerges: "Man, oh not men! a chain of linked thought, / Of love and might to be divided not" (IV.394–95). Men and women become their own masters, labor becomes fulfillment, and dreams of Paradise become the simple produce of the common day:

> Man, one harmonious Soul of many a soul
> Whose nature is its own divine controul
> Where all things flow to all, as rivers to the sea;
> Familiar acts are beautiful through love;
> Labour and Pain and Grief in life's green grove
> Sport like tame beasts—none knew how gentle they could be! (IV.400–405)

My allusion above to Hegel's greatest disciple is meant in all seriousness, for the writings of the young Marx present several significant analogues to *Prometheus Unbound.* Marx redefined Hegel's master-slave relation as one brought about by the estrangement of labor entailed by growing industrialization, somewhat as Shelley felt that the "cultivation of those sciences which have enlarged the limits of the empire of man over the external world" had exacerbated the "inequality of mankind"; that "man, having enslaved the elements, remains himself a slave."[34] For Marx, ending such "estrangement" would enable humankind to participate in the "consciousness of species," a transformation that would bring with it "the true resurrection of nature—the naturalism of man and the humanism of nature brought to fulfillment." Man "unclassed . . . and nationless" would also be freed from the "religious estrangement" caused by the projection of his displaced power into an authoritarian heaven.[35] Shelley's conception of an interpersonal consciousness that would bring with it a humanized nature appears far less mystical or "poetic" when placed in the context of Marx's thought.

Coupling the names of Marx and Shelley inevitably raises, all the same, the specter of Arnold's "beautiful and ineffectual angel": Marx's writings are a continual call to action, but how does one actualize the visionary species-consciousness depicted in *Prometheus Unbound?* Shelley was, in fact, one of the first to express such qualms regarding his "favorite poem" among his own works. His remark in the preface that his poetry addresses "the more select classes of poetical readers" was stated more bluntly in a letter to his publishers: " 'Cenci' is written for the multitude, and ought to sell well. I think, if I may judge by its merits, the 'Prometheus' cannot sell beyond twenty copies."[36] And yet, comparing in the preface his use of mental imagery to that of the Greek tragedians, he praised them—as he would again in the *Defence*—as "writers to whom no resource of awakening the sympathy of their contemporaries was unknown." And the concessive passage on his limited readership goes on to state that, "until the mind can love, and admire, and trust, and endure, reasoned principles of moral conduct are seeds cast upon the highway of life which the unconscious passenger tramples into dust, although they would bear the harvest of his happiness."[37] The readers of *Prometheus Unbound* would, though few, become more fit to take up the work Promethean. More than one critic sympathetic to Shelley's political views has noted that *Prometheus Unbound* was shortly followed by the highly pragmatic and popularly written *Philosophical View of Reform*, a tract applying the drama's "beautiful idealisms" directly and with unexpected political foresight and common sense to the actual situation of the English working class in 1820.[38]

Prometheus Unbound has itself been read, moreover, as an "invitation" for each reader to work through its conflicts and "celebrate" its redemptive program: "Prometheus is potential in you. His problem is your problem."[39] Here we recognize again a central aim of Romantic mental theater, the strategic implication of the reader in the dramatic struggle, confronting her or him with a conceptual need to resolve its restless casuistry. As in *The Cenci*, Shelly provides in *Prometheus Unbound* a scene that presents the reader with an image of engagement, and, in this case, implicitly discountenances a half-hearted response. Asia's journey of self-discovery begins with her active interpretation of the two dreams transmitted by Panthea, each of which she "reads," the first figuratively ("that I may read his written soul"), the second literally, as the message "O follow, follow" is "stamped" on the leaves (which evoke, as in the "Ode to the West Wind," the leaves of a book).[40] The scene that follows introduces, apparently for no reason, two "young Fauns" who do not appear again, and who overhear a chorus of spirits describing the sisters' passage to Demogorgon's cave.

The Fauns take up a short and seemingly irrelevant dialogue on the nature of the spirits they have just heard. The second Faun cites "those more skilled in spirits," who theorize that the "bubbles which the enchantment of the sun" raises from "the oozy bottom" of lakes and pools—in other words, hydrogen gas—become the vehicles of spirits, bursting to form *ignis fatui* and returning as fire to the swamp bottoms (II.2.70–82). The passage, a very lovely one, has been read both as an index of Shelley's enthusiasm for science and as an incidental and precious "fairy tale."[41] But the most striking aspect of the passage, which in its apparent irrelevance begs for interpretation, is the allusion to Banquo's similar theory about the Witches in response to Macbeth's bewilderment: "The earth hath bubbles, as the water has, / And these are of them" (I.3.79–80).

The allusion to *Macbeth* serves to remind the reader that interpretation can be fatal: Macbeth's careless and self-gratifying reading, in contrast to the interpretive caution of the "self-uninterested Banquo" (Coleridge's phrase),[42] begins the process that eventually destroys his psychic integrity. The Fauns, however, fall victim to the opposite error. Their reading is passive and detached, the echo of an uncertain hermeneutic tradition, and they readily give over their dialogue in favor of the myths of "thwart Silenus":

> those wise and lovely songs
> Of fate and chance and God, and Chaos old,
> And love and the chained Titan's woful doom
> And how he shall be loosed, and make the Earth
> One brotherhood—(II.2.91–95).

While Asia persists in her dialogue with Demogorgon until she brings forth the active truth within her, the Fauns yield, like Kierkegaard's Platonist, to a myth that, far from resolving the dilemma, merely fills up the interpretive vacuum. Their version of the Prometheus myth (and indeed the entire brief scene) anticipates the elegiac tone that characterizes the benevolent but outmoded deities of Act III. It reduces them to passive spectators of a millennial vision that human beings will realize. The scene provides a negative exemplum, highlighting through contrast the portrayal of Asia (whose status as a reader has been repeatedly stressed in the previous scene) as an active and actualizing interpreter. One could add that the very difficulty of *Prometheus Unbound*—ranging from the paradoxical conception of Demogorgon to the rarefied and conceptually challenging imagery that makes a first reading so formidable—draws in the sympathetic reader by demanding a greater than usual commitment.

Shelley's implication of the reader in the drama constitutes yet another aspect of the work's continual transcending of conventional, artificial boundaries, a program that finally calls into question the genre of "drama" itself. The first act, concerned with the struggle between Jupiter and Prometheus, takes a form not far removed from Aeschylus or *Samson Agonistes*;[43] the more obtrusive elements find analogues in Shakespearean tragedy, as the formal allusion to the Witches in *Macbeth* suggests. Once the complex struggle with Jupiter is resolved, first for Prometheus and Asia and then in the experience of humankind, the tragic mode yields to forms not based on dramatic tension. As the action progresses, tragedy is replaced by pastoral, masque, pageant; dialogue by hymn, lyric and choric song, leading to the "complicated and uncontrollable splendour" of Act IV.[44] Shelley's oxymoronic subtitle, "A Lyrical Drama," suggests a fusing of the private lyric voice with the interpersonality of dramatic exchange, and points from the outset toward the dynamic sympathy that enables self-consciousness to transcend the struggle for psychic autonomy.

Until he had written *The Cenci*, Shelley felt that *Prometheus Unbound* was complete in three acts.[45] After elaborating a struggle very much like that of Prometheus and Jupiter in his tragedy, however, Shelley may well have wished to extend the lyrical drama further beyond the portrayal of psychic conflict. Act IV is still more studiously undramatic than Act III; with Panthea and Ione appropriately cast as spectators from their cave, it presents a pageant of the liberated, expanding consciousness of humanity, and a densely symbolic epithalamium of the marriage of contrary principles exemplified by the moon and the earth.

A number of themes that recur throughout mental theater feature here in redeemed contexts. The abyss that functions so often as an emblem of the gulf between minds, or of the void that overwhelms an isolated psyche, is bridged by the outpourings of sympathy and the growth of a species-consciousness:

> And our singing shall build,
> In the Void's loose field,
> A world for the Spirit of Wisdom to wield;
> We will take our plan
> From the new world of man
> And our work shall be called the Promethean. (IV.153–58)

In place of the psychic imperialism of an Oswald or Lucifer, the spirits of the human mind "colonize" the "Deep" (IV.143) through widening, not raiding, the borders of consciousness, building (in terms that recall Wordsworth's "Prospectus" to *The Recluse*) "a new earth and sea / And a Heaven where yet Heaven never could be" (IV.164–65). The concept of mastery itself returns as collective mastery over the individual will and over a nature humanized through sympathy: "Compelling the elements with adamantine stress"; "one harmonious Soul of many a soul / Whose nature is its own divine controul" (IV.396, 400).

The wedding hymns sung by the Earth and Moon to one another are so generous in symbolic evocation that another chapter could easily be devoted to them alone. Much of the imagery, however, can be read in light of a single pervasive strategy, concerned with breaking down contraries in an ecstatic intermingling.[46] Panthea sees in their nuptial encounter a complicated spectacle "Embleming Heaven and Earth united now" (IV.273); her interpretation, like her characterization of Asia, needs only to be elaborated. Heaven and Earth are one of a number of paired contraries that meet here to dissolve. Masculine and feminine, matter and spirit, actual and potential, sense and imagination, nature and consciousness reveal themselves as arbitrary oppositions rendered obsolete by a force that eradicates conventional boundaries:

> The joy, the triumph, the delight, the madness,
> The boundless, overflowing bursting gladness,
> The vaporous exultation, not to be confined! (IV.319–21)

The Earth, who speaks these lines, takes on and universalizes the history and attributes of Prometheus. He pronounces an end to the "Sceptred Curse" of Jupiter, and celebrates Love "filling" the God's "void annihilation" (IV.338, 354). Like the Titan's, however, his regeneration remains incomplete until the Moon, his Asia, overflows into the void within:

> O gentle Moon, thy chrystal accents pierce
> The caverns of my Pride's deep Universe,
> Charming the tyger Joy, whose tramplings fierce
> Made wounds, which need thy balm. (IV.499–502)

Like Prometheus and Asia, the Earth and the Moon can approach completeness only through an androgynous fusion, one that, by a complex network of emblematic associations, collapses with it a number of the drama's thematic oppositions.[47]

The memory of the past, so often in mental theater a crippling force, yields in the form of "the melancholy ruins of cancelled cycles" to the liberating consciousness of the age; Shelley's vision sustains even the weight of the ruins of prior earths that had brought Cain, like Keats's Endymion, to despair:

> The wracks beside of many a city vast,
> Whose population which the Earth grew over
> Was mortal but not human. (IV.296–98)[48]

Similarly, reflection, which elsewhere in mental theater conveys the imposition of one mind onto another in a confining, specular relation, finds its corrected form through the transformations that

> Leave Man, who was a many-sided mirror
> Which could distort to many a shape of error
> This true fair world of things—a Sea reflecting Love.
> (IV.382–84)

From the pernicious shadows and reflections of Act I, akin to the "distorting mirror" of *The Cenci,* reflexive consciousness takes on a new form in the final act of *Prometheus Unbound* and a redeemed function. It comes to assist the ripening of a liberating vision through the undiscouraged contemplation of that vision: "To love, and bear; to hope, till Hope creates / From its own wreck the thing it contemplates" (IV.574–75).[49] The fragility of the revolutionary vision becomes a part of its strength, as its inevitable crisis leads not to despair but, in the Promethean tradition which Demogorgon bequeaths to humanity at the drama's close, to action.

Shelley's lyrical drama may well strike us as the most formally innovative longer poem of its period, and yet in its very uniqueness lies a part of its quintessential Romanticism. Shelley remarked on his work's participation in the "endowment of the age" in its preface; discussing originality, he stresses that, although indebted to no one living writer, he would not defend the integrity of the individual poetic voice. Like his protagonist, Shelley refuses to set himself on a pedestal removed from the shared life and thought of a community.[50] He argues instead that the greatest English writers were not splendid solitaries figured against the bleak tapestry of history, but rather participants in the main currents of intellect and feeling of their times. Shakespeare and Milton themselves are distinguished by their immersion in "that fervid awakening of the public mind," the Reformation, to which later ages owe their works.[51] As he would write later in the *Defence,* poetry is neither the simple product of social factors nor independent of them. At once responsive to social conditions, an ideological force in shaping them and, through participating in the spirit of events, able to prophesy their outcome, poetry is the "herald, companion, and follower of the awakening of a great people."[52] For Shelley, "the connection of poetry and social good is more observable in the drama than in whatever other form,"[53] making part of its attractiveness for a revolutionary writer, and of its power as an index to and call for social change.

Turning to his own time, Shelley saw an awakening like that of the Reformation at work: "The great writers of our own age are, we have reason to suppose, the companions and forerunners of some unimagined change in our social condition or the opinions which cement it. The cloud of mind is discharging its collected lightning, and the equilibrium between institutions and opinions is now restoring, or about to be restored."[54] A related image for collective ideological renewal occurs in Asia's celebrated metaphor for the "sun-awakened avalanche,"

whose mass
Thrice sifted by the storm, had gathered there
Flake after flake, in Heaven-defying minds
As thought by thought is piled, till some great truth
Is loosened, and the nations echo round
Shaken to their roots: as do the mountains now.
(II.3.37–42)

Shelley abjures the pose, too often for later readers a definitive Romantic image, of the alienated artist. He celebrates instead his part in the electric cloud of mind that he would name, in the *Defence,* the "spirit of the age."[55] In *Prometheus Unbound,* his most challenging work, Shelley transcends the limitations of a private vision by appealing without fear to the strong influences of his tradition and the awakened spirit of his own historical moment. Through his creative engagement with the literary past, and through sympathy with the living minds of his age, Shelley made one of the great original poems of the nineteenth century.

8

Death's Jest-Book: "Shadows of Words"

In 1825 Thomas Lovell Beddoes, an English poet studying anatomy in Germany, began the dramatic poem he would continue to work at until his suicide a quarter of a century later. That year, in a letter to Thomas Kelsall—his future literary executor and first editor—he wrote of combining his medical and his dramatic pursuits in terms that suggest a definition of mental theater:

> The science of psychology, & mental varieties, has long been used by physicians, in conjunction with the corresponding corporeal knowledge, for the investigation & removal of immaterial causes of disease; it still remains for some one to exhibit the sum of his experience in mental pathology & therapeutics, not in a cold technical dead description, but a living semiotical display, a series of anthropological experiments, developed for the purpose of ascertaining some important psychical principle—i.e. a tragedy.

He ends "this unnecessary subject" by remarking that "Death's Jest-book goes on like the tortoise—slow & sure"; and after closing the letter adds a postscript: "Could you find a Prometheus unbound and a Cenci and send them straight and fearlessly?"[1]

The "living semiotical display" on which Beddoes's posthumous reputation has precariously rested, *Death's Jest-Book* hangs tantalizingly beyond conventional literary boundaries: neither a stage-play nor the collection of lyrics anthologists have made of it, relentlessly derivative in language and formidably original in conception, Romantic in form and bitterly post-Romantic in sensibility. Read in the context of mental theater, however, the "spectral dramatic fantasia" that Arthur Symons exiled to a "place apart in English poetry"[2] reveals its uneasy status as the last great work of a Romantic genre. Working from Shelley's dramatic poems of 1819, Beddoes extended the tradition of mental theater and pushed it to extremes that have left its handful of readers intrigued but, like Symons, bewildered.[3] Caught up by Shelley's dramatic vision while despairing of anything approaching his moral and political idealism, Beddoes at once emulates and parodies his models; *Death's Jest-Book* follows *Cain, The Cenci,* and *Prometheus Unbound* like the goat-play following a Greek trilogy.[4]

Like the Romantics before him, Beddoes had "lived in Shakespeare,"[5] but to label him, as did Strachey, the "Last Elizabethan," or even to associate him too narrowly with the Elizabethan Revival of his acquaintances Darley and Procter, would be misleading.[6] When Beddoes wrote critically of his contemporaries' reliance on Elizabethan models—"we had better beget than revive—attempt to give the literature of this age an idiosyncrasy & spirit of its own"—he meant it;[7] while his blank verse often reads like a masterful pastiche of the finest Jacobean tragedies, his poetic arguments are rooted in the mental theater of Shelley, whom he frankly idolized, and Byron, whom he affected to despise. For Beddoes, Shakespeare was an "imaginary universe," and the "Shakespearian form of drama" the "only English one." But beginning from Shakespeare did not keep Beddoes (any more than it did Shelley himself) from the Shelleyan intuition that "at certain periods of the world, some secret influence in nature was acting universally on the spirit of mankind."[8] As a dramatist Beddoes held to the waning spirit of the Romantic age. He valued Shakespeare primarily for his mastery of the "sciences of the affections and passions," and he rejected the contemporary stage—his disgust with the melodrama of his day once resulted in a drunken attempt to ignite the Drury Lane Theater with a burning five-pound note.[9] But Beddoes adapted the conventions and themes of mental theater to his own cynical, post-Romantic vision.

In *The Second Brother* (1824–25), which he abandoned after drafting three acts and beginning a fourth, Beddoes experimented unsuccessfully with a drama of psychic conflict conceived along Byronic lines. Built on the Cain theme of warring brothers, the work sets Orazio, a *soi-disant* "deity's son" (I.1.82) who scorns the quotidian world, against Marcello, a wanderer who returns to his brother's court as a "Prae-adamite skeleton" (I.1.63), self-exiled from humanity. Their unexpected exchange of fortunes only aggravates the social estrangement marking both brothers into an extreme, unviable autonomy. Orazio courts a Satanic fate mediated by *Manfred* as he falls "Deeper than Lucifer . . . Into a place made underneath all things, / So lost and horrible that hell's its heaven" (I.2.175–77), claiming Manfred's proud self-torment as his own:

> Thou canst not drag me deeper, wrap me darker,
> Or torture me as my own thoughts have done. (II.2.216–17)

Marcello grows equally inhuman. He invokes Lady Macbeth's infernal spirits—

> Undo these human veins that tie me close
> To other men, and let your servant griefs
> Unmilk me of my mother (I.1.223–25)—

and adopts the psychic imperialism of Milton's Satan and Byron's Lucifer, desiring to "stretch [his] dukedom through men's souls" (III.1.65). But however promising as an elaboration of Byronic motifs, *The Second Brother* approaches neither the subtlety nor the daring of Beddoes's masterpiece. Only with *Death's Jest-Book* does his poetic voice gain both its full powers of mimicry and its inimitable idiosyncrasy, as his relation to Romantic models grows more critical and more complex.

Death's Jest-Book might be described initially, borrowing Byron's term for *Manfred* and *Cain*, as a "metaphysical" drama. The setting—ostensibly fourteenth-century Egypt and Silesia—suggests an atmosphere of ghosts, necromancy, graveyards; Beddoes could have called its world, as he did its style, the "florid Gothic,"[10] the fictive, atemporal Gothic invented by Walpole, Radcliffe, and Lewis. As the action unfolds, however, another period and genre altogether—the Elizabethan revenge tragedy—are brought to mind. Isbrand, who vies with the Silesian Duke Melveric as the work's anti-hero, enters claiming "Revenge and blood" in atonement for a father and sister, and he berates his virtuous brother Wolfram for putting off their vengeance in his growing admiration and friendship for the Duke, their intended victim. Disguised as Melveric's court fool, Isbrand awaits his revenge with the quasi-erotic anticipation that marks Vindice in *The Revengers Tragedy* (a major influence, with Marston, on Beddoes's wonderfully anachronistic prose passages). But Isbrand's first soliloquy lays claim to yet another tradition, the Romantic heritage explored in *The Second Brother:*

> But I will turn my bosom now to thee,
> Brutus, thou saint of the avenger's order;
> Refresh me with thy spirit, or pour in
> Thy whole great ghost. (I.1.311–14)[11]

Like the protagonists of Beddoes's earlier *Bride's Tragedy* and his unfinished dramas, Isbrand is a literary descendant of Byron's Manfred, the brooding victim of a compulsion to fall, self-tempted and eventually self-condemned. And the price he pays for a dehumanized and pseudo-autonomous character is, again, the tragic isolation suffered by Manfred:[12]

> Isbrand, thou tragic fool,
> Cheer up. Art thou alone? Why so should be
> Creators and destroyers.

Unlike Byron's protagonist, however, Isbrand, the "tragic fool," possesses throughout much of the drama an ironically detached perspective on his own progressive degeneration. Isbrand's unsettling capacity to mock his own dissolution underscores his perverse investment in it. And such self-directed irony is characteristic of the author as well, in his pervasively cynical attitude toward his dramatic subject. Writing a drama of "satiric pathos,"[13] Beddoes never loses sight of his Romantic heritage, but he casts on it an inexorably cold eye.

Melveric, Isbrand's dramatic opposite and thematic double, is introduced in the next scene. He has just escaped the North African prison from which Wolfram intends to free him and, complicating a plot which is unabashedly baroque from the start, has rescued his fellow captive Sibylla, beloved by Wolfram when he happened to find himself in the same prison a year or so back. Sibylla initially plays a reluctant Miranda to Melveric's Prospero. She wishes to shun "cruel mankind" and remain with "kinder Nature" (I.2.113–14); the Duke promises her a "godliker mankind" in Europe once they leave the pagan shores. Melveric's vaunted humanism, however, soon rings as hollow as his pretended disinterest. He desires Sibylla only for himself, and falls into worried musing the moment he learns that rescue—Wolfram's expeditionary force—is imminent:

> how palely, with what careless lips
> Do we salute this unhoped change of fortune!
> Thou art so silent, lady; and I utter
> Shadows of words, like to an ancient ghost,
> Arisen out of sea-wrapt centuries
> Where none can speak his language. (I.2.176–81)

Ezra Pound cannily singled out these lines as encapsulating Beddoes's failure to find a niche in the accepted literary canon, his commitment to Jacobean diction rendering him, despite his originality, finally unable to make it new.[14] But the passage is only the most striking of many concerned with the disjunction between language and social context, language and desire. Speech constitutes in *Death's Jest-Book* an unsatisfactory, fallen medium: "My friend and I have need to use those words," Melveric declares shortly afterwards, "Which are bequeathed unto the miserable" (I.2.267–68). Language functions less to reveal than to entomb the world: "Methinks there's nothing in the world but names: / All things are dead" (II.3.325–26). And while speech fails as transparent communication—

> You put questions to me
> In an Egyptian or old magic tongue
> Which I can ill interpret (II.4.137–39)—

its opacity does not render it stable. A purely incidental dialogue between some clownish fishermen, who at first seem to have walked in from *Pericles*, suggests an implicit commentary on the slippage of words that evokes *Finnegans Wake* more than Shakespeare:

> —'Twere a right evening to die in.
> —Of the ailing of availing ale: let thy nose die in purple on strong beer, and stout be thy porter to paradise. Death shall not catch me in his gin till the swallow comes again. (I.4.126–29)

For Beddoes, the insufficiency and instability of language underscore the gulf between the visionary, death-transcending faith with which he began *Death's Jest-Book* and the bitter, parodic expression that remained after his vision's collapse. His commitment to archaic diction reflects less a naive infatuation with Shakespeare than a continual acknowledgment of his painful distance from the spirit of the Romantic age. His characters are in turn isolated from one another and divided within themselves, speaking a language that neither reaches the other nor expresses the self.

When Wolfram appears in North Africa, the Cain theme, hinted at in his earlier quarrel with Isbrand, is taken up in earnest. Melveric has sworn himself a "brother" knight to Wolfram (I.2.203), but he seizes at once on his jealous, though evanescent, love for Sibylla as an excuse to break with his rescuer and begin plotting his death. Far from struggling with his change of heart, the Duke plunges headlong into moral collapse. Like Isbrand, Melveric seems to have been courting all along an occasion through which to abandon his humanity in favor of a monstrous, isolated pose. Along with his love for Wolfram, Melveric puts off "Friendship, esteem, faith, hope, and sympathy" (I.3.307); he leaves himself, as did Manfred and Cenci, only "hell's embrace." Much in the fashion of Cenci plotting his daughter's rape, or Beatrice her father's murder, Melveric grows obsessed with an unutterable thought—"shapeless and shadowy" (I.3.364)—that becomes an irresistible compulsion the moment he speaks it. Not Sibylla but the "fair fascinating fiend" that suddenly inhabits his mind as the sign of its division lures him toward "one triumphant crime" (I.3.347), the act that will seal his now manifest psychic disintegration. In contrast to Beatrice, or Cain, or Wordsworth's Marmaduke, Melveric requires no temptation in order to fall; typical of Beddoes's anti-heroes, he has stood all along on the verge of an abyss, awaiting a simple push.

His crime is set off, as so often in mental theater, by references to *Othello*. Echoing Brabantio's disbelieving charges against the Moor, the Duke accuses Wolfram of having "subdued" Sibylla with "spells and adjurations" (I.3.289); he orders the murder with words resonant of Othello: "One light on't / Must be put out" (I.3.386–87). When his first attempt fails, and Wolfram so far forgives him as to save his life, Melveric remains inexorable: "Murderer / My thought has christened me, such must I remain" (I.4.184–85); like Wordsworth's Oswald, he would rather lose his social identity than live as the grateful "bondslave" (I.4.183) of his preserver. In an earlier version of the first act, another correspondence with *The Borderers* (which Beddoes could not have read) occurs when the Duke ironically seals the curse uttered by one of Wolfram's followers on the unknown murderer:

> He is cursed
> And from this moment shut up in a hell
> Far from all earthly things. (1833.I.4.91–93)

Again the parallel is significant but only partial. Like the protagonists of earlier mental theater, Melveric locks himself through his crime into an enclosed, private hell. But, as Beddoes's concern with the limitations of speech underscores throughout, the crime merely confirms an isolation and a self-division that Melveric, no less than his fellow characters, seems doomed to in any case.

Wolfram and Sibylla alone attempt to escape such a fate, and both fail. They strive to maintain a Shelleyan conviction in the spirit's triumph over death, but their faith grows increasingly untenable as the drama progresses. When Wolfram dies at the close of the first act, allusions to Shelley proliferate, comprising a sort of farewell to the vision that Beddoes found so tantalizingly evanescent. Wolfram's dying words recapitulate the conclusion of the elegy for Adonais, whose soul, in Shelley's lines, "like a star, / Beacons from the abode where the Eternal are":

> Yet, can man die? Ay, as the sun doth set:
> The earth it is that falls away from day;
> Fixed in the heavens, although unseen by us
> The immortal life and light remains triumphant.
> (I.4.251–54)

And the following "Song from the Waters," Wolfram's dirge, picks up the imagery and millennial spirit of Shelley's anthem to the deathless power of the prophetic voice, the "Ode to the West Wind":

> The wind dead leaves and snow
> Doth hurry to and fro;
> And, once, a day shall break

O'er the wave,
When a storm of ghosts shall shake
The dead, until they wake
In the grave. (I.4.266–72)

But Beddoes's intimations of apocalypse, which emerge in several other songs as well, fail to effect the drama they ornament; instead, they function as teasing contrasts to the work's pervasive despair. With Wolfram dies the only considerable voice of Shelleyan idealism; Sibylla quietly champions Wolfram's faith but grows increasingly ethereal until she dies of sheer unearthliness. As Isbrand says of his role of fool, she becomes a mere "commentator" on the "text" of the drama's world (II.1.67).

Allusions to Romantic themes elsewhere in *Death's Jest-Book* invite either dismissal or parody. Speaking of his own versifying, Isbrand illustrates his "romantic humour" with a song composed "One night a-strewing poison for the rats / In the kitchen corner" (III.3.309–10).[15] The character most often given to debunking Romantic themes, whether in words or through parodic action, is the "zany," Homunculus Mandrake, whose name doubly implies a dwarfed, attenuated humanity. Mandrake's irrepressible satire appropriately begins as the drama opens. In the first scene—a masterpiece of the camp tradition in English drama that reaches from Marlowe's *Dido* to Ashbery's *Heroes*—Mandrake announces his determination to "live no longer like a retired cream-jug in the broken China Shop of History." Instead he takes up the "arts and sciences spagiric, necromantic, hierophantical, black, occult," arts once practiced by his near namesake Manfred, who similarly eschews history and loses "his title to humanity" (I.1.59).

Mandrake returns as the protagonist of a comic subplot that bears a relation to the main action remarkably different from those characteristic of Renaissance drama. Rather than qualifying the principal events with a tempered irony like that, say, of the subplots in *As You Like It,* or providing a comic gloss and alternative conclusion like that in *The Changeling,* Mandrake's appearances deflate altogether the succeeding action in advance. In the opening scene his fatuous posing underscores the absurdity of Isbrand's following attempt to glory in Manfred's pride. As the second act begins, Mandrake returns from Egypt as a mock ghost, having accidentally drenched himself in a "linament of invisibility" which he concocted from "all manner of mummy" with alchemical skill. "Viewless" but "palpable" (II.1.121), he parodically evokes the formless Demogorgon (in turn modeled on Milton's shapeless Death). When Wolfram, returning from the dead as a legitimate ghost, tries to inject something of Demogorgon's oracular detachment into the drama, his inevitable failure has already been made comically evident. Though alive, Mandrake cannot begin to convince his friends of his substantiality: They beat him out of his wife's tavern for presuming to haunt it. Wolfram in turn consistently fails to affect Melveric and the others as the representative of another, transcendent realm.

When the action (such as it is) shifts to Silesia, the fraternal strife of the first act repeats itself in the political and amorous struggle between the Duke's sons, ostensibly opposites but in fact as interchangeable as their names, Athulf and Adalmar, suggest. (Those readers who at first confuse the two can empathize with their common beloved, Amala, who grants one and then the other her affection without much noticing the change.) Their inheritance of the Duke's and Wolfram's fraternal strife constitutes another parallel with earlier works of mental theater: Marmaduke's reenactment of Oswald's crime, Cain's unwitting imitation of Lucifer and Eve, Cenci's fatal transference of his burden to Beatrice. But repetition in *Death's Jest-Book* does not complete an intricate process of seduction; rather, as in *Heaven and Earth,* it reflects the degeneracy of the characters and their world. As a result, *Death's Jest-Book* manifests some of the dramatic weakness of Byron's "oratorio," but Beddoes's ingeniousness in varying his Romantic themes, the relentless daring of his Romantic and self-parodies, along with his brilliant manipulation of Jacobean devices and tonalities, give his work an intensity that Byron rarely attains in *Heaven and Earth.*

Though Athulf, Cain to Adalmar's rather sanguinary Abel, needs little prodding, Isbrand does not hesitate to add the seducer's role to his increasingly demonic repertoire. Isbrand's existence has become entirely subordinate not so much to his revenge as to the venom that feeds it—"My life is hate of him" (II.4.30)—and he sees in the brothers' feud another path toward destroying their father while furthering his own ducal ambitions. Athulf, less naive—perhaps because already possessed of a criminal mentality—than Marmaduke or Cain, quickly perceives in Isbrand

> the snaky opening
> Of a dark cavern, where one may converse
> With night's dear spirits. (II.4.134–36)

Here is the cavern, or gulf, or chasm that throughout mental theater signifies the tragic self-estrangement rendered permanent and inescapable by the protagonist's crime; Isbrand tells his intended victim that, though invocation cannot raise the devil, "Bold deeds and thoughts, / What men call crimes, are his loved litany" (II.4.156–57). But the temptation has more to do with filling out the drama's thematic structure than moving its plot. Athulf has already declared himself "born to be a fratricide" (II.3.231), and has invited Milton's Sin into a breast made void by Amala's betrayal:

> Great and voluptuous Sin now seize upon me,
> Thou paramour of Hell's fire-crowned king,
> That sowedst the tremulous fairness of thy bosom
> In heaven, and so didst ravish the best angels. (II.4.118–21)

Born in *Paradise Lost* from Lucifer's cloven skull—parodying the birth of Athena—Sin becomes here, as in *The Cenci*, the patron devil of psychic division.[16] Athulf betters his would-be mentor, invoking *his* demon in words that underscore the self-alienating gesture with the proper literary archetype.

The alien selves fashioned by Isbrand and Athulf are tragic counterparts to Mandrake's farcical invisibility. Both conditions point up a split between mind and body that harrows in one manner or another all of the principal characters. Even for a virtuous character, such as the living Wolfram, mind and body form an uneasy, unstable union. As a revenger he was, like his brother, "doubly souled / With murder and [his] own cold ghost" (I.1.227–28); his redeeming but misplaced love for Melveric makes of them a "double-bodied soul" (II.4.45). In neither state can Wolfram remain simply himself. Melveric in turn, haunted by his crime, becomes "stuffed / With an o'erwhelming spirit" (II.3.332–33), and in context even his amorous invitation to Sibylla—"Come, let me pour my heart out into thine" (I.2.85)—takes on a sinister tone. Mandrake's lament for his lost body parodies the transformations undergone by his betters (not to mention their precedents in *Richard III* and *Othello*): "I am not what I was—for

I am what I was not; I am no more I, for I am no more: I am no matter, being out of all trouble, and nobody at all, but poor Mandrake's essence" (II.2.70–73). The drifting of spirit from body, like the gap between language and world, represents the cleavage within, the abyss without each individual that darkens Beddoes's worldview.

Death most obviously renders the schism between body and soul manifest, leaving a disembodied spirit or a vacant corpse. The eventual resurrection of the body is a doctrine that Beddoes wistfully evokes (as in the first "Song from the Waters" preceding Wolfram's death) but cannot ultimately accept. Beddoes sought through both his anatomical studies and his dabblings in "Rabbinic" lore to substantiate such a notion, and initially hoped in *Death's Jest-Book* to make "a mock, a fool, a slave of him / Who was the planet's tyrant: dotard Death."[17] But the regenerative "bone of Luz" became for him not an esoteric secret but an "excellent joke," worthy of Mandrake's "spagiric" nonsense.[18] Growing again tyrannical, mocking the pretensions of men and women, emphasizing their aloneness and disintegrity, death triumphs in a hollow apocalypse in which all perish and none await resurrection. Death remains a fool, but the bitter fool that undercuts all hope; as Isbrand puts it in one of his splendid moments of Jacobean railing:

> I will yield Death the crown of folly. He hath no hair, and in this weather might catch cold and die: besides he has killed the best knight I knew, Sir Wolfram, and so is doubly deserving. Let him wear the cap, let him toll the bells; he shall be our new court-fool: and, when the world is old and dead, the thin wit shall find the angel's record of man's works and deeds, and write with a lipless grin on the innocent first page for a title, "Here begins Death's Jest-book." (II.3.110–17).

In these lines Beddoes both laments and celebrates the development of his poetic stance. The innocent first page of his initial, Shelleyan vision yielded to the force of despair, but its fragments—and *Death's Jest-Book* is ultimately both a fragment and a series of fragments—persistently clustered around its ruin.

One of the starkest and most compelling scenes in the drama features a resurrection that resolves nothing and is travestied in advance. It opens with Mandrake—who has decided to consider himself dead since no one around him will believe otherwise—exposing death as a "take in":

> as soon as gentlemen have gained some 70 years of experience they begin to be weary of the common drudgery of the world, lay themselves down, hold their breath, close their eyes and are announced as having entered into the fictitious condition by means of epitaphs and effigies. But, good living people, don't you be deceived any more: It is only a cunning invention to avoid paying poor's rates and the reviewers. (III.3.4–10)

If death leads to no higher state, neither does it hold any mystery or transcendent value in itself.[19] As the scene progresses, the insufficiency of language and the division between body and soul, motifs established throughout the first two acts, are explicitly related to the overarching theme of death. Soon losing all interest in Sibylla, the Duke grows subject to his "body-bursting spirit's yearnings" for his dead wife, herself an "oversouled creation" too ethereal for the world (III.3.228, 221). When his retainer Thorwald offers Christian consolation, Melveric breaks out with his most moving speech, stressing the inconceivability of a spirit "pure from all earth":

> I loved no desolate soul: she was a woman,
> Whose spirit I knew only through those limbs,
> Those tender members thou dost dare despise;
> By whose exhaustless beauty, infinite love,
> Trackless expression only, I did learn
> That there was aught yet viewless and eternal;
> Since they could come from such alone. Where is she?
> (III.3.227–33)

At this point Melveric's mysterious servant, the Egyptian Ziba—who boasts such occult knowledge as Mandrake has rendered absurd—offers to raise the Duchess from her tomb through one of the "chinks" in death. Thorwald has already expressed anxiety at the Duke's wish to violate the border between death and life: "this breaking through the walls, that sever / The quick and cold, led never yet to good" (III.3.198–99). Melveric himself does not dare hope, and scorns Ziba for pretending that "words of human speech" (404) could draw a soul from dust.

Ziba, however, claims that he can traverse the several chasms entrapping the other characters. His posthumous birth—"My birth was an arising from the dead, / The grave my nurse" (III.3.495–96)—gives him claim to a liminal status that, together with his "skill in language" (III.1.42), empowers him even to make "grave-piled caverns"—the pervasive abyss once more—"throb with the pangs of birth" (III.3.258–59). Isbrand enters in time to mock Ziba's boasts with a macabre song about an aborted soul—"A bodiless childful of life in the gloom"—repelled by all natural bodies, and remarks that: "Methinks the earth and heaven have grown bad neighbors, / And have blocked up the common door between them" (III.3.384–85). But in fact Ziba's partial success harms his cause more effectively than Isbrand's unbelieving sarcasm.

Ziba's incantation recalls *Cain* in its evocation of a world "Ere our grey ancestors wrote history" and approaches Blake in its depiction of bodily creation: "Marrow fill bone, and vine-like veins run round them" (III.3.533, 544). But its immediate effect punctures the moment's solemnity: When Ziba first hears steps on "Jacob's ladder-rungs" and then the "staircase echo" of Hell, Mandrake stumbles out of the crypt, still alive and hiding among the dead for safety (it seems his invisibility has worn off). Beddoes's self-parody here becomes disturbingly comic as Ziba's awful commands—"Draw on thy body, take up thy old limbs, / And then come forth tomb-born"—are answered by Mandrake's inanities: "I have drawn on my stockings, and taken up my old jerkin: but before I go out, can't you give me some water to shave with?" (561–65). And the parallel between Homunculus and the returned Wolfram becomes comically obvious as well. In echt-Jacobean fashion, Isbrand had earlier deposited his brother's corpse in the Duke's vault, so that instead of reposing with his wife he would spend eternity "Embracing his damnation" (II.4.94). (The grave switching, along with the risen ghost, recalls another late Romantic given to the florid Gothic, Emily Brontë.) When Ziba withdraws disgusted ("Death is a hypocrite"), Mandrake announces a second arrival: "If you want to speak to another ghost of longer standing, look into the old lumber room of a vault again. Some one seems to be putting himself together there" (III.3.597–600). As Wolfram's resurrection takes place, the Duke muses on the betweenness of things, a border state that leads neither forward nor backward, a vagueness at the heart of the world incapable of resolution:

> 'Tis still, and cold, and nothing in the air
> But an old grey twilight, or of eve or morn
> I know not which, dim as futurity,
> And sad and hoary as the ghostly past,
> Fills up the space. (III.3.616–20)

The dramatic irony of Wolfram's return works on at least three levels. The Duke inadvertently summons his enemy instead of his beloved; he mistakes the living Mandrake for the returning dead; and he himself has made the abhorred return possible through a pact made with Wolfram in the days of their friendship. Hoping to gain assurance of an afterlife, the two had pledged that the first to die would haunt the survivor. But Wolfram's appearance inspires his murderer only with rage and disbelief: "Thou art not truer than a mirror's image, / Nor half so lasting" (III.3.657–58).

Wolfram has in fact become the reflection of a dehumanized Melveric, who acknowledges as much in the next scene:

> I do begin to feel
> As if I were a ghost among the men,
> As all I loved are; for their affections
> Hang on things new, young, and unknown to me:
> And that I am is but the obstinate will
> Of this my hostile body. (IV.1.65–70)

Affectless, barren of human sympathy, and driven on by a compulsion to beat Wolfram in a renewed struggle from which neither has anything to gain, Melveric recognizes his radically alienated condition, imaged once more as a division between mind and body. If their pact made "full Hell / Boil over" and spill Wolfram as the "topmost damned" (III.3.666), the Duke has made his own world a hell, "a face made up / O'er graves and fiery depths; and nothing's true / But what is horrible" (IV.1.7–9). Again his "fellow soul" (IV.1.61), Wolfram objectifies not so much Melveric's guilt or remorse as the psychic disintegration manifested in his crime.

Athulf, who sends his brother to "Abel's grave" (IV.3.342) in this act, functions as yet another likeness of the Duke. It is appropriate that the murder follows his attempt at suicide, for Athulf's hatred for his double Adalmar ultimately expresses his self-estrangement: "I hate and will have vengeance on my soul" (IV.3.17). Instead of dispatching himself "living into hell" (IV.3.128) he creates, like his father, a hell on earth, taking on a demonic shadow life: "Humanity is taken from my form . . . I am unsouled, dishumanized, uncreated" (IV.3.377–79). His literary genealogy stretches back through Cenci and Manfred to Satan and to the Macbeths: "sleep my soul," he mutters before the deed, "And walk not in thy sleep to do the act / Which thou must ever dream of" (IV.2.13–15). Like that of his father, and of the typical protagonist of mental theater, his crime is a mere copy, a repetition that destroys his human character and leaves him with an inherited psychic torment.

Mandrake no longer appears after Act III, for his satiric role has become superfluous: Isbrand, Melveric, Athulf have all degenerated into self-parodies, growing more like one another in the process. Even the returned Wolfram, who claims to act for Death and not from private vengeance or desire, takes on a role both "dishumanized" and diabolic. When Sibylla—forgotten by Melveric—calls for "comfort from the grave," Wolfram appears, and tempts her to join him in death in spite of his compassionate misgivings. In a passage echoing Beatrice's description of the murderous precipice in *The Cenci*, he cautions Sibylla using tones calculated to make resistance seem powerless:

> I have a fascination in my words,
> A magnet in my look, which drags you downwards,
> From hope and life. You set your eyes upon me,
> And think I stand upon this earth beside you:
> Alas! I am upon a jutting stone,
> Which crumbles down the steeps of an abyss;
> And you, above me far, grow wild and giddy:
> Leave me, or you must fall into the deep. (IV.2.66–73)

The drama's last representative of a hopeful perspective, Sibylla has by now seen enough to find the abyss inevitable; surrounded as she is by unsympathetic and indeed inhuman characters, her isolation is still more unbearable than theirs because it is inflicted and not chosen. Wolfram tempts her further by recounting the mythos that Byron elaborates in *Heaven and Earth,* and Shelley and Keats invert in such works as *Alastor* and *Endymion:*

> There are histories
> Of women, nature's bounties, who disdained
> The mortal love of the embodied man,
> And sought the solitude which spirits cast
> Around their darksome presence. (IV.2.100–104)

Wolfram's version of the demon-lover scenario stresses once more the tragic rift between the "embodied" and the spiritual, and the inevitable lure of solitude, that inform the drama's thematic structure. Following Wolfram, who now reveals himself, into death, Sibylla is in turn "dishumanized"; she chooses at the end merely between death and death-in-life.

Beddoes was in his youth an ardent democrat and took a sometimes prominent part in various radical movements on the Continent—another cause for his feeling of descent from Shelley. In *Death's Jest-Book,* however, political ideals, including that of a democratic revolution, do not escape Beddoes's pervasive devaluation of Romantic values. Isbrand furthers his revenge and ambition through infiltrating a conspiracy against the Duke, intended to bring about a more equable regime. Its principles are exemplified by Mario, a "Roman in unroman times" (III.3.115) who ardently dreams of the Republican glory of his city. Describing his vision of revolution, he celebrates the tyrannicide Brutus—Isbrand's personification of revenge. The connection foreshadows the conspiracy's fate. Though Isbrand's rhetoric gives the revolution millennial proportions—"Noah's world washing shower," "a new creation / In our old dukedom" (III.3.66, 71)—the millennium proves as hollow as Wolfram's resurrection or Isbrand's Apocalypse ending in "Death's Jest-book." Isbrand urges his accomplices with the image, echoing Athulf's invocation of Sin, of a parodic Athena-birth: "a hatchet-stroke, to free / The Pallas of your Jove-like headaches" (IV.1.75–76). And his rebellion brings no more equality than did Lucifer's, the morning star to whom he implicitly compares himself:

> O you small star-mob, had I been one of you,
> I would have seized the sky some moonless night,
> And made myself the sun. (IV.4.196–98)

The temporary success of the revolt merely allows him to put a new garb on his inhumanity. "Tired of being no more than human," he would grow "heavenly" and, as he says, "sleep off / This old plebian creature that I am" (IV.4.188–200).

Isbrand functions at the end as the collective seducer of the conspirators: "You looked on him, and saw your looks reflected," Melveric tells them, "Because his soul was in a dark deep well, / And must draw down all others to encrease it" (V.2.21–23). Like Lucifer or Cenci, his literary avatars, he strives to counterbalance his fiendish isolation by wielding power over others, and also like them he seeks psychic as well as political empire. Early on he recommends to Athulf "swords that pierce the mind" (II.4.190); he boasts to the disguised Duke of his penetration into the "labyrinthine home of the still soul," the "little hiding holes of cunning thought" (III.3.78, 82). In keeping with the pervasive suspicion of language, Melveric derides him for claiming to interpret the "alphabet" of the "hieroglyphic human soul" (III.3.91–92).

His turn at political ascendancy encourages in Isbrand a deific self-view and the illusion—the occupational hazard of Romantic villains—of unconditioned autonomy: "I have a bit of FIAT in my soul, / And can myself create my little world" (V.1.38–39). But Isbrand's pursuit of boundless power rests, again typically, on self-estrangement:

> It was ever
> My study to find out a way to godhead,
> And on reflection soon I found that first
> I was but half created; that a power
> Was wanting in my soul to be its soul,
> And this was mine to make. Therefore I fashioned
> A will above my will, that plays upon it,
> As the first soul doth use in men and cattle. (V.1.47–54)

Isbrand tyrannizes over himself even as he attempts to master his world. His strategy follows the fatal parting advice given Byron's Cain by his seducer:

> form an inner world
> In your own bosom—where the outward fails;

> So shall you nearer be the spiritual
> Nature, and war triumphant with your own. (*Cain*, II.2.464–67)

In either case, the attempt to rise above others demands a psyche continually at war with itself, unresting (Isbrand sleeps no more than do his antecedents), inauthentic. At the end, Isbrand himself perceives the emptiness of his pretended autonomy. Manfred at least could defy hell with a greater, preemptive self-torment, outfacing Satan as the greater fiend. Isbrand dies acknowledging the opposite fate:

> I jest and sing, and yet alas! am he
> Who in a wicked masque would play the Devil;
> But jealous Lucifer himself appeared,
> And bore him—whither? I shall know tomorrow,
> For now Death makes indeed a fool of me. (V.4.281–85)

Even the forced, ambivalent heroism that uneasily concludes *Manfred* is too strong to fit Beddoes's villain; Isbrand's sense of self-alienation emerges once more in the unsettling shift from first to third person in his final speech.

Shelley facilitated his resolution of the master and slave struggle in *Prometheus Unbound* with the introduction of Demogorgon, a figure able by definition (or suggestive lack of definition) to remain outside the circular psychic and political conflict. Wolfram's reappearance initially seems to promise a bleak resolution of Beddoes's own. He claims to act for his "master" Death (IV.2.310), called elsewhere "King Death" (V.4.148) and the "King of the grave" (II.4.218), with the dead his "subject spirits" (II.4.63). But the reign of Death is no more certain than that of the Duke. Wolfram's resurrection figures as a "rebellion" against Death even as the political rebellion takes shape (III.3.688), and Ziba's incantation follows on the heels of the conspirators' meeting in the same scene. As Mandrake's mock death suggests, death offers not even a shadowy transcendence of the struggles that poison life; if Wolfram can be taken as a fair sample, the dead retain their desires, both erotic and vengeful, and with less hope than ever of their fulfillment. Rather than ceasing, the master-slave struggle vacillates to the end. Isbrand sings to the Duke at the close of the fourth act, "Thou'rt slave to him, who was thy fool," and near that of the fifth, "He fetches thee, who should be dead": In either case, the "tyrannous fun" begun by the Duke goes round. Mandrake, Isbrand, Wolfram, Death have all in turn taken the part of Fool. By the end, no position remains undeflated by irony, no stance unshaken by satire.

Death's Jest-Book can be placed as one of the first major responses to English Romanticism, anticipating a tradition that embraces *The City of Dreadful Night* and *The Waste Land, The Dynasts* and *The Comedian as the Letter* C. But Beddoes's imagination remained locked in the Romantic vision he could not sustain. Occasionally he describes himself as caught in a period not marked, like that preceding it, for greatness: "Read only an act of Shakespear, a bit of Milton, a scene or two of the admirably true Cenci . . . and then take to these Jestbooks—you will feel at once how forced, artificial, insipid, etc., etc. all such things are. To keep me up, you must be a daily reader of Walker, Sheil and the Lit. Gaz. Parnassians."[20] Uncomfortable with his inherited tradition but powerless—partly from temperament, partly no doubt from his early and long exile—to join in forging a new one, Beddoes held to his Romantic material, but held it at arm's length. Like Carlyle he was formed by an English and German Romanticism out of tune with his era; but when Beddoes closed his Byron, he found no new heroes to take up.

One factor in Beddoes's disillusionment was certainly his political disgust. For Shelley, the dilemma of an egoistic self-consciousness could ultimately be resolved only in the context of political and social revolution; and the age of Metternich could inspire Shelley himself—one thinks of *The Triumph of Life*—with bitter despair. Beddoes saw enough repression at first hand to fuel a lasting cynicism. He sums up the millennial conclusion to *Prometheus Unbound*—man and nature reconciled through a regenerative species-consciousness—as "matrimonial night-caps for old Goody Nature and Gaffer Mankind to play Punch and Judy in" (I.1.81–82); humankind collectively plays the fool in the "puppet show" of Prometheus (I.1.117). (This much from Mandrake; Isbrand echoes both images at the beginning of Act V: "Well done, Prometheus! / Thou'st pitied Punch and given him a soul, / And all his wooden peers.") Another factor lies in his exceptional embarrassment before the literary past. In a verse letter he describes his own writing with a mixture of elation and modesty as exorcising

With strange black marks and inky wild devices
The witch of words, the echo of great verse
About the chasms of the universe,
Ringing and bounding immortality.

The self-portrait, dating from 1825, was prophetic of his last, great work.[21] Dense with Romantic and Jacobean echoes, constantly aware of the world's pervasive "chasms," self-mocking and yet confident of its own, bounded immortality: *Death's Jest-Book.* The work can be ignored or relegated outside the canon, but once encountered—as Browning, Symons, Strachey, Pound, and others have attested—it cannot be forgotten. Beddoes's response to the preceding generation may be less vital than Carlyle's, but it is no less vivid. The problematic nature of his masterpiece, its difficulty, can finally be considered one of its greatest attractions, as we continue to explore our own response to the Romantic tradition.

Epilogue

No work written after *Death's Jest-Book* could be said to belong to the Romantic genre I have called "mental theater." This is neither to say, however, that poetic dramas were no longer written nor that the iconoclastic program behind the Romantic fusion of drama and lyric was spent. Tennyson, Browning, and Swinburne wrote between them some twenty-five verse plays, and there were also experimental works like Tennyson's "monodrama," *Maud;* Browning's dramatic narrative, *Sordello;* and Hardy's "epic-drama," *The Dynasts*. The plays, mostly historical or period tragedies, were usually written with an eye to the stage, and a few—Tennyson's *Becket,* for example—were produced with considerable success.[1] For the most part, these works show only faint and incidental resemblances to the works of mental theater. It was in the Victorians' generic experiments, particularly their fusion of genres in the "dramatic lyric," that the energies of mental theater persisted.

Looking over the nineteenth century as a whole, one can discriminate two modes of poetic drama, both inspired by the example of Shakespeare. One school descends from Shakespeare's chronicle plays and historical tragedies and is characterized by historical subjects, conventional dramaturgy, and (often) the poet's desire, however ambivalently expressed, for stage production. This group would include Byron's historical tragedies, Keats's *Otho the Great* and fragmentary *King Stephen,* Darley's *Thomas à Becket,* Tennyson's "historical trilogy" (*Queen Mary, Harold,* and *Becket*), and Swinburne's "Scots trilogy" (*Mary Stuart, Chastelard,* and *Bothwell*). The other, rooted in Shakespeare's "tragedies of consciousness," is the tradition of mental theater.[2] The central concern with a developing or degenerating consciousness, the interplay of self and other, and the fusion of lyric and dramatic modes characteristic of mental theater reappear in the dramatic lyric or dramatic monologue of the Victorian period. Although the relation of Romantic lyrical drama to the Victorian dramatic lyric has more to do with shared tendencies than with direct imitation,[3] certain works by Tennyson and Browning show that the development of a "dialogized" lyric mode was in part directly inspired by the mental theater of Byron and Shelley. The interrelations may emerge more clearly, however, if the Romantic works are briefly considered from a new perspective.

Partly in reaction to the stock characterization of the Romantic drama as "monodrama," this study has emphasized throughout its dialectical character. Another response to the tendency to lyricize the genre would draw on the work of Bakhtin and his recent explicators and emphasize the dialogical character of mental theater. Although Bakhtin's writings are mainly concerned with the novel, his remarks on the "novelization" of other genres in the nineteenth century leave space for the transposition of his theoretical models; Bakhtin himself mentions "the whole of Naturalist drama" and Romantic epics like *Don Juan* and *Eugene Onegin* as dialogical works.[4]

A number of dialogical strategies that Bakhtin identifies in the novel recur throughout mental theater as well. The phenomenon of "novelization" in itself brings out a disregard for generic boundaries common to the novel and to Romantic writing in general; the novel originates as a "new and large multi-genred genre . . . an encyclopedia of genres."[5] Bakhtin uses the term "border-violation" for the novel's incursions into "extraliterary genres," including such "ideological" modes as the moral confession, the philosophical tract, and the political manifesto,[6] discourses which insert themselves equally into mental theater through such characters as Oswald in *The Borderers* and Lucifer in *Cain*. Although such intrusions might be deplored in more conventional drama as leading to "set speeches," in a mental theater they function to underscore the poet's engagement with political and religious ideologies without undermining stage illusion. Another feature common to Romantic drama and the early novel is the exoticism and particularly the Orientalism which, in several works, initially seems gratuitous. Bakhtin situates the origins of the dialogic novel in the impact of "oriental" cultures and ideologies on Greece: "The world has already opened up; one's own monolithic and closed world . . . has been replaced by the great world of one's own plus 'the others'."[7] The English Romantics' nineteenth-century Orientalism similarly participates in the dialogizing of lyric drama, setting received ideologies into relief and relativizing the conventional assumptions of character and contemporary reader alike. One finds it not only in the heterodox Asiatic mythologies of *Manfred* and *Prometheus Unbound*, but in the North African scenes and Egyptian "necromancy" of

Death's Jest-Book, in the setting of Oswald's ideological awakening in Palestine and Syria, and in the Near Eastern settings of Byron's revisionary biblical dramas.

Bakhtin's recognition of the interrelation of languages (or styles) and ideologies similarly helps elucidate the larger issue of style in mental theater. The Romantic drama has often been faulted for stylistic irregularities and particularly for its archaisms.[8] But in a genre concerned with portraying developing and antagonistic belief systems, such irregularities reflect literary sophistication, not naivete. Archaism for Bakhtin can signify a revolutionary or "decentralizing" tendency in literary language, rather than a puerile attempt to revive an outdated style;[9] Romantic archaism is less concerned with reviving Elizabethan diction than with unsettling the conventional assumptions embedded in the accepted language of the contemporary stage. A related assault on monological discourse is posed by parody and "quotation" of (allusion to) earlier literary works, a phenomenon that, again, occurs throughout mental theater, especially in regard to Shakespeare and Milton.[10]

More profoundly, Bakhtin's analysis of the "politics of style" provides another perspective from which to situate the dialogical rhetoric of mental theater in its dialectical approach to consciousness. We have seen throughout mental theater that the imposition of a master consciousness can succeed only through the disciple's implication in a master discourse. The rhetorical struggles of the heroes and seducers of mental theater always involve a conflict of two styles and the eventual domination of one: Marmaduke inherits Oswald's Godwinian accents along with his crime, and Adah quickly spots the Luciferian tonalities reflecting Cain's deformed consciousness ("Thou hast not spoken well, nor is that thought / Thy own, but of the spirit that was with thee"). Similarly, the curse that Prometheus literally revokes is articulated not only by a double of Jupiter but in his imperial diction as well, a vocabulary of mastery and servitude that Prometheus divests himself of only gradually, the same vocabulary that signals Cenci's reflected presence in Beatrice's violated psyche. For Bakhtin, an individual's "ideological becoming"—cognate with the emergence of self-consciousness in Romantic terms—arises through and is complicated by just such a struggle: "Another's discourse performs here no longer as information, directions, rules, models and so forth—but strives rather to determine the very bases of our behavior: it performs here as *authoritative discourse*, and as *internally authoritative discourse.*" The dialogical relation of speakers, that is, proceeds through a struggle of wills much like the dialectical relation of master and slave as developed by Hegel. The rhetorical conflict of speakers in both the novel and in mental theater is political not only in its embodiment of competing ideologies but in its agonistic dynamics as well: "Language is not a neutral medium that passes freely and easily into the private property of the speaker's intentions; it is populated—overpopulated—with the intentions of others. Expropriating it, forcing it to submit to one's own intentions and accents, is a difficult and complicated process."[11]

Features which have troubled readers as irregularities in Romantic drama emerge in relation to the novel as part of an intentional, sophisticated program for problematizing literary conventions and received ideas, for more deeply engaging and more directly challenging the reader. But an outline of dialogism in mental theater serves also to help relate the Romantics' resistance to what Bakhtin calls the "single-personed hegemony" of the lyric voice to the similarly iconoclastic practice of the Victorians.[12] The dramatic monologue has been described as an "eminently Romantic form" precisely in its insistence on dialogizing the lyric; the same genre and tendency come to characterize the dominant voice of modern poetry as well: "poetry became modern again in the historically responsive dialogized mode that Browning, Tennyson, and others had brought forward from the Romantics."[13] The Romantics' awareness of the presence of the other in lyric consciousness leads directly to the Victorians' implication of the other in their experimental poetic modes.

The relation between lyrical drama and dramatic lyric does not lie only within shared tendencies, however; in dialogizing the lyric, the Victorians were responding not only to the literary climate established by Romantic poetry, but to particular Romantic texts, including those of mental theater, as well. Many related motifs characteristic of mental theater—the painfully restless self-consciousness, the determining crime, the will to mastery, the abyss underlying isolated autonomy—recur singly or together in such dramatic monologues as Browning's "Porphyria's Lover," "My Last Duchess," and "The Bishop Orders His Tomb" and Tennyson's "Ulysses" and "Tithonus." But the most direct awareness of the Romantic lyrical drama tends to be found in more extended studies of "Action in Character" (to quote Browning's phrase for *Strafford*). Tennyson's "monodrama" *Maud* (1855), a monologue which concentrates and extends his earlier experiments with a dramatized lyric mode, perhaps most clearly shows the extent of the Victorians' response to Romantic drama.

Arthur Hallam described Tennyson's "new" poetic mode as "a graft of the lyric on the dramatic,"[14] and while Tennyson's monologues are sometimes considered more lyrical than those of Browning,[15] such works as *Maud*, "The Two Voices," and "Tithonus" bear out much more than the later plays the soundness of Hallam's characterization. *Maud* has been read as a Symbolist poem, a proto-modern anticipation of *The Waste Land*, or as a generic monodrama extending a minor tradition shaped by Rousseau and Southey, but its rootedness in mental theater has not been explored.[16] As an attempt to recapture Shakespeare's portrayal of consciousness in a lyricized, nontheatrical dramatic mode—Tennyson called *Maud* "a little Hamlet"—the "monodrama" clearly evokes the Romantic lyrical drama.[17]

Tennyson's own explication of the subtitle, "a monodrama," stresses the portrayal of a single character's consciousness as it is formed and transformed through confrontations with silent but present others: "successive phases of passion in one person take the place of successive persons,"[18] a practice evoking both *Manfred* and the first act of *Prometheus Unbound*. Equally reminiscent of mental theater is the anonymous hero's continual mental restlessness, and his fear of repeating an earlier crime, his brooding, betrayed father's suicide:

> What! am I raging alone as my father raged in his mood?
> Must *I* too creep to the hollow and dash myself down and
>   die
> Rather than hold by the law that I made, nevermore to
>   brood
> On a horror of shattered limbs and a wretched swindler's
>   lie? (I.53–56)[19]

Maud develops a concern with psychic isolation and restlessness apparent throughout Tennyson's earlier experiments with the dramatized lyric. The "damned vacillating state" portrayed in the "Supposed Confessions of a Second-Rate Sensitive Mind," Mariana's endless, isolated waiting, the Lady of Shalott's introspective weaving "by night and day" all figure an unhappy, sleepless consciousness. The speakers of Tennyson's first dramatic monologues are similarly restless, isolated figures, his Ulysses an eternal wanderer—a Wandering Jew with nothing to expiate—and Tithonus condemned to a "cruel immortality" of reproach and remorse. The night-long debate of "The Two Voices," an explicitly dialogical work, records the struggle between a Tennysonian persona and the "still, small voice" of hypercritical, unsleeping self-awareness. In all of these works, with the possible exception of "Ulysses,"[20] the portrayal of a socially detached, intensified self-consciousness is qualified by a recognition of its contradictions and limitations. In *Maud*, his most fully developed study of self-consciousness, Tennyson attempts to emulate *Prometheus Unbound* in contrasting a self-limiting introspection with a regenerative love, and the mixture of various lyrical measures owes something to Shelley's precedent as well. But the emphasis on repetition, on a crime that deforms consciousness, which owes more to the example of Byron in *Manfred*, *Cain*, and *Werner*, renders Tennyson's attempt at resolution extremely problematic.

An early stanza of *Maud* (I.6.8) relates the protagonist intertextually to some of Tennyson's earlier studies in psychic restlessness. Like Mariana, he lives "alone in an empty house," listening to the "shrieking rush of the wainscot mouse"; like Tithonus, he has endured "many a summer"; and, like the Lady of Shalott, his sleepless solitude—"the wakeful ear in the hush of the moonless nights" (I.42)—is self-reflective, as he repeatedly hears his "own sad name in corners cried." Though he lacks the worldliness of a Manfred or an Oswald, he shares their self-determined social alienation: "a morbid hate and horror have grown / Of a world in which I have hardly mixt" (I.264–65). He does not lack a Gothicized Satanic ambience: His inner restlessness is figured as a devil's familiar spirit—"a raven ever croaks, at my side, / Keep watch and ward"—and he describes his mental state as a "lonely hell" (I.678). The "Spirit of Cain," which the hero first names (I.23) in order to deny, plays nevertheless a more integral part. Like Cain, a self-divided outcast, he is "At war with [himself] and a wretched race / Sick, sick to the heart of life" (I.364–65). Like Byron's Cain, he is obsessed with "inherited sin" (I.484), the self-destructive gloom inherited from his father, and the blood-guilt Maud's brother has inherited for the lucrative "scheme" by which Maud's father, the "wretched swindler," ruined his associate and precipitated his suicide. The protagonist fears that, like Cain, he lives under a curse; and the figure of Maud, who suddenly emerges into his life, bears an oddly double relation to that curse.

As his love for Maud grows, a love which is relentlessly self-regarding, the hero hopes that "her beauty" will ward from him the repetition of his father's crime he so obsessively fears:

> I know it the one bright thing to save
> My yet young life in the wilds of Time,
> Perhaps from madness, perhaps from crime,
> Perhaps from a selfish grave. (I.556–59)

Yet he has earlier wondered of Maud, "She may bring me a curse" (I.73), and his growing obsession with her is rather alarmingly signaled by the "rook's caw,"[21] "Maud, Maud, Maud" (I.414), a call too reminiscent of his familiar raven's croak. His love for Maud seems to promise escape from his tragic inheritance, yet that love was itself foreordained by their fathers, a fact which emerges in the crucial dream section which Rossetti found so incomprehensibly gratuitous.[22] "Men were drinking together, / Drinking and talking of me" (I.285–86); before their break, the fathers agree on a match between the infant son and unborn daughter. The passage ominously suggests that in loving Maud the hero is accepting rather than escaping his father's heritage, and inevitably with that heritage come the crime and madness he ironically tries to displace through his love.

The slaying of Maud's brother, who embodies for the hero "the whole inherited sin," marks the fulfillment of a curse as it repeats, in reverse, the crimes of both fathers. The duel takes place at the primal scene of the original crime, the "red-ribbed hollow" that echoes with death and repetition:

> For front to front in an hour we stood,
> And a million horrible bellowing echoes broke
> From the red-ribbed hollow behind the wood,
> And thundered up into Heaven the Christless code,
> That must have life for a blow. (II.23–27)

If Maud's love for the protagonist is a "duty done to the tomb" (I.732), a healing, unexpected fulfillment of the broken betrothal agreement, his murder of her brother, so inextricably tied to the consummation of that love, finally appears as equally determined:

> For the prophecy given of old
> And then not understood,
> Has come to pass as foretold. (II.280–82)

Like Cain, the hero is doomed to carry out a curse of death, and in performing the ritual crime he sees himself bringing death and Hell into the Garden:

> O dawn of Eden bright over earth and sky,
> The fires of Hell brake out of thy rising sun,
> The fires of Hell and of Hate. (II.8–10)

The parallel is posed more directly in his mad raving: "An old song vexes my ear; / But that of Lamech is mine" (II.95–96). Lamech, a direct descendant of Cain, himself reenacts Cain's crime—"I have slain a young man to my wounding"—and recognizes his inheritance of the curse and mark of Cain: "If Cain shall be avenged sevenfold, truly Lamech shall be avenged seventy and sevenfold" (Genesis 4:24). And the names of Lamech's wives, Adah and Zillah, supply Byron with names for the wives of Cain and Abel in *Cain*.

Love functions, in works like *The Borderers* and *Cain*, as the last bastion (or, if one prefers an existential reading, the last infirmity) of a mind on the verge of Romantic self-consciousness; yet its most striking feature is its total ineffectuality in averting the repetition of the seducer's crime. Tennyson's editor, W. J. Rolfe, wrote that *Maud* celebrates love as "*the* influence which rescues the soul from the prison, or the madhouse, of self,"[23] and seems to have hit close to Tennyson's Shelleyan intention. But Tennyson's resolution bears only an oblique relation to the radical transformation of self-consciousness in the dissolution of the self in Act IV of *Prometheus Unbound*. The recovery from madness of Tennyson's hero proceeds not through a renewed vision of social love, but by means of an entire society's acceptance of the "Christless code" in waging a war of retribution. The protagonist abdicates rather than recovers his moral freedom and accepts his curse in the tradition of Cain and Marmaduke: "I embrace the purpose of

God, and the doom assigned." The transition is less one from Satan to Prometheus than from Hamlet to Tamerlane.

In discussing the "Supposed Confessions of a Second-Rate Sensitive Mind," Hallam wrote of its "deep insight into human nature, and into those particular trials, which are sure to beset men who think and feel for themselves at this epoch of social development." The greatest of those trials was "that return of the mind upon itself" that Hallam, relating Tennyson to Keats and Shelley, held inescapable for the modern poet seeking to restore the imaginative intensity of Shakespeare and Milton.[24] *Maud* sets forth the problem of a Romantic self-consciousness without resolving it; like *Death's Jest-Book*, it can be seen as both a response to and late flowering of Romantic drama, but Beddoes's relentless parody gives his work a critical distance from its models which *Maud* finally lacks.

Browning's early *Pauline* (1833) resembles Tennyson's *Maud* in its attempt to internalize the psychic conflict portrayed in mental theater. His first attempt at "poetry always dramatic in principle"[25] manifests an indebtedness to Romantic models not only in its fusion of lyric and drama but, again like *Maud*, in its thematic matrix as well. The anonymous protagonist defines himself in terms clearly shaped by *Manfred*, *Cain*, *The Cenci*, and *Prometheus Unbound*:

> I am made up of an intensest life,
> Of a most clear idea of consciousness
> Of self, distinct from all its qualities,
> From all affections, passions, feelings, powers;
> And thus far it exists, if tracked at all:
> But linked, in me, to self-supremacy,
> Existing as a centre to all things,
> Most potent to create and rule and call
> Upon all things to minister to it;
> And to a principle of restlessness
> Which would be all, have, see, know, taste, feel, all—
> This is myself.[26]

The passage reads like a brief catalogue of motifs from mental theater: intensified self-consciousness, social estrangement, the dependence of "self-supremacy" on the mastery of others, psychic restlessness elevated (as in Tennyson's "Ulysses") to a principle. *Pauline*, along with

Maud and Arnold's *Empedocles*, demonstrates the difficulties of working through (let alone moving beyond) the Romantic dialectic of self and other without the other's at least tacit presence. Although the title itself gestures dramatically toward the awareness of an auditor, at once recipient and subject of the speaker's confessions, Pauline remains much more vague and shadowy even than Astarte in *Manfred* (which *Pauline* insistently evokes).

Browning attempted in a number of formal experiments to move beyond the monologism of *Pauline:* by divesting the "Dramatic Poem" of its references to stage dramaturgy in *Paracelsus* (1835), by contextualizing the hero's perspective in the narrative dramatic mode of *Sordello* (1840), by provocatively juxtaposing the single-voiced lyrics of Pippa with conventional dramatic scenes in *Pippa Passes* (1841). Browning also entertained hopes for the contemporary stage, writing for the actor-manager Macready verse tragedies such as *Strafford* (1840) and *A Blot in the 'Scutcheon* (1843). *Strafford* belongs with the historical trilogies of Tennyson and Swinburne as an attempt to revive the Shakespearean history play for a Victorian audience. *A Blot in the 'Scutcheon* bears a closer relation to the Romantic tradition as a study of crime and criminal self-consciousness with undertones of sibling incest, but Browning's reliance on "well-made play" dramaturgy gives the work a foreshortened quality, barely allowing its Romantic themes to develop as it moves remorselessly toward the next tableau.[27] More interesting is Browning's experimental *A Soul's Tragedy* (1846), with the first act in verse and the second in prose, reflecting the degeneration of its protagonist. The hero, Chiappino, is a would-be Promethean revolutionary who decides between the acts to collaborate, allegedly as his "soul's capacity to love widens," with the Pope, the play's Jupiter;[28] Ogniben, the Pope's legate, functions as his seducer, a brilliant and relentlessly ironic talker whose demonic original is Mephistopheles rather than Satan. As in *A Blot in the 'Scutcheon,* however, Browning's straitened, schematic approach leaves little room for development, and both works lack the complexities and subtleties of the Romantic mental theater. It was with the dramatic lyric that Browning was able to preserve and extend the Romantic tradition from which he worked; in collections like *Dramatic Lyrics, Dramatic Romances and Lyrics,* and *Dramatis Personae,* Browning perfected a dialogized lyric mode in which the presence of a silent or even absent other—Porphyria in "Porphyria's Lover," Gandalph in "The Bishop

Orders His Tomb," Lucrezia in "Andrea del Sarto"—informs the monologue with a dramatic intensity missing from Browning's nearer approaches to conventional drama.[29]

Prometheus Unbound inspired several nineteenth-century adaptations of Greek dramatic form and subjects, beginning with Mary Shelley's *Proserpina* and *Midas* (1820), the latter remembered for the "Song of Apollo" and "Song of Pan" that Percy Shelley wrote for it. Swinburne's *Atalanta in Calydon* (1865) and *Erectheus* (1876) are more considerable works, and both show a verbal indebtedness to Shelley, but (as Swinburne stated in regard to *Atalanta*) his conjunction of lyric and drama proceeds from Athenian, not Romantic, principles: "I think it is pure Greek, and the first poem of the sort in modern times, combining lyric and dramatic work on the old principle. Shelley's *Prometheus* is magnificent and un-Hellenic, spoilt too in my mind by the infusion of philanthropic doctrinaire views and 'progress of the species'."[30] Arnold's *Merope* (1858) has been found a still more "complete reproduction of the form and conventions of Sophoclean tragedy,"[31] but his earlier *Empedocles on Etna* (1852), subtitled (like *Manfred*) "a dramatic poem," owes a great deal more to the Romantic tradition.

Although Empedocles attempts, in the first act, to counter the eternal "burden of ourselves" with a stoic optimism ("Life still / Leaves human effort scope"), our first view of Empedocles aligns him with the hero of *Maud*, with Manfred, with the unregenerate Prometheus, and with Milton's Satan as "half mad / With exile, and with brooding on his wrongs" (I.2.128, I.1.23–24).[32] Act II places him on the "Summit of Etna," a setting that combines the familiar chasm or abyss of mental theater with the mountaintop equally associated with an isolated, illusory psychic autonomy: Satan on Niphates, Manfred on the Jungfrau, Prometheus on the Indian Caucasus. Empedocles' self-reduction to "Nothing but a devouring flame of thought— / But a naked, eternally restless mind" (II.329–30) seems inevitable simply given the location. Although he strives to escape self-consciousness—to "rid him of the presence of himself"—through social reintegration, he is doomed to repeat perpetual "oscillations" between his appeals to others and a return to a domineering psychic autonomy: "Mind is the spell which governs earth and heaven" (II.223, 233; I.2.27). The lyrist Callicles supplies, like Browning's Pippa, an integrated, univocal mode in contrast to Empedocles' post-Romantic "dialogue of the mind with itself";[33] but, as with Pippa, his physical distance from Empedocles reflects the absence of any dialectical relation between the two modes. Instead, Empedocles internalizes the psychic conflict of mental theater, engaging in a struggle for mastery with his own alienated consciousness, the "imperious lonely thinking-power" (II.376):

> But mind, but thought—
> If these have been the master part of us—
> Where will *they* find their parent element . . .
> . . . .
> And they will be our lords, as they are now;
> And keep us prisoners of our consciousness . . .
> . . . .
> Slave of sense
> I have in no wise been;—but slave of thought? (II.345–91)

His one consolation is that, unlike the Satanic minds of mental theater, he at least recognizes his social estrangement and "bonds" to a dominating, alienated self:

> And who can say: I have been always free,
> Lived ever in the light of my own soul?—
> I cannot; I have lived in wrath and gloom.
> Fierce, disputatious, ever at war with men,
> Far from my own soul, far from warmth and light.
> But I have not grown easy in these bonds—
> But I have not denied what these bonds were. (II.390–96)

Empedocles' dilemma was, for Arnold, the dilemma of a distinctly modern sensibility; his resort in *Merope* to a slavishly imitative mode can be seen as the nostalgic retreat from an impasse he could delineate but not penetrate.

Swinburne's remark on the "old principle" for combining lyric and drama implies that the new mode, that of mental theater, was recognized as such and was a working concept for the Victorian poets. By the time (1903) that Hardy writes his preface to *The Dynasts* ("Complete Edition," 1910), a work "intended simply for mental performance" and addressed to the "mental spectator," an established tradition of mental theater can be taken as precedent: "by dispensing with the theatre altogether, a freedom of treatment was attainable in this form that was denied where the material possibilities of stagery had to be rigorously remembered."[34] *The Dynasts*, an "Epic-Drama of the War with Napoleon, in Three Parts, Nineteen Acts, & One Hundred & Thirty Scenes," bears more than a generic relation to Romantic drama. Like *The Borderers* and *Prometheus Unbound*, it was written in reaction to the French Revolution and ensuing Napoleonic wars, the "vast international tragedy" still a common topic for conversation in the "Wessex" of Hardy's boyhood. The poem's machinery—the "Overworld" introduced in the "Fore Scene" and reappearing as a choric device throughout—is inspired by *Prometheus Unbound*; the "Spirit of the Years" and the "Shade of the Earth" are taken from it almost wholesale, and the unconscious "Immanent Will" behind the action—the "pulsion of the Byss"—owes more than a little to Demogorgon. In addition, the verbal war in heaven between the Spirit Sinister and the Spirit of the Pities reflects, though palely and obliquely enough, the central conflict in mental theater.

Despite its debts to the Romantic drama, however, *The Dynasts* is very much a work *sui generis*. Hardy mingles not only lyric, drama, and epic, but draws heavily on the chronicle play tradition as well, appealing to "oral tradition" and to "the historian, the biographer, and the journalist, English and Foreign," as direct and scarcely modified sources. And the dramaturgy is as much influenced by new technologies like the diorama as by the conventional or the mental stage.[35] In conception, the work seems the ultimate expression of the nineteenth-century dialogic imagination; and the verbal pyrotechnics of the "Fore Scene" embody heteroglossia at its most carnivalesque:

> You'll mark the twitchings of this Bonaparte
> As he with other figures foots his reel,
> Until he twitch him into his lonely grave:
> Also regard the frail ones that his flings
> Have made gyrate like animalcula
> In tepid pools.—Hence to the precinct, then,
> And count as framework to the stagery
> Yon architraves of sunbeam-smitten cloud.—
> So may ye judge Earth's jackaclocks to be
> Not fugled by one Will, but function-free.

Hardy's lexical daring, even more so than Beddoes's, hovers between the breathtaking and the absurd: He brings Jacobean, Shelleyan, and Miltonic diction, colloquialisms, scientific and military terminology, neologisms, archaisms, and nonce words that few but Hardy would ever have retained into a dazzling, unsettling, dissonant multivocality. Unfortunately, the body of the work is marked by static, unwieldy dramaturgy (almost every speech is set); the sources are sometimes scarcely absorbed; and the human characters speak a language which reminds us that, if archaic diction can be a sign of linguistic sophistication, it can also be simply derivative, outmoded, and flat.

Hardy allowed himself to speculate, in his "Preface" to *The Dynasts*, "whether mental performance alone may not eventually be the fate of all drama other than of contemporary or frivolous kind,"[36] but the following decades saw profound changes in the theater and in what Hardy called "stagery." The growing influence of Wagner's Bayreuth Festivals, Diaghilev's revolutionary approach to staging dance, Gordon Craig's innovations in set design and the use of masks, and the discovery of Noh drama all contributed to a new theater freed from the constraints of naturalistic dramaturgy. By the late 1930s Yeats could bring elements from mental theater into a poetic drama designed for the Abbey Stage. *Purgatory* (1939) builds, more surely than Tennyson's *Maud*, on the Romantic motifs of crime, inheritance, and repetition. Against a setting in which souls "Re-live / Their transgressions, and that not once / But many times," an itinerant peddler—a post-Romantic wanderer—murders his son, repeating his prior murder of his father, to prevent the son himself repeating the crime and engendering yet another cycle of recurrence: "I finished all that consequence."[37] Drawing on a variety of avant-garde conventions, Yeats could embody an essentially Romantic conception of psychological drama on the stage.

Yeats was not the only playwright to look to mental theater in developing alternatives to nineteenth-century stage conventions. The emergence of an experimental dramaturgy freed from the constraints of naturalistic representation meant that effects once available only to the "mental spectator" could be retooled for the stage. Though the relation of twentieth-century drama to the Romantics demands a study of its own,[38] a single example here may suggest how a feature of mental dramaturgy could be appropriated by an avant-garde stage. The Romantic interpolation (especially marked in *Prometheus Unbound*) of various lyric modes into a reader-oriented drama allowed poetic form to enhance, if not sometimes take the place of, characterization; Shelley's Earth and the Moon (in Act IV) speak their lyrical ecstasy in a form part ode, part song, that underscores their shared distance from the work's dramatic and choric characters. Browning and Arnold introduce an all but disembodied lyrical consciousness antithetical to the dominant voices of their poetic plays in the characters of Pippa and Callicles; their songs express a sensibility, an ideology unavailable to the dramatic characters, who overhear the lyrics without comprehending or fully responding to them. This detached lyrical mode comes to represent in twentieth-century theater an integral, univocal, prelapsarian consciousness, and characterizes utterances overheard but disregarded by the others on stage. Yeats uses lyric in this way in *Cathleen ni Houlihan* (1902): The Old Woman's traditional nationalistic songs cannot be understood until the hero, Michael, undergoes a change of political consciousness (and then can no longer hear the other dramatic characters). In later twentieth-century drama, a lyrically charged prose—marked by "poetic" imagery, by metaphor and other tropes, especially by repetition—conveys the nostalgic reveries of characters who step back into edenic pasts (imagined or otherwise) and out of the immediate dramatic context: Hamm in Beckett's *Endgame*, Eddie in Sam Shepard's *Fool for Love*, Hugh (a character steeped in Latin elegy) in Brian Friel's *Translations*.

If drama found a place for the univocal lyric, however, lyric poetry was in turn dramatized in the wake of the Romantic tradition. Yeats wrote, "I wanted all my poetry to be spoken on a stage or sung";[39] Pound further developed Browning's dialogized monologue in *Personae*; Eliot's *Waste Land* is our brief epic of hetero- and polyglossia ("He do the police in different voices"). The dramatic lyric has persisted as the dominant mode of English and American poetry, while more ambitious generic experiments, like James Merrill's mingling of lyric, dramatic, and epic modes in *Divine Comedies*, continue to be written. Here the influence of mental theater must be subsumed in its larger Romantic context, the dialogizing of lyric and epic represented not only by lyrical drama but by such iconoclastic works as Coleridge's "conversation poems," Wordsworth's experimental ballads and *Excursion*, Keats's odes and the two Hyperion poems, Shelley's *Julian and Maddalo* and *The Triumph of Life*. Once this context has been recognized, however, we can no longer afford to think of the Romantic drama as peripheral. The interleaving of lyric and drama developed in mental theater has left both genres profoundly and lastingly changed.

Notes

Chapter 1

1. Friedrich Schlegel, *Lucinde and the Fragments*, trans. Peter Firchow (Minneapolis: University of Minnesota Press, 1971), fragment 16 (p. 175). For a recent study of the Romantic critique of genre, see Lacoue-Labarth and Nancy, "Genre."

2. For frankly dismissive criticism, see Nicoll, A *History of English Drama 1660–1900*, vol. 4: *Early Nineteenth-Century Drama*, esp. pp. 191–207; and Ernest B. Watson, *Sheridan to Robertson*. For a more sympathetic, yet ultimately no less condescending, approach, see Steiner, *The Death of Tragedy*, esp. pp. 106–50. For studies which develop Steiner's anatomy of Romantic verse drama, see Otten, *The Deserted Stage;* and Gottleib, *Lost Angels of a Ruined Paradise*. The tradition of setting the shortcomings of Romantic drama against those of the contemporary stage begins with Walter Scott, "Essay on the Drama" (1819), and is the principal apology offered by Richard M. Fletcher in *English Romantic Drama 1795–1843*.

3. See, for example, Swingle, "On Reading Romantic Poetry"; Christensen, " 'Thoughts That Do Often Lie Too Deep for Tears' "; and Rajan, "Romanticism and the Death of Lyric Consciousness."

4. See Ball, *The Central Self*, ch. 2: "The Romantics as Dramatists." Her views are allied to those of Bloom, Hartman, and Langbaum discussed below.

5. See, for example, Joseph W. Donohue's objections against separating dramatic from theatrical qualities in *Dramatic Character in the English Romantic Age*, pp. 157–62.

6. John Bayley, *Shakespeare and Tragedy* (London: Routledge & Kegan Paul, 1981), p. 164.

7. Charles Lamb, "On the Tragedies of Shakespeare Considered with Reference to Their Fitness for Stage-Representation," in *The Complete Works and Letters* (New York: Modern Library, 1935), p. 292.

8. Lamb, p. 302. For a detailed and informative consideration of Lamb's dramatic theory in relation to the contemporary stage, see Ades, "Lamb, Shakespeare, and Early Nineteenth-Century Theater."

9. Lamb, "On the Tragedies of Shakespeare," p. 291.

10. See the studies by Scott, Fletcher, and Nicoll cited above.

11. See Jacobus, " 'That Great Stage Where Senators Perform.' "

12. Quoted in Cox, "Melodrama, Monodrama and the Forms of Romantic Tragic Drama," p. 24.

13. Butler, *Romantics, Rebels and Reactionaries*, p. 65.

14. For a recent and important study of this problem, see Rzepka, *The Self as Mind*.

15. Margaret Cooke argues the strongest case for the influence of German drama in "Schiller's 'Robbers' in England." One could argue that much of the weakness of *Remorse* follows from Coleridge's very ambitions for its representation on the stage of his time. Keats's *Otho the Great* similarly reflects the stilted melodrama and heroic flatulence of the contemporary stage play.

16. Such a tendency emerges even in Henry Mackenzie's "Account of the German Theatre" (1788), which introduced English readers to Schiller. Mackenzie celebrated the new German drama for its healthy "disregard for the regularities and decorum of the stage," coupled with a bent for scenes of passion and sublimity recalling "the ancient English Tragedy." He continues: "They call for deeper and more impressive scenes, scenes of high passion and strong emotion. The Germans have accordingly adapted, with the greatest eagerness, the English tragedies most celebrated to please this turn of mind. Shakespeare is their favorite author, and the model of some of their most popular tragedies." Mackenzie, "Account of the German Theatre," p. 159.

17. See Bertrand Evans, *Gothic Drama from Walpole to Shelley*; and Babcock, *The Genesis of Shakespeare Idolatry, 1766–1799*, p. 226.

18. This is not to say that the portrayal or revelation of character in neoclassical drama is undramatic; rather that character in itself is conceived of in static, not dynamic, terms. One need only contrast Shakespeare's Antony and Cleopatra with Dryden's, or with Otway's related Jaffeir and Belvidera, for this fundamental difference in characterization to become apparent.

19. Joanna Baillie, *A Series of Plays*, 2nd ed. (London: Cadell and Davies, 1799), p. 38.

20. See William Richardson, *Essays on Shakespeare: Dramatic Characters*, 6th ed. (London: Bagster, 1812), "of Macbeth," pp. 35–68. Babcock writes that the "procedure applied *passim* by the critics in analyzing Shakespeare's characterization psychologically with regard to the passions is first to describe the passion in general and then to apply this description to a Shakespearean character" (*Genesis*, p. 158).

21. William Hazlitt, *The Round Table; Characters of Shakespear's Plays* (London: Dent, 1906; rpt. 1969), pp. 187, 188.

22. Helen Gardner discusses the parallels between *Macbeth* and *Paradise Lost* in "Milton's 'Satan' and the Theme of Damnation in Elizabethan Tragedy," *Essays and Studies* 1 (1948): 46–66. See also J. H. Hanford, "The Dramatic Element in *Paradise Lost*," *Studies in Philology* 14 (1917): 178–95; Grant McColley, "*Macbeth* and *Paradise Lost*," *Shakespeare Association Bulletin* 13 (1938): 146–50; and Alwin Thaler, *Shakespeare's Silences* (Cambridge: Harvard University Press, 1929), pp. 139–208.

23. Hazlitt, *The Round Table*, p. 191.

24. Thomas De Quincey, "On the Knocking at the Gate in *Macbeth*," in *Confessions of an Opium Eater and Other Writings*, ed. Aileen Ward (New York: Signet, 1966), pp. 327, 328.

25. *Paradise Lost* IV.800. All references to Milton follow the text in Merrit Y. Hughes, *John Milton: Complete Poems and Major Prose* (Indianapolis: Bobbs-Merrill, 1975). For bestial imagery in *Othello*, see Wolfgang Clemen, *The Development of Shakespeare's Imagery* (Cambridge: Harvard University Press, 1951), pp. 131–32.

26. Hazlitt, *The Round Table*, p. 207.

27. William Hazlitt, *Lectures on the English Poets; The Spirit of the Age* (London: Dent, 1910; rpt. 1967), p. 64.

28. Bloom, introductory note, *Romanticism and Consciousness*, p. 1.

29. See especially Bloom, "The Internalization of Quest-Romance"; and Thorslev, "The Romantic Mind Is Its Own Place."

30. Hartman, *Wordsworth's Poetry 1787–1814*, p. 125.

31. Hartman, p. 126.

32. Hartman, p. 125.

33. Hartman, p. 130.

34. This debt is largely unacknowledged but glaringly obvious to anyone who happens to read Freud's essay alongside of Hartman's "Synopsis: The Via Naturaliter Negativa." See Hartman, "Synopsis," pp. 31–72 in *Wordsworth's Poetry;* Sigmund Freud, *Beyond the Pleasure Principle*, trans. James Strachey (New York: Norton, 1961), esp. chapters 1 and 4. (The discussion of "repetition compulsion" begins on p. 149.)

35. This model is not, of course, characteristic of Freud's theories in general, but results from his vast simplification of the child's world—into a hostile field that delimits and reacts against his development—for the purposes of his argument in *Beyond the Pleasure Principle.* One can draw a very different, interpersonal model for psychic development from other of Freud's works; see, for example, Terry Eagleton's reading of Freud in *Literary Theory* (Minneapolis: University of Minnesota Press, 1983), pp. 151–61.

36. Hartman, *Wordsworth's Poetry*, p. 125.

37. Bloom, "Internalization," p. 6.

38. Bloom is aware of these limitations but holds that they are inherent in the English Romantic poetic stance. See his discussion of Romantic "love" in "Internalization," esp. p. 24.

39. Langbaum, *The Poetry of Experience*, p. 25. In his later work Langbaum dissociates himself from this approach, citing Erikson's criticism of Freud's "mechanistic model" in *The Mysteries of Identity* (New York: Oxford University Press, 1977), p. 11.

40. Langbaum, *The Poetry of Experience*, p. 64.

41. G. F. W. Hegel, *Hegel on Tragedy*, ed. Anne and Henry Paolucci (New York: Harper and Row, 1975), p. 4.

42. Quoted in Walter Kaufmann, *Philosophy and Tragedy* (1968; rpt. New York: Anchor, 1969), p. 332. Cf. A. W. Schlegel on Shakespeare: "This is the very summit of dramatic characterization . . . we must see [a man] in his relations with others; and it is here that most dramatic poets are deficient." *A Course of Lectures on Dramatic Art and Literature*, p. 298.

43. *Hegel on Tragedy*, p. 6. I should stress that, while I make use of a Hegelian model, I am not engaged in a work of "Hegelian" dramatic criticism. For what such an enterprise might look like, see (besides Hegel) Georg Lukacs, "The Metaphysics of Tragedy," in *Soul and Form*, trans. Anna Bostock (Cambridge: MIT Press, 1974); and Lucien Goldmann, *The Hidden God*, trans. Philip Thody (London: Routledge & Kegan Paul, 1964).

44. Since the latter is meant to supplement Freud's psychoanalytic account of the development of self-consciousness, Lacan's turn to Hegel forms a still more appli-

cable precedent for my resort to it here. See Jacques Lacan, "The Mirror Stage as Formative of the Function of the I," in *Ecrits*, trans. Alan Sheridan (New York: Norton, 1977). R. D. Laing, who approaches Hegel both directly and through Sartre, supplements Freudian theory in a similar manner in *The Divided Self* (1959; rpt. Harmondsworth: Penguin, 1965); see esp. ch. 7, "Self-consciousness," in which Laing discusses his own version of the "mirror" stage. Compare also D. W. Winnicott, "Mirror-role of Mother and Family in Child Development," in *Playing and Reality* (London: Tavistock, 1971). For the use of Hegel's account of the development of self-consciousness as a model for literary studies, cf. René Girard, *Deceit, Desire, and the Novel*, trans. Yvonne Freccero (Baltimore: Johns Hopkins Press, 1965), esp. ch. 4, "Master and Slave."

45. Because his use of the terms "master and servant" rather than the usual "lord and bondsman" for Hegel's "*Herr und diener*" better conveys the kinship of Hegel's metaphors to those of the English Romantics, I have here relied on Carl J. Friedrich's revision of J. B. Baillie's translation of the "Master and Servant" section of the *Phenomenology*, in *The Philosophy of Hegel*, ed. Carl J. Friedrich (New York: Modern Library, 1954). Elsewhere I have preferred the A. V. Miller translation, *Hegel's Phenomenology of Spirit* (New York: Oxford, 1977). For critical interpretation, I have relied most on Charles Taylor, *Hegel* (Cambridge: Cambridge University Press, 1975).

46. Friedrich, *The Philosophy of Hegel*, p. 399.

47. Friedrich, p. 400.

48. Friedrich, p. 402.

49. Friedrich, pp. 402–3.

50. Friedrich, p. 406.

51. See, however, Hartman's important discussion of these limitations in "Romanticism and Anti-Self-Consciousness," in Bloom, *Romanticism*.

52. In a recent article, Ross Woodman relates the autonomous or "apocalyptic" self-consciousness in Wordsworth's poetry—including *The Borderers*—to the implicit figure of Satan; see "Milton's Satan in Wordsworth's 'Vale of Soul-making.' "

53. Robert Southey, preface to "A Vision of Judgement," in *Poetical Works*, 10 vols. (Boston: Little, Brown, 1864), 10.194–97.

54. David Lee Clark, ed., *Shelley's Prose* (Albuquerque: University of New Mexico Press, 1954), pp. 284–85.

55. Samuel Johnson, *Rambler* 140, in *The Rambler*, ed. W. J. Bate (New Haven: Yale University Press, 1969), vol. 4, p. 305.

56. R. D. Havens's study, *The Influence of Milton on English Poetry*, is a good (and pertinent) example of the "source study" approach, although his chapter on Wordsworth, in which he departs from his usual attention to "peculiarities of style and diction" to consider a "temperamental similarity" (p. 177), is a partial exception. For a representative discussion of intertextuality, see Julia Kristeva, "The Bounded Text," in *Desire and Language*, trans. Leon S. Roudiez (New York: Columbia University Press, 1980).

57. Hollander, *The Figure of Echo*, p. 62. I have tried to keep Hollander's distinction between "echo" and "allusion" (see esp. pp. 62–64) in mind throughout this study.

58. Bloom, *Poetry and Repression*, p. 2.

59. See the essays, especially those by James Rieger and Stuart Curran, in Wittreich, *Milton and the Line of Vision*. Their approach is not, of course, altogether a new one; twenty years earlier, for example, Ants Oras coined the term "imaginal condensation" for Shelley's "integration of Milton's lines into a new frame of reference." See "The Multitudinous Orb," p. 255. More recent approaches which seek to depart from both models, some taking intertextuality into account, can be found in Hôsek and Parker, *Lyric Poetry;* see especially the essays by Cynthia Chase, Barbara Johnson, David Bromwich, and Jonathan Arac.

60. Longinus, "On the Sublime," in *Aristotle, Horace, Longinus: Classical Literary Criticism*, T. S. Dorsch, trans. (Harmondsworth: Penguin, 1965), pp. 119–20.

61. Since I use his phrase here, I should stress that Bloom himself would draw the opposite conclusion, as the later poet's "repression" of his memory of the earlier text would attest to a stronger "defense" against the blocking power of influence. See, for example, *Poetry and Repression*, p. 72.

62. Bate, *The Burden of the Past*, pp. 76–77 and 112–13; see also Steiner (whom Bate cites), *Death of Tragedy*, pp. 108–9.

63. Bate, *The Burden of the Past*, p. 4.

64. De Quincey, "On the Knocking at the Gate in *Macbeth*," p. 327.

65. William Hazlitt, *Lectures on the English Comic Writers*, in *The Complete Works of William Hazlitt*, ed. P. P. Howe, 21 vols. (London: Dent, 1931), 6.31. For an overview of the German Romantics' similar emphasis on "the reader as a fellow labourer," see Kathleen Wheeler's introduction to *German Aesthetic and Literary Criticism: The Romantic Ironists and Goethe* (Cambridge: Cambridge University Press, 1984), pp. 11–13.

66. I refer, of course, to the argument of Stanley Fish's *Surprised by Sin* (1967; rpt. Berkeley: University of California Press, 1971), an approach Fish later repudiates as assuming a reader too "strictly controlled by the features of the text" in *Is There a Text in This Class?* (Cambridge: Harvard University Press, 1980), p. 7.

67. Clark, *Shelley's Prose*, p. 327.

68. Clark, p. 323.

Chapter 2

1. "1842 Note" in *The Borderers*, ed. Robert Osborn (Ithaca: Cornell University Press, 1982), p. 813. All citations of *The Borderers* refer to this parallel text edition of the published 1842 version and the unpublished early version (cited in the text as "EV").

2. Osborn, p. 814.

3. E. L. Griggs, ed., *Collected Letters of Samuel Taylor Coleridge*, 2 vols. (Oxford: Clarendon, 1956), 1.325.

4. Osborn, *The Borderers*, pp. 63–64. For Hazlitt's analysis of Iago, see *Characters*, pp. 206–9.

5. Osborn, *The Borderers*, p. 66.

6. See de Selincourt, "Wordsworth's Preface to 'The Borderers,' " esp. pp. 173–74; Charles J. Smith, "The Effect of Shakespeare's Influence on *The Borderers*"; Thorslev, "Wordsworth's *Borderers* and the Romantic Villain-Hero"; and Osborn, "Meaningful Obscurity." See also the annotations in Osborn's edition, and in that of de Selincourt in the first volume of *The Poetical Works of William Wordsworth* (London: Oxford University Press, 1940). Some of the textual parallels I discuss are noted in one or more of these works.

7. Next to the lines in *Macbeth* that recount this moment (I.4.35–42) Coleridge notes simply, "Messiah-Satan." See T. M. Raysor, ed., *Coleridge's Shakespeare Criticism*, 2 vols. (Cambridge: Harvard University Press, 1930), 1.64.

8. Hartman notes Oswald's "repetition-compulsion" in *Wordsworth's Poetry*, p. 130. His view of Oswald is in some respects similar to that advanced here, although he sees Oswald's interaction with Marmaduke in a very different light.

9. One thinks also, of course, of the murder of Hamlet's father, but the dramatic situation is in this case quite different. For a provocative discussion of this image in the context of *Hamlet*, see Stanley Cavell's essay "Hamlet's Burden of Proof," in *Disowning Knowledge: In Six Plays of Shakespeare* (Cambridge: Cambridge University Press, forthcoming).

10. *Othello* I.3.292 and III.3.360.

11. This parallel is touched on by Osborn in the introduction to his edition of *The Borderers*, p. 24.

12. For an influential discussion of Othello's sexual horror, see Stanley Cavell, *The Claim of Reason* (New York: Oxford University Press, 1979), pp. 481–96.

13. Osborn, *The Borderers*, p. 65.

14. Such sentiments have inspired a great deal of speculation as to whether Oswald is intended as a spokesman for the ideas of William Godwin, and, if so, whether Wordsworth embraces, rejects, or parodies these views in his drama. For an examination and bibliography of such interpretations, see Sharrock, "*The Borderers*." These various criticisms suffer generally from the more widespread lack of attention to Oswald's dramatic role. Any examination of Godwin's thought and *The Borderers* should begin with the fact that, whatever Oswald *says*, the relation he forms with Marmaduke is explicitly and roundly condemned by Godwin himself. "But, when I make the voluntary surrender of my understanding, and commit my conscience to another man's keeping . . . I then become the most mischievous and pernicious of animals. I annihilate my individuality as a man, and dispose of my force as an animal to him among my neighbors who shall happen to excel in imposture and artifice, and to be least under restraint from the scruples of integrity and justice." *Political Justice* (Harmondsworth: Penguin, 1976), pp. 243–44. For all Oswald's mimicry of Godwinian argument, these seem to me the lines in *Political Justice* most applicable to the action of *The Borderers*.

15. See Emile Legouis, *The Early Life of William Wordsworth* (London: Dent, 1921), p. 272; and Hartman, *Wordsworth's Poetry*, p. 125.

16. For a related point, see Pipkin, "*The Borderers* and the Genesis of Wordsworth's Spots of Time."

17. The phrase is Alvin Kernan's from "*Othello:* An Introduction," in *Modern Shakespeare Criticism*, ed. Kernan (New York: Harcourt, Brace, 1970), pp. 351–59.

Sharrock relates the "symbolic border" to Wordsworth's experience with the French Revolution in his above-mentioned article.

18. "Thy letters have transported me beyond / The ignorant present, and I feel now / The future in an instant." (I.5.57–59)

19. See Hartman, *Wordsworth's Poetry*, p. 130.

20. Algernon Charles Swinburne, *Miscellanies* (London: Chatto and Windus, 1911), pp. 117–19.

21. Hartman suggests the applicability of the *Phenomenology* to *The Borderers* in a footnote to his very different reading of the drama in *Wordsworth's Poetry*, p. 129.

22. Hartman, p. 129.

23. See Osborn's Introduction, pp. 27–28, and his note, p. 80.

24. This repetition is discussed briefly by both Hartman (*Wordsworth's Poetry*, p. 130 f.n.) and Osborn (Introduction, pp. 34–35).

25. Osborn, *The Borderers*, p. 814.

26. Thorslev notes this parallel (of which the phrase is only a part) in "Wordsworth's *Borderers*," p. 86.

Chapter 3

1. Byron frequently described *Manfred* and *Cain* as "metaphysical" dramas: see, for example, his letter to Douglas Kinnaird, 11 September 1821, in *Byron's Letters and Journals*, ed. Leslie A. Marchand, 12 vols. (Cambridge: Harvard University Press, 1982), 8.205.

2. David V. Erdman discusses Byron's ambivalence toward the stage in "Byron's Stage Fright." Note that Erdman confines his argument to the "regular" dramas (see esp. pp. 240–41). For "reform the stage," see pp. 228 and 241. Margaret Howell argues in *Byron Tonight* that Byron consistently wrote for the reader rather than the stage, and that his plays are better read than performed (see esp. pp. 1–11).

3. From Goethe's 1817 review of *Manfred* (publ. 1820), trans. R. B. Hoppner and rpt. in *Byron: The Critical Heritage*, ed. Andrew Rutherford (New York: Barnes and Noble, 1970), p. 119.

4. Letter to Murray, 23 August 1821, *Letters and Journals* (hereafter "*L&J*") 8.186–87.

5. Letter to Lady Byron, 14 September 1821, *L&J* 8.210.

6. Paul West, *Byron and the Spoiler's Art*, p. 119.

7. Francis Jeffrey, review of *Manfred* in *Edinburgh Review* 28 (1817), rpt. in *Critical Heritage*, p. 116.

8. Byron claimed to have known *Faust* at the time of composing *Manfred* only through a *viva voce* translation of "most of it" by M. G. Lewis. See Byron's letter to Murray, 7 June 1820, *L&J* 7.113. All quotations from Byron's poems, except for *Cain*, follow the text of *The Poetical Works of Byron*, ed. Robert F. Gleckner (Boston: Houghton Mifflin, 1975).

9. See, for example, Twitchell, "The Supernatural Structure of Byron's *Manfred.*" Twitchell finds that the spirits "reflect psychological changes in the protagonist" (p. 602), and yet they "exist both within and without" (p. 609).

10. Bloom, *The Visionary Company*, p. 250.

11. Rutherford, *Byron: A Critical Study*, p. 89.

12. G. Wilson Knight first discussed the importance of Shakespearean echoes in *Manfred*, which he read as a "commentary" on *Macbeth*, in "Shakespeare and Byron's Plays," pp. 82–83. Knight points out, incidentally, that Manfred's "Destinies" are linguistically (and mythographically) cognate with Macbeth's "Weird" sisters. See also Knight's *Byron and Shakespeare*, pp. 174–77.

13. Jon Galt, *Life of Lord Byron*, 2nd ed. (London: Colburn, 1830), p. 214; Bertrand Evans, "Manfred's Remorse and Dramatic Tradition."

14. Cf. Peter J. Manning's contention in *Byron and His Fictions* that "Manfred does not so much seek for Astarte as a separate, independent being as he searches for a state prior to identity, the state in which mother and child form one organic unit. Astarte is an ideal, mirror image, a reflection in which the self can discover and ground itself, or, in this instance more accurately, a vision of wholeness imagined by a being in discord" (p. 83).

15. See Claude Lévi-Strauss, *The Elementary Structures of Kinship*, rev. ed., trans. James Bell et al. (Boston: Beacon Press, 1969). For a discussion of incest in *Manfred* in a broader context, see my "The Dangers of Sympathy: Sibling Incest in English Romantic Poetry," *SEL* 25 (1985): 737–54.

16. Jacques Lacan relates this passage to Hegel's account of self-consciousness in "Desire and the Interpretation of Desire in *Hamlet*," in *Literature and Psychoanalysis*, ed. Shoshana Felman (Baltimore: Johns Hopkins University Press, 1982), p. 31.

17. Hegel, *Philosophy* (Friedrich), p. 114.

18. Hegel, *Phenomenology* (Miller), p. 125.

19. Peter L. Thorslev, Jr., discusses Manfred's kinship to Cain and the Wandering Jew in *The Byronic Hero*, pp. 165–76. For the relation of those figures to Milton's Satan, see the chapters devoted to each in the same work.

20. Thorslev discusses the importance of this locus for Romantic poetry in detail in "The Romantic Mind Is Its Own Place."

21. Bloom, *Visionary Company*, p. 249.

22. See Byron's letter to Murray, 14 April 1817, *L&J* 5.211–12.

23. Stuart M. Sperry, in "Byron and the Meaning of *Manfred*," writes that "what the climax of *Manfred* dramatizes is Byron's confrontation with his own persona."

24. See "genius" in the *OED* and C. S. Lewis's remarks on the daemon or genius in *The Discarded Image* (Cambridge: Cambridge University Press, 1964), p. 42. See also Sperry, "Byron," p. 198.

25. In a significant parallel, Freud (probably inspired by *Manfred*) imagines a Rome in which the city's various past forms would coexist with the modern city as an emblem for the persistence of infantile drives and early memories in the adult psyche. See *Civilization and Its Discontents*, trans. James Strachey (New York: Norton, 1961), pp. 16–18.

26. Byron's phrase "the language of another world" itself echoes Milton's "The secrets of another World" (5.569), which Raphael appropriately uses to describe "th' invisible exploits / Of warring Spirits."

27. See Bostetter, *The Romantic Ventriloquists*, p. 278; Sperry, "Byron," p. 201; Bloom, *Visionary Company*, p. 249.

28. Jeffrey in *Critical Heritage*, p. 117.

Chapter 4

1. Letter to Moore, 19 September 1821, *L&J* 8.216.

2. Letter to Hobhouse, 27 September 1821, *L&J* 8.224.

3. See Thorslev, *Byronic Hero*, pp. 92–107.

4. My text for *Cain* is Truman Guy Steffan, *Lord Byron's Cain: Twelve Essays and a Text with Variants and Annotations* (Austin: University of Texas Press, 1968).

5. Walter Scott, letter to John Murray, 17 December 1821, rpt. in Rutherford, *Critical Heritage*, p. 214; Shelley, letter to John Gisborne, 26 January 1822, *The Letters of Percy Bysshe Shelley*, ed. Frederick L. Jones, 2 vols. (Oxford: Clarendon, 1964), 2.388; Leigh Hunt, "Letter" on *Cain* in *The Examiner*, 2 June 1822, rpt. in *Critical Heritage*, p. 227.

6. Letter to Murray, 8 February 1822, *L&J* 9.103.

7. Jeffrey, review of *Cain* in *The Edinburgh Review* 36 (1822), rpt. in *Critical Heritage*, pp. 233–34.

8. Stavrou, "Milton, Byron, and the Devil," p. 153; Cantor, "Byron's *Cain*," p. 50. Cantor's study appears in a slightly different form as chapter 5 of *Creature and Creator*.

9. Letter to Moore, 8 March 1822, *L&J* 9.123.

10. For a detailed and balanced discussion of Byron's religious views in relation to his "mysteries," see McGann, *Fiery Dust*, pp. 248–53.

11. Each view has been espoused by a number of critics: see Steffan's useful survey of twentieth-century approaches to *Cain* in his edition, pp. 453–69. It is Marchand who calls Lucifer a "defender" of mankind: *Byron's Poetry*, p. 86. Several more recent studies should be noted as well: Terry Otten calls Lucifer "Promethean" but views his influence as a "threat," *Deserted Stage*, pp. 50–51; Cantor similarly sees Lucifer as a reliable purveyor of devastating conceptions, "Byron's *Cain*," pp. 50–71; A. P. Whitmore describes the "essential conflict between Cain and Lucifer" in *The Major Characters of Byron's Dramas*, pp. 98–104.

12. "Thoughts for a Speech of Lucifer, In the Tragedy of 'Cain,' " in Gleckner, *The Poetical Works of Byron*, p. 237.

13. Letter to Murray, 3 November 1821, *L&J* 9.53–54.

14. Cf. I.540–43; II.1.16–20; III.80–86; III.318–20.

13. Letter to Murray, 3 November 1821, *L&J* 9.53–54.

14. Cf. I.540–43; II.1.16–20; III.80–86; III.318–20.

15. Byron has too often been seen as falling uncritically into the very dilemma he delineates with such clarity in *Cain*. Typical is Stuart Curran's assertion that "it fell to the least systematic or philosophically learned of the three members of Southey's 'Satanic school' openly to avow the heretical implications" of a sympathetic view of Satan. "The Siege of Hateful Contraries," p. 220. Jerome J. McGann has gone far toward clearing the ground of such a misapprehension—which depends on the tiresome view that Byron was less intellectually sophisticated than Blake or Shelley—in his "Milton and Byron," in which he emphasizes the "problematic" character of Byron's Satanic heroes, whose portrayals "prove nothing; rather, they raise questions" (p. 15).

16. Thorslev emphasizes Lucifer's inability to love, *Byronic Hero*, p. 180, as does Cantor, "Byron's *Cain*," pp. 68–70.

17. I am thinking here of Kierkegaard's critique of Plato's use of Socrates in *The Concept of Irony*, which I return to at some length in the chapter on *Prometheus Unbound*.

18. Quoted by E. H. Coleridge in *The Works of Lord Byron*, rev. ed. (London: John Murray, 1901), *Poetry* 5.224. Coleridge also notes the scriptural echo.

19. Cicero, *De Re Publica* VI, esp. sections 11–17; Dante, *Paradiso* XXII.151; Chaucer, *Troilus and Criseyde* V.1815.

20. *Endymion* III.129–39. All citations of Keats follow the edition of Jack Stillinger, *The Poems of John Keats* (Cambridge: Harvard University Press, 1978).

21. *Endymion* IV.646–48.

22. For this view of Keats's romances (though without reference to Platonism), see Perkins, *The Quest for Permanence*, esp. pp. 259–76; and Jack Stillinger, "The Hoodwinking of Madeline: Scepticism in *The Eve of St. Agnes*," *Studies in Philology* 58 (1961): 533–55.

23. See Cantor, "Byron's *Cain*," p. 63.

24. W. H. Auden, *The Dyer's Hand* (New York: Vintage, 1968), p. 388.

25. Cf. Wordsworth:

A motion and a spirit, that impels
All thinking things, all objects of all thought,
And rolls through all things.

26. Bloom, *Visionary Company*, p. 254.

27. Bloom, *Visionary Company*, p. 253; Hartman, *Wordsworth's Poetry*, p. 128.

28. Letter to Gisborne cited above. Cantor contrasts the absence of apocalyptic vision in Byron's works to its importance in Shelley's in "Byron's *Cain*," p. 63.

29. "The Ghost of Abel," in *The Complete Poetry and Prose of William Blake*, ed. David V. Erdman, rev. (Berkeley: University of California Press, 1982), pp. 270–72. For discussions of Blake's scene in relation to *Cain*, see Frye, *Fearful Symmetry*, pp. 198–99; and Bloom, *Blake's Apocalypse*, pp. 434–35.

30. Letter to Murray, 3 November 1821 (cited above).

Chapter 5

1. This interpretive tradition begins in the New Testament with 2 Peter 3:6–7: "Whereby the world that then was, being overflowed with water, perished; But the heavens and earth, which are now, by the same word are kept in store, reserved unto fire against the day of judgment and perdition of ungodly men."

2. Hazlitt, *Spirit of the Age*, p. 240.

3. Cited By E. H. Coleridge in *Works, Poetry* 5.281–82.

4. John Wilson, "Byron's 'Heaven and Earth,' " *Blackwoods' Edinburgh Magazine* 13 (Jan. 1823); rpt. in Reiman, *The Romantics Reviewed*, Part B: *Byron and Regency Society Poets* 1.196.

5. Francis Jeffrey, review of *Heaven and Earth* and Moore's "Loves of the Angels," *Edinburgh Review* 38 (Feb. 1823); rpt. in Reiman, 2.945.

6. Letter to Kinnaird, 14 December 1821, *L&J* 9.81.

7. Readers who enjoy parody should see Swinburne's travesty of Byron's lyrical style in *Miscellanies*, p. 83.

8. Chew, *The Dramas of Lord Byron*, p. 141.

9. Wordsworth, *Prelude* (1850) XI.143–44.

10. E. H. Coleridge remarks on this passage that "Byron said that it was difficult to make Lucifer talk 'like a clergyman.' He contrived to make Noah talk like a street-preacher." *Works, Poetry* 5.309.

11. Cited by Rutherford in *Critical Heritage*, p. 218.

12. *Prelude* (1850) XI.143–44; *Logic*, ed. J. R. de J. Jackson (Princeton: Princeton University Press, 1981), p. 42.

13. De Quincey, "The Literature of Knowledge and the Literature of Power," in *Confessions*, p. 331.

14. Isaiah 11:6.

15. Medwin's *Conversations of Lord Byron*, ed. Ernest B. Lovell, Jr. (Princeton: Princeton University Press, 1966), p. 156.

16. Thomas McFarland gives a brilliant overview of the significance of the Romantic fragment in *Romanticism and the Forms of Ruin*, pp. 3–55.

17. See T. H. Vail Motter's thorough study, "Byron's 'Werner' Re-Estimated."

18. See George Steiner's remarks on Byron's sketch for completing *The Deformed Transformed* in *Death of Tragedy*, pp. 211–12.

Chapter 6

1. Letter to Keats, 27 July 1820, *The Letters of Percy Bysshe Shelley*, ed. Frederick L. Jones, 2 vols. (Oxford: Clarendon, 1964), 2.221.

2. Shelley's preface to *The Cenci* in *Shelley's Poetry and Prose*, ed. Donald H. Reiman and Sharon B. Powers (New York: Norton, 1977), p. 241; and Mary Shelley's "Note" in *The Cenci*, ed. Roland A. Duerkson, p. 111. (All citations of *The Cenci* refer to Reiman and Powers.) For an account of Shelley's relation to the theater, see Joseph W. Donohue, Jr., "Shelley's Beatrice and the Romantic Conception of Character," rev. as chapter 7 of *Dramatic Character*. Shelley's ambivalence is evident in the choice of a subject—incest—which he feared would not "be admitted on the stage" (Letter to Peacock, c. 20 July 1819, *Letters* 2.102).

3. A number of studies dealing with Shelley's use of either Shakespeare or Milton have appeared over the years. For Shelley and Shakespeare, see Clark, "Shelley and Shakespeare"; S. R. Watson, "Shelley and Shakespeare"; Langston, "Shelley's Use of Shakespeare"; Cantor, " 'A Distorting Mirror' "; and Harrington-Lueker, "Imagination versus Introspection." For Shelley and Milton, see Baker, "A Note on Shelley and Milton"; Jones, "Shelley and Milton"; Oras, "The Multitudinous Orb"; Wittreich, "The 'Satanism' of Blake and Shelley Reconsidered"; Curran, "The Siege of hateful contraries" and *Shelley's Annus Mirabilis*, pp. 54–60; and Cantor, *Creature and Creator*, pp. 77–102.

4. *The Wandering Jew* has in the past been partly attributed to Thomas Medwin, mainly on Medwin's own authority, and is now usually considered wholly Shelley's. See Bertram Dobell, *The Wandering Jew* (London: Shelley Society, 1887), pp. xxiv–xxx; Neville Rogers, *The Complete Poetical Works of Percy Bysshe Shelley*, 4 vols. (Oxford: Clarendon, 1972), 1.374–75; S. G. Andrews, "Shelley, Medwin, and *The Wandering Jew*," *Keats-Shelley Journal* 20 (1971): 78–86. My quotations from this poem follow Rogers's edition.

5. Paulo's Cain-like stigma—a bloody cross on his forehead—is also related to Satan through the epigraph to Canto III (". . . but his face / Deep scars of thunder had intrenched . . .") from *Paradise Lost* I.600–601.

6. Preface, p. 239; Wordsworth in Osborn, p. 814.

7. Shaw's review of the Shelley Society production of *The Cenci*, *Our Corner* 7 (1886): 372.

8. Hazlitt, *Characters*, p. 18.

9. See, for example, Cantor, "Distorting Mirror," pp. 101–2.

10. Cited in Richard Ellmann, *James Joyce* (New York: Oxford University Press, 1959), p. 692.

11. Representative is Whitman, "Beatrice's 'Pernicious Mistake' in *The Cenci*."

12. Cantor discusses this point and cites a number of supporting critical views in "Distorting Mirror," p. 97. Two more recent studies define Cenci's transformation of Beatrice's character in terms quite different from my own: see Lemoncelli, "Cenci as Corrupt Dramatic Poet"; and Twitchell, "Shelley's Use of Vampirism in *The Cenci*."

13. Shelley, of course, does not affirm, but rather criticizes, such antifeminist concepts as "chastity" and "deflowering" in *The Cenci*. Beatrice reacts to the rape—and Cenci counts on this—as a woman formed by the profoundly sexist ideology of sixteenth-century Catholic Italy. See Shelley's remarks on Catholicism in the Preface, pp. 240–41; the point is amplified (and perhaps overstated) by Harry White in "Beatrice Cenci and Shelley's Avenger." Nathaniel Brown has studied Shelley's feminism

in *Sexuality and Feminism in Shelley.*

14. Shelley's "Dedication," p. 237 in Reiman and Powers. For comparisons of Beatrice and Prometheus, see Whitman, "Beatrice's 'Pernicious Mistake,' " pp. 250–52; Milton Wilson, *Shelley's Later Poetry,* pp. 78–92; Rieger, *The Mutiny Within,* pp. 125–28; Woodman, *The Apocalyptic Vision in the Poetry of Shelley,* pp. 116–17; Wasserman, *Shelley: A Critical Reading,* pp. 98–99; Curran, *Shelley's Annus Mirabilis,* pp. 120–30; and Jean Hall, "The Socialized Imagination: Shelley's *The Cenci* and *Prometheus Unbound,*" *Studies in Romanticism* 23 (1984): 339–50.

15. Preface, p. 240; and Clark, *Shelley's Prose* (hereafter cited as "*Prose*"), p. 282.

16. Preface, p. 241.

17. Compare also Hazlitt's reading of *Macbeth:* "It moves upon the verge of an abyss," *Characters,* p. 191.

18. Raymond Williams, for example, assigns the introduction into the English language of "the unconscious" to Coleridge and of "subconscious" to De Quincey in *Keywords* (New York: Oxford University Press, 1976), pp. 271–72.

19. In the (one hopes temporary) absence of such a reading, see Richard Onorato's remarks on the image of the abyss in his psychoanalytic study of Wordsworth in *The Prelude* in *The Character of the Poet,* esp. pp. 19–22 and 116–20.

20. One imagines, for example, the application of statements such as Paul de Man's in "Criticism and Crisis": "Here the human self has experienced the void within the self and the invented fiction, far from filling the void, asserts itself as pure nothingness, *our* nothingness stated and restated by a subject that is the agent of its own instability." *Blindness and Insight,* p. 19.

21. Preface, p. 238.

22. *Macbeth* II.2.12–13; *Borderers* 966–67: "The features of Idonea lurked in his face." It is significant that Marmaduke, through his shared childhood with Idonea, thinks of Herbert as a father (*Borderers* 86–97).

23. Preface, p. 242. On the system of patriarchal tyranny in *The Cenci,* see Hammond, "Beatrice's Three Fathers."

24. Preface, p. 240. Several critics take pains to justify Beatrice. Notably sympathetic readers include Curran, *Shelley's Cenci,* pp. 138–41; and James D. Wilson, "Beatrice Cenci and Shelley's View of Morality."

25. Note also the strong echo of Othello's "Put out the light" speech in Giacomo's anxious words during the first murder attempt (III.2.10–20 and 51–52), which parallels the allusions to Duncan's murder that mark Beatrice's attempt.

26. Preface to *Prometheus Unbound* in Reiman and Powers, p. 133. James Rieger notes the parallel with the preface to *The Cenci* in *The Mutiny Within,* pp. 125–26. Compare also Shelley's description of Godwin's Falkland (yet another literary avatar of Milton's Satan): "Falkland, whom the author, with that sublime casuistry which is the parent of toleration and forbearance, persuades us personally to love, whilst his actions must forever remain the theme of our astonishment and abhorrence." *Prose,* p. 309.

27. *Prose,* p. 290.

28. *Prose,* p. 285.

29. Reiman and Powers, p. 133.

Chapter 7

1. For Shelley's critique of Milton's Satan, see Wittreich, "The 'Satanism' of Blake and Shelley Reconsidered"; and Curran, "The Siege of Hateful Contraries."

2. N. I. White, *Shelley*, 2 vols. (New York: Knopf, 1940), 1.278.

3. See Bloom, *Shelley's Mythmaking*, p. 109; Curran, "Siege"; and Cantor, *Creature and Creator*, pp. 77–78.

4. The parallels between Jupiter and Satan were first noted by Carlos Baker in *Shelley's Major Poetry*, p. 98; see also Bloom, *Shelley's Mythmaking*, pp. 107–10.

5. My text for *Prometheus Unbound* is that in Reiman and Powers.

6. For an influential reading of Act I describing Prometheus's repentance as an elaborated process, rather than a simple change of heart, see Woodman, *Apocalyptic Vision*, pp. 110–16.

7. Stuart Sperry finds a parallel between the curses of Prometheus and the Seventh Spirit in "Byron and the Meaning of *Manfred*," pp. 191–92.

8. The close relation of Jupiter's shade to Prometheus's former self is discussed both by Wasserman, *Shelley: A Critical Reading*, p. 260; and by Milton Wilson, *Shelley's Later Poetry*, p. 64.

9. Cf. Ross Woodman's contention that in Act I "Prometheus rules over the Jupiter within himself, thereby merely perpetuating the master-slave relationship in another guise." "The Androgyne in *Prometheus Unbound*," p. 229.

10. Cantor discusses "loathsome sympathy" in *Creature and Creator*, pp. 81–82. The phrase echoes Milton's "horrid sympathy," which describes the devils' transformation into serpents mirroring Satan's own unwilling metamorphosis as he announces his successful temptation of Eve (*Paradise Lost* X.540).

11. The Furies allude, of course, to both the Witches' own words, "Fair is foul, and foul is fair" (I.1.11), and to Macbeth's ominous echo shortly afterwards, "So fair and foul a day I have not seen" (I.3.38).

12. Osborn, *The Borderers*, p. 814.

13. Harold Bloom forcefully summarizes the second pageant, "even Christ at last becomes the tyrant of the upper sky," *Visionary Company*, p. 300.

14. Clark, *Shelley's Prose*, p. 314. (Hereafter cited as "*Prose*.")

15. See Sperry, "Necessity and the Role of the Hero in Shelley's *Prometheus Unbound*."

16. Sympathy theory in the eighteenth century and its importance for English Romanticism have been studied by W. J. Bate, "The Sympathetic Imagination in Eighteenth-Century English Criticism," *ELH* 12 (1945): 144–64, rev. as chapter 5 of *From Classic to Romantic*; Roy Male, Jr., "Shelley and the Doctrine of Sympathy"; and James Engell, *The Creative Imagination*, chapter 11.

17. Male, "Shelley and the Doctrine of Sympathy," p. 185.

18. Adam Smith, *The Theory of Moral Sentiments*, ed. D. D. Raphael and A. L. Macfie (Oxford, 1976; rpt. Indianapolis: Liberty Classics, 1982), p. 9.

19. *Prose*, p. 282.

20. *Prose*, p. 283.

21. *Prose*, p. 285.

22. Adam Smith, *The Theory of Moral Sentiments*, pp. 109–10. Nathaniel Brown draws attention to these passages in *Sexuality and Feminism*, p. 30.

23. *Prose*, p. 220. See also Shelley's remarks on the "social sympathies" in the *Defence*, p. 278 in *Prose*.

24. *Prose*, p. 170. Since discussions of love tend to grow as slippery in theoretical as they do in intimate contexts, precisely what Shelley means by "love" is sometimes arguable; when, for example, it can be identified with "sympathy" and when not. See the chapters on Shelley's various conceptions of love in Beatty, *Light from Heaven*; Brown, *Sexuality and Feminism*; and Singer, *The Nature of Love*, vol. 2, "Courtly and Romantic." I have tried scrupulously, however, not to distort Shelley's remarks on love and sympathy when taking them out of the context of his prose works.

25. Quoted in Abrams, *Natural Supernaturalism*, p. 294. The entire chapter ("Romantic Love") in which Hegel is cited bears on my discussion of sympathy theory in Shelley.

26. On this point, see Fogle, "Image and Imagelessness," esp. p. 28.

27. Demogorgon's Socratic method is noticed by Woodman, *Apocalyptic Vision*, p. 125.

28. Søren Kierkegaard, *The Concept of Irony*, trans. L. M. Capel (Bloomington: Indiana University Press, 1965), pp. 203, 213, 173 and (on Plato) 139, 205. As Gregor Malantschuk points out in *Kierkegaard's Thought*, ed. and trans. Howard V. Honig and Edna H. Honig (Princeton: Princeton University Press, 1971), Kierkegaard "in his dissertation limits Socrates' position to the standpoint of irony"; elsewhere Kierkegaard credits Socrates' "abstract dialectic" with establishing the conditions for an "infinite" ethical existence (pp. 191–202). From this larger perspective, Socrates resembles Demogorgon more than Oswald.

29. Since Demogorgon's phrase arises through his response to Asia's insistent questions on the master-slave relation, I find it all the more appropriate that Michael Rosen, in defining the "nature of thought" as conceived of by Hegel, cites Shelley: "Its deep truth is imageless." *Hegel's Dialectic and Its Criticism* (Cambridge: Cambridge University Press, 1982), p. 93.

30. See Wasserman, *Shelley's Prometheus Unbound* (Baltimore: Johns Hopkins University Press, 1965), p. 32.

31. A number of such complaints are cited in Zillman, *Shelley's Prometheus Unbound*, pp. 151–52.

32. The parallel is noted by Reiman and Powers, p. 187.

33. *Prose*, p. 227. Compare Shelley on Bacon's prose in the *Defence*: "it is a strain which distends and then bursts the circumference of the hearer's mind and pours itself forth together with it into the universal element with which it has perpetual sympathy" (*Prose*, p. 281).

34. *Prose*, p. 293.

35. Karl Marx, *Economic and Philosophic Manuscripts of 1844*, ed. D. J. Struik (New York: International, 1964), pp. 132–46. For a reading of *Prometheus Unbound* in its contemporary political setting that lends weight to this parallel, see Cameron,

"The Political Symbolism of *Prometheus Unbound*"; also Woodring, *Politics in English Romantic Poetry*, pp. 278–310; and Curran, "The Political Prometheus." Marx's early Romanticism, and the relation of his later work to Romantic thought, are discussed briefly by Abrams in *Natural Supernaturalism*, pp. 313–16; and (with thorough annotations of related studies) by Paul Breines, "Marxism, Romanticism, and the Case of Georg Lukacs," *Studies in Romanticism* 16 (1977): 473–89.

36. Preface, p. 135; letter to Charles and James Ollier, 6 March 1820 (*Letters* 2.551).

37. Preface, pp. 133, 135.

38. Woodring, *Politics*, pp. 307–10; Richard Holmes, *Shelley: The Pursuit* (New York: Dutton, 1975), pp. 568–69; Paul Foot, *Red Shelley* (London: Sidgwick and Jackson, 1980), pp. 191–202.

39. Woodring, *Politics*, p. 297.

40. Tilottama Rajan discusses these "interpretive interludes" in "Deconstruction or Reconstruction."

41. Zillman, *Shelley's Prometheus Unbound*, pp. 440–41.

42. T. M. Raysor, ed., *Coleridge's Shakespeare Criticism*, 2 vols. (Cambridge: Harvard University Press, 1930), 1.69.

43. See Hurt, "*Prometheus Unbound* and Aeschylean Dramaturgy."

44. The phrase is from C. S. Lewis, "Shelley, Dryden, and Mr. Eliot," *Rehabilitations* (1959); rpt. in M. H. Abrams, ed., *English Romantic Poets*, 2nd ed. (London: Oxford University Press, 1975), p. 335.

45. See the letters to Hunt, 15 August 1819, and Ollier, 6 September 1819 (*Letters* 2.508, 513).

46. For more extended discussions that help substantiate my point here, see Knight, *The Starlit Dome*, pp. 218–24; and Rapf, "A Spirit in Search of Itself."

47. See Woodman, "Androgyne."

48. See V. A. DeLuca's intricate and persuasive reading of the "cancelled cycles" passage in "The Style of Millennial Announcement in *Prometheus Unbound*," pp. 95–99.

49. Here I have drawn on William Keach's important study, "Reflexive Imagery in Shelley."

50. Daniel Hughes sees this comparison working within the drama: "Shelley lets the rest of the poem use him up; he is sacrificed, like the Bard of the West Wind, in order that the great images of millennium and apocalypse can come to consciousness. Even as he becomes a capable poet, he yields to his creations." "Prometheus Made Capable Poet in Act One of *Prometheus Unbound*," p. 4.

51. Preface, p. 134.

52. *Prose*, p. 297. Shelley often stresses the interdependence of poetry and social conditions; for example, in *A Philosophical View of Reform* (*Prose*, pp. 231, 263), *A Discourse on the Manners of the Ancient Greeks* (*Prose*, p. 217), the Preface to *Laon and Cythna* (*Prose*, p. 318), and elsewhere in the *Defence* (see esp. p. 283).

53. *Prose*, p. 285.

54. Preface, p. 134.

55. *Prose*, p. 297.

Chapter 8

1. H. W. Donner, *The Works of Thomas Lovell Beddoes* (London: Oxford University Press, 1935), p. 609. All citations of Beddoes's works follow this edition, hereafter referred to in the notes as "*Works*."

2. Symons, "Thomas Lovell Beddoes," p. 126.

3. Northrop Frye, who devotes a third of his *Study of English Romanticism* to Beddoes, is a notable exception; but his modernist emphasis on what he calls "the Romantic rejection of the social process as the center of human reality" results in a perspective on *Death's Jest-Book* and its relation to earlier Romantic works vastly different from my own.

4. Bloom writes, in his brief consideration of Beddoes in *The Visionary Company*, that "Beddoes' imagination is a grotesque version of his master Shelley's" (p. 437).

5. "Fragment of a Preface," *Works*, p. 530.

6. Strachey, "The Last Elizabethan," *New Quarterly* 1907; rpt. in *Books and Characters*. More recent criticism of Beddoes locates his work instead as proto-Modernist, comparing him especially to Eliot; see, for example, Ricks, "Thomas Lovell Beddoes," pp. 32–48, and Frye *passim*. Oddly, neither critic discusses Pound's interest in Beddoes, or his lines in *The Cantos*—

> Curious, is it not, that Mr Eliot
> has not given more time to Mr Beddoes
> (T. L.) prince of morticians
> Where none can speak his language . . . (Canto 80)—

although Ricks, in a revised version of his Beddoes essay in *The Force of Poetry*, credits Charles Tomlinson with drawing his attention to this passage in Pound.

7. Letter to Kelsall, 11 January 1825, *Works*, p. 595.

8. Letter to Bryan Waller Procter, 3 March 1824, *Works*, p. 581; 1829 preface to *Death's Jest-Book*, *Works*, p. 534; letter to Procter, 19 April 1829, *Works*, p. 643.

9. Donner, *Thomas Lovell Beddoes* (Oxford: Blackwell, 1935), pp. 375–76. Beddoes's remark that the stage is "the highest aim of the dramatist, & I should be very desirous to get on it" (letter to Kelsall, 27 February 1829, *Works*, p. 640) has sometimes been read as evidence that *Death's Jest-Book* was intended for the stage; rather it refers to the "right Tragedy" which Beddoes thought of beginning later (letter to Kelsall, 13 November 1844, *Works*, p. 676). Beddoes expresses his misgivings about the contemporary stage in his preface to *The Bride's Tragedy* (*Works*, pp. 528–29) and in his letter to Procter, 9 October 1826 (*Works*, pp. 624–25).

10. 1829 preface to *Death's Jest-Book*, *Works*, p. 534.

11. Donner gives two versions of the first act on facing pages; all citations are from the later version unless otherwise noted.

12. John Agar identifies the theme of "power purchased by an alienation of human sympathy" in an important article, "Isbrand and T. L. Beddoes' Aspiring Hero," p. 374.

13. Verse letter to Procter, March 1826, *Works*, p. 87.

14. Pound, "Beddoes and Chronology," p. 351.

15. One might object that, in English, the term "romantic" did not yet convey the meaning I make it bear here. But Beddoes was steeped in German literature and thought—indeed German was his principal language for most of his adult life—and *Romantische* had long signified the "modern" tradition that Beddoes would have associated as much with Wordsworth and Shelley as with the Schlegels and Tieck.

16. Cf. *The Cenci* IV.1.119–20.

17. Verse letter to Procter, March 1826, *Works*, p. 87.

18. See Beddoes's note on "Luz," *Works*, pp. 487–88; and his letter to Kelsall, 12 February 1829, *Works*, p. 640.

19. Frye takes a very different view, seeing death as a privileged state for Beddoes (*Study*, pp. 52ff.).

20. Letter to Kelsall, 30 April 1829, *Works*, p. 645.

21. Verse letter to Procter, May 1825, *Works*, p. 84.

Epilogue

1. For discussions of these poets, their dramas, and their relations to the contemporary stage, see Hallam Tennyson, *Alfred Lord Tennyson: A Memoir, By His Son*, 2 vols. (London: MacMillan, 1897), 2.173–199; Jerome Hamilton Buckley, *Tennyson: The Growth of a Poet* (Cambridge: Harvard University Press, 1960), pp. 195–215; Otten, *The Deserted Stage*, pp. 108–42; Samuel C. Chew, *Swinburne* (London: John Murray, 1931), pp. 185–227.

2. The distinction is heuristic rather than absolute: *The Cenci* belongs to the historical group in formal and to mental theater in thematic terms, and Browning's dramatic works tend also to fall somewhere between the two traditions, though more nearly to the history plays. Certain other works—like Coleridge's *Sturm und Drang* play *Remorse* and Swinburne's Greek Revival tragedies *Atalanta in Calydon* and *Erectheus*—appeal to other traditions altogether.

3. See Langbaum, *The Poetry of Experience*, pp. 9–74.

4. M. M. Bakhtin, *The Dialogic Imagination: Four Essays*, ed. Michael Holquist, trans. Caryl Emerson and Michael Holquist (Austin: University of Texas Press, 1981), pp. 5–6, 405.

5. Bakhtin, p. 65.

6. Bakhtin, p. 33.

7. Bakhtin, p. 29.

8. See esp. Prior, *The Language of Tragedy*, pp. 231–64.

9. "The novel fights for the renovation of an antiquated literary language, in the interests of those strata of the national language that have remained (to a greater or lesser degree) outside the centralizing or unifying influence of the artistic and

ideological norm established by dominant literary language." Bakhtin, *The Dialogic Imagination*, p. 67.

10. That commentary has often divided in finding certain allusions, particularly in *Manfred*, *Cain*, and *Prometheus Unbound*, expressive of either parody or emulation also finds a parallel in Bakhtin's remarks on medieval literature: "the role of the other's word was enormous at the time: there were quotations that were openly and reverently emphasized as such, or that were half-hidden, completely hidden, half-conscious, unconscious, intentionally distorted, unintentionally distorted, deliberately re-interpreted and so forth. The boundary lines between someone else's speech and one's own speech were flexible, ambiguous, often deliberately distorted and confused." Bakhtin, p. 69.

11. Bakhtin, pp. 342, 294.

12. Bakhtin, p. 297. See also Rajan, who in "Romanticism and the Death of Lyric Consciousness" relates the lyrical drama to a pervasive tendency within the period: "The movement in Shelley's play from lyric to drama is one instance of a larger movement in Romanticism toward making the lyric interdiscursive, by intertextualizing it, narrating, or dramatizing it" (p. 206).

13. Tucker, "Dramatic Monologue and the Overhearing of Lyric," pp. 236–37, 239.

14. A. H. Hallam, "On Some of the Characteristics of Modern Poetry, And on the Lyrical Poems of Alfred Tennyson," *The Englishman's Magazine* 5 (1831): 626.

15. See, for example, Tucker, "Dramatic Monologue," p. 229.

16. E. D. H. Johnson, "The Lily and the Rose: Symbolic Meaning in Tennyson's *Maud*," *PMLA* 44 (1949): 1222–27; Clyde de L. Ryals, "Tennyson's *Maud*," *Connotation* 1 (1962): 12–32; A. Dwight Culler, "Monodrama and the Dramatic Monologue," *PMLA* 90 (1975): 366–85 and *The Poetry of Tennyson* (New Haven: Yale University Press, 1977), pp. 190–213.

17. Hallam Tennyson, *Memoir*, 1.196.

18. Quoted in Alfred Tennyson, *Complete Poetical Works*, Cambridge edition, ed. W. J. Rolfe (Cambridge: Houghton Mifflin, 1898), p. 198.

19. My text for *Maud* is *The Poems of Tennyson*, ed. Christopher Ricks (London: Longman, 1969).

20. But see Langbaum's reading in *The Poetry of Experience*, pp. 89–91.

21. Hallam Tennyson, *Memoir*, 1.403.

22. M. L. Howe, "Dante Gabriel Rossetti's Comments on 'Maud,' " *Modern Language Notes* 49 (1934): 290–93.

23. De Ryals, "Tennyson's *Maud*," pp. 12–14.

24. Hallam, "Modern Poetry," pp. 626, 619–20.

25. Browning's preface to the 1867 edition of his collected poems, cited in *The Poetical Works of Robert Browning*, ed. Horace E. Scudder, rev. G. Robert Strange (Boston: Houghton Mifflin, 1974), p. 1.

26. Lines 268–79 from *Pauline*, ed. John Berkey, in *The Complete Works of Robert A. Browning*, vol. 1 (Athens: Ohio University Press, 1969).

27. See Otten, *The Deserted Stage*, pp. 111–21.

28. II.190 from *A Soul's Tragedy*, ed. Allan C. Dooley, in *Complete Works*, vol. 5 (Athens: Ohio University Press and Waco: Baylor University, 1981).

29. See Tucker, "Dramatic Monologue and the Overhearing of Lyric." I rely here also on the work in progress of Ashton Nichols, particularly his as yet unpublished essay "Dialogism in the Dramatic Monologue: The Example of Browning."

30. Letter to Lady Trevelyan, 15 March 1865, quoted in Bush, *Mythology and the Romantic Tradition in English Poetry*, p. 332.

31. Bush, *Mythology*, p. 260; Swinburne's judgment, expressed in the letter cited above, was that "the clothes are well enough, but where has the body gone?"

32. My text for Arnold is *The Poetical Works of Matthew Arnold*, ed. C. B. Tinker and H. F. Lowry (London: Oxford University Press, 1950).

33. Arnold's "Preface" to *Poems*, 1853, in *Poetical Works*, p. xvii. The parallel with Browning is suggested by Bush in *Mythology*, p. 255.

34. Thomas Hardy, *The Dynasts: An Epic-Drama of the War with Napoleon, in Three Parts, Nineteen Acts, & One Hundred & Thirty Scenes, The Time Covered by the Action Being About Ten Years* (London: Macmillan, 1920).

35. See Susan Dean, *Hardy's Poetic Vision in The Dynasts: The Diorama of a Dream* (Princeton: Princeton University Press, 1977), pp. 36–42.

36. Hardy, *The Dynasts*, p. x.

37. *Purgatory*, line 204, in *The Variorum Edition of the Plays of W. B. Yeats*, ed. Russell K. Alspach (New York: Macmillan, 1966).

38. See the related essays in Cave, *The Romantic Theatre*.

39. From Yeats's 1937 "An Introduction to My Plays," in *Essays and Introductions* (1961; rpt. New York: Collier, 1968), p. 529.

Selected Bibliography

Abrams, M. H. *Natural Supernaturalism: Tradition and Revolution in Romantic Literature*. New York: Norton, 1971.

Adams, Charles L. "The Structure of *The Cenci*." *Drama Survey* 4 (1965): 139–48.

Ades, John I. "Lamb, Shakespeare, and Early Nineteenth-Century Theater." *PMLA* 85 (1970): 514–26.

Agar, John. "Isbrand and T. L. Beddoes' Aspiring Hero." *Studia Neophilologica* 45 (1973): 372–91.

Babcock, Robert W. *The Genesis of Shakespeare Idolatry, 1766–1799*. Chapel Hill: University of North Carolina Press, 1931.

———. "The Inception and Reception of Byron's 'Cain.' " *South Atlantic Quarterly* 25 (1927): 178–88.

Baker, Carlos. "A Note on Shelley and Milton." *Modern Language Notes* 55 (1940): 585–89.

———. *Shelley's Major Poetry: The Fabric of a Vision*. Princeton: Princeton University Press, 1948.

Ball, Patricia M. *The Central Self: A Study in Romantic and Victorian Imagination*. London: University of London Press, 1965.

Bate, W. J. *The Burden of the Past and the English Poet*. 1970. Reprinted New York: Norton, 1972.

———. *From Classic to Romantic: Premises of Taste in Eighteenth Century England*. Cambridge: Harvard University Press, 1946.

Bates, E. S. *A Study of Shelley's Drama "The Cenci."* New York: Columbia University Press, 1908.

Beaty, Frederick C. *Light from Heaven: Love in British Romantic Literature*. DeKalb: Northern Illinois University Press, 1971.

Bennett, James R. "*Prometheus Unbound*, Act I, 'The play's the thing.' " *Keats-Shelley Journal* 23 (1974): 32–51.

Bloom, Harold. *Blake's Apocalypse*. Garden City: Doubleday, 1963.

———. *Poetry and Repression*. New Haven: Yale University Press, 1976.

———. Introduction to *Romanticism and Consciousness*. New York: Norton, 1970.

———. "The Internalization of Quest-Romance." In *Romanticism and Consciousness*, edited by Harold Bloom, pp. 3–23.

———. *Shelley's Mythmaking*. 1959. Reprinted Ithaca: Cornell University Press, 1969.

———. *The Visionary Company: A Reading of English Romantic Poetry*. Revised edition. Ithaca: Cornell University Press, 1971.

Bostetter, Edward E. "Byron and the Politics of Paradise." *PMLA* 75 (1960): 571–76.

———. *The Romantic Ventriloquists: Wordsworth, Coleridge, Keats, Shelley, Byron*. Revised edition. Seattle: University of Washington Press, 1975.

Brisman, Susan H. " 'Unsaying His High Language': The Problem of Voice in *Prometheus Unbound*." *Studies in Romanticism* 16 (1977): 51–86.

Brooke, Stopford. "Byron's 'Cain.' " *Hibbert Journal* 18 (1919): 74–94.

Brown, Nathaniel. *Sexuality and Feminism in Shelley*. Cambridge: Harvard University Press, 1979.

Bush, Douglas. *Mythology and the Romantic Tradition in English Poetry*. 1937. Reprinted New York: Norton, 1963.

Butler, Marilyn. *Romantics, Rebels and Reactionaries: English Literature and Its Backgrounds 1760–1830*. Oxford: Oxford University Press, 1981.

Calvert, William. *Byron: Romantic Paradox*. Chapel Hill: University of North Carolina Press, 1935.

Cameron, K. N. "The Political Symbolism of *Prometheus Unbound*." *PMLA* 58 (1943): 728–53.

Cantor, Paul. " 'A Distorting Mirror': Shelley's *The Cenci* and Shakespearean Tragedy." In *Shakespeare: Aspects of Influence*, edited by G. B. Evans, pp. 91–108.

———. "Byron's *Cain*: A Romantic Version of the Fall." *Kenyon Review* (n.s.) 2 (1980): 50–71.

———. *Creature and Creator: Mythmaking and English Romanticism*. Cambridge: Cambridge University Press, 1984.

Cave, Richard Allen, editor. *The Romantic Theatre: An International Symposium*. New York: Barnes and Noble, 1987.

Chew, Samuel C. *The Dramas of Lord Byron*. In *Hesperia*, heft 3. Göttingen, 1915.

Christensen, Jerome. " 'Thoughts That Do Often Lie Too Deep for Tears': Toward a Romantic Concept of Lyrical Drama." *The Wordsworth Circle* 12 (1981): 52–64.

Clancy, Charles J. A *Selected Bibliography of English Romantic Drama*. Norwood, Pa.: Norwood Editions, 1976.

Clark, David Lee. "Shelley and Shakespeare." *PMLA* 54 (1939): 261–87.

Cooke, Margaret. "Shiller's 'Robbers' in England." *Modern Language Review* 11 (1916): 156–75.

Cox, Jeffrey N. "Melodrama, Monodrama and the Forms of Romantic Tragic Drama." *Within the Dramatic Spectrum* 6 (1986): 20–29.

Coxe, Louis O. "Beddoes: The Mask of Parody." *Hudson Review* 6 (1953): 252–65.

Craig, Gordon, editor. *Essays in Dramatic Literature*. Princeton: Princeton University Press, 1935.

Culler, A. Dwight. "Monodrama and the Dramatic Monologue." *PMLA* 90 (1975): 366–85.

Curran, Stuart. "The Political Prometheus." *Studies in Romanticism* 25 (1986): 429–55.

———. *Shelley's Annus Mirabilis: The Maturing of an Epic Vision*. San Marino: Huntington Library, 1975.

———. *Shelley's Cenci: Scorpions Ringed with Fire*. Princeton: Princeton University Press, 1970.

———. "The Siege of hateful contraries: Shelley, Mary Shelley, Byron." In *Milton and the Line of Vision*, edited by Joseph Wittreich, pp. 209–30.

DeLuca, V. A. "The Style of Millennial Announcement in *Prometheus Unbound*." *Keats-Shelley Journal* 28 (1979): 78–101.

De Man, Paul. *Blindness and Insight: Essays in the Rhetoric of Contemporary Criticism*. Revised 2nd edition. Minneapolis: University of Minnesota Press, 1983.

De Selincourt, Ernest. "Wordsworth's Preface to 'The Borderers.' " In *Oxford Lectures on Poetry*. London: Oxford University Press, 1934.

Donner, H. L. *Thomas Lovell Beddoes: The Making of a Poet*. Oxford: Blackwell, 1935.

Donoghue, Denis. *The Third Voice*. Princeton: Princeton University Press, 1959.

Donohue, Joseph W. *Dramatic Character in the English Romantic Age*. Princeton: Princeton University Press, 1970.

———. "Shelley's Beatrice and the Romantic Conception of Character." *Keats-Shelley Journal* 17 (1968): 55–73.

Duerkson, Roland A., editor. *The Cenci*. Indianapolis: Bobbs-Merrill, 1970.

Elledge, W. P. "Imagery and Theme in Byron's *Cain*." *Keats-Shelley Journal* 15 (1966): 49–57.

Engell, James. *The Creative Imagination: Enlightenment to Romanticism*. Cambridge: Harvard University Press, 1981.

Erdman, David V. "Byron's Stage Fright: The History of His Ambition and Fear of Writing for the Stage." *ELH* 6 (1939): 219–43.

Evans, Bertrand. *Gothic Drama from Walpole to Shelley*. Berkeley: University of California Press, 1947.

———. "Manfred's Remorse and Dramatic Tradition." *PMLA* 62 (1947): 752–73.

Evans, G. B., editor. *Shakespeare: Aspects of Influence*. Cambridge: Harvard University Press, 1976.

Fletcher, Richard M. *English Romantic Drama 1795–1843: A Critical History*. New York: Exposition Press, 1966.

Fogle, R. H. "Image and Imagelessness: A Limited Reading of *Prometheus Unbound.*" *Keats-Shelley Journal* 1 (1952): 23–36.

Frye, Northrop. *Fearful Symmetry.* Boston: Beacon Press, 1947.

———. *A Study of English Romanticism.* Chicago: University of Chicago Press, 1968.

Gleckner, Robert F. *Byron and the Ruins of Paradise.* Baltimore: Johns Hopkins University Press, 1967.

Gottleib, Erica. *Lost Angels of a Ruined Paradise: Themes of Love and Strife in Romantic Tragedy.* Victoria: Sono Nis Press, 1981.

Hammond, Eugene R. "Beatrice's Three Fathers: Successive Betrayal in Shelley's *The Cenci.*" *Essays in Literature* 8 (1981): 25–32.

Harrington-Leuker, D. "Imagination versus Introspection: *The Cenci* and *Macbeth.*" *Keats-Shelley Journal* 32 (1983): 172–89.

Hartman, Geoffrey. "Romanticism and Anti-Self-Consciousness." In *Romanticism and Consciousness,* edited by Harold Bloom, pp. 46–56.

———. *Wordsworth's Poetry 1787–1814.* New Haven: Yale University Press, 1964.

Havens, R. D. *The Influence of Milton on English Poetry.* Cambridge: Harvard University Press, 1922.

Heath-Stubbs, John. *The Darkling Plain: A Study of the Later Fortunes of Romanticism in England from George Darley to W. B. Yeats.* London: Eyre and Spottiswoode, 1950.

Hollander, John. *The Figure of Echo.* Berkeley: University of California Press, 1981.

Hôsek, Chaviva, and Patricia Parker, eds. *Lyric Poetry: Beyond New Criticism.* Ithaca: Cornell University Press, 1985.

Howell, Margaret. *Byron Tonight: A Poet's Plays on the Nineteenth-Century Stage.* Windlesham: Springwood, 1982.

Hughes, Daniel J. "Potentiality in *Prometheus Unbound.*" *Studies in Romanticism* 2 (1963): 107–26.

———. "Prometheus Made Capable Poet in Act One of *Prometheus Unbound.*" *Studies in Romanticism* 17 (1978): 3–11.

Hurt, James R. "*Prometheus Unbound* and Aeschylean Dramaturgy." *Keats-Shelley Journal* 15 (1966): 43–48.

Jacobus, Mary. " 'That Great Stage Where Senators Perform': *Macbeth* and the Politics of Romantic Theatre." *Studies in Romanticism* 22 (1983): 353–87.

Jones, F. L. "Shelley and Milton." *Studies in Philology* 49 (1952): 488–519.

Jordan, Frank, editor. *The English Romantic Poets: A Review of Research and Criticism.* 4th edition. New York: Modern Language Association of America, 1985.

Keach, William. "Reflexive Imagery in Shelley." *Keats-Shelley Journal* 24 (1975): 49–69.

Knight, G. Wilson. *Byron and Shakespeare*. London: Routledge, 1966.

———. "Shakespeare and Byron's Plays." *Shakespeare Jahrbuch* 95 (1959): 82–97.

———. *The Starlit Dome: Studies in the Poetry of Vision*. London: Oxford University Press, 1941.

Lacoue-Labarth, Phillipe, and Jean-Luc Nancy. "Genre." *Glyph* 7 (1980): 1–15.

Langbaum, Robert. *The Poetry of Experience: The Dramatic Monologue in Modern Literary Tradition*. 1957. Reprinted New York: Norton, 1963.

Langston, Beach. "Shelley's Use of Shakespeare." *Huntington Library Quarterly* 12 (1949): 163–90.

Lemoncelli, Ronald L. "Cenci as Corrupt Dramatic Poet." *English Language Notes* 16 (1978): 103–16.

McFarland, Thomas. *Romanticism and the Forms of Ruin: Wordsworth, Coleridge, and Modalities of Fragmentation*. Princeton: Princeton University Press, 1981.

McGann, Jerome J. *Fiery Dust: Byron's Poetic Development*. Chicago: University of Chicago Press, 1968.

———. "Milton and Byron." *Keats-Shelley Memorial Bulletin* 25 (1974): 9–25.

McGill, M. S. "The Role of Earth in Shelley's *Prometheus Unbound*." *Studies in Romanticism* 7 (1968): 117–28.

Mackenzie, Henry. "Account of the German Theatre." *Transactions of the Royal Society of Edinburgh* 2 (1790): 154–92.

Male, Roy, Jr. "Shelley and the Doctrine of Sympathy." *Studies in English* 29 (1950): 183–203.

Manning, Peter J. *Byron and His Fictions*. Detroit: Wayne State University Press, 1978.

Marchand, Leslie A. *Byron's Poetry: A Critical Introduction*. London: Murray, 1965.

Marshall, William H. *The Structure of Byron's Major Poems*. Philadelphia: University of Pennsylvania Press, 1962.

Mathur, Om Prakesh. *The Closet Drama of the Romantic Revival*. Salzburg: Institut für Englische Sprache und Literatur, 1978.

Motter, T. H. Vail. "Byron's 'Werner' Re-Estimated." In *Essays in Dramatic Literature*, edited by Hardin Craig, pp. 243–75.

Neufeldt, L. N. "Poetry as Subversion: The Unbinding of Shelley's Prometheus." *Anglia* 95 (1977): 60–86.

Nicoll, Allardyce. *A History of English Drama 1660–1900*, Vol. 4, *Early Nineteenth-Century Drama*. 2nd edition. Cambridge: Cambridge University Press, 1955.

Onorato, Richard. *The Character of the Poet: Wordsworth in "The Prelude."* Princeton: Princeton University Press, 1971.

Oras, Ants. "The Multitudinous Orb: Some Miltonic Elements in Shelley."

Modern Languages Quarterly 16 (1955): 247–57.

Osborn, Robert. Introduction to *The Borderers*. Edited by Robert Osborn. Ithaca: Cornell University Press, 1982.

———. "Meaningful Obscurity: The Antecedents and Character of Rivers." In *Bicentenary Wordsworth Studies*. Edited by Jonathan Wordsworth. Ithaca: Cornell University Press, 1970.

Otten, Terry. *The Deserted Stage: The Search for Dramatic Form in Nineteenth-Century England*. Athens: University of Ohio Press, 1972.

Peacock, Ronald. *The Poet in the Theatre*. 1946. Reprinted New York: Hill and Wang, 1960.

Perkins, David. *The Quest for Permanence: The Symbolism of Wordsworth, Shelley, Keats*. Cambridge: Harvard University Press, 1959.

Pipkin, James W. "*The Borderers* and the Genesis of Wordsworth's Spots of Time." *Tennessee Studies in Literature* 24 (1979): 111–19.

Pottle, Frederick A. "The Role of Asia in the Dramatic Action of Shelley's *Prometheus Unbound*." In *Shelley: A Collection of Critical Essays*, edited by George M. Ridenour, pp. 133–43.

Pound, Ezra. "Beddoes and Chronology." In *Selected Prose*, edited by William Cookson, pp. 348–53. London: Faber and Faber, 1973.

Prior, Moody E. *The Language of Tragedy*. New York: Columbia University Press, 1947.

Purkayastha, Pratyush Ranjan. *The Romantics' Third Voice: A Study of the Dramatic Works of the English Romantic Poets*. Salzburg: Institut für Englische Sprache und Literatur, 1978.

Rader, Ralph W. "The Dramatic Monologue and Related Lyric Forms." *Critical Inquiry* 3 (1976): 131–51.

Rajan, Tilottama. "Deconstruction or Reconstruction: Reading Shelley's *Prometheus Unbound*." *Studies in Romanticism* 23 (1984): 317–38.

———. "Romanticism and the Death of Lyric Consciousness." In *Lyric Poetry*, edited by Chaviva Hôsek and Patricia Parker, pp. 194–207.

Rapf, Joanna. "A Spirit in Search of Itself: Non-Narrative Structure in Act IV of Shelley's *Prometheus Unbound*." *Keats-Shelley Memorial Bulletin* 30 (1979): 36–47.

Reiman, Donald H. *Percy Bysshe Shelley*. New York: Twayne, 1969.

———. *The Romantics Reviewed: Contemporary Reviews of British Romantic Writers*. 5 vols. New York: Garland, 1972.

Ricks, Christopher. *The Force of Poetry*. Oxford: Clarendon Press, 1984.

———. "Pilgrim Misery: Thomas Lovell Beddoes (Part II)." *Grand Street* 2 (1984): 90–102.

———. "Thomas Lovell Beddoes." *Grand Street* 1 (1982): 32–48.

Ridenour, George M., editor. *Shelley: A Collection of Critical Essays*. Englewood Cliffs: Prentice-Hall, 1965.

Rieger, James. *The Mutiny Within: The Heresies of Percy Bysshe Shelley*. New York: George Braziller, 1967.

Rutherford, Andrew. *Byron: A Critical Study*. Stanford: Stanford University Press, 1961.

Rzepka, Charles J. *The Self as Mind: Vision and Identity in Wordsworth, Coleridge, and Keats*. Cambridge: Harvard University Press, 1986.

Schlegel, A. W. *A Course of Lectures on Dramatic Art and Literature*. Translated by John Black. Philadelphia: Hogan and Thompson, 1833.

Scott, Sir Walter. "Essay on the Drama." In *The Prose Works of Sir Walter Scott, Bart*. Vol. 6. Edinburgh: Cadell, 1943.

Sharrock, Roger. "*The Borderers*: Wordsworth on the Moral Frontier." *Durham University Journal* 56 (1964): 170–83.

Singer, Irving. *The Nature of Love*, Vol. 2, "Courtly and Romantic." Chicago: University of Chicago Press, 1984.

Smith, Charles J. "The Effect of Shakespeare's Influence on *The Borderers*." *Studies in Philology* 50 (1953): 625–39.

Smith, Paul. "Restless Casuistry: Shelley's Composition of *The Cenci*." *Keats-Shelley Journal* 13 (1964): 77–85.

Sperry, Stuart M. "Byron and the Meaning of *Manfred*." *Criticism* 16 (1974): 189–202.

———. "The Ethical Politics of Shelley's *The Cenci*." *Studies in Romanticism* 25 (1986): 411–27.

———. "Necessity and the Role of the Hero in Shelley's *Prometheus Unbound*." PMLA 96 (1981): 242–54.

Stavrou, Constantine N. "Milton, Byron, and the Devil." *University of Kansas City Review* 21 (1955): 153–59.

Steffan, Truman Guy. *Lord Byron's Cain: Twelve Essays and a Text with Variants and Annotations*. Austin: University of Texas Press, 1968.

Steiner, George. *The Death of Tragedy*. 1961. Reprinted New York: Oxford University Press, 1980.

Stokoe, F. W. *German Influence in the English Romantic Period 1788–1818*. Cambridge: Cambridge University Press, 1926.

Strachey, Lytton. "The Last Elizabethan." 1907. Reprinted in *Books and Characters*, pp. 235–65. New York: Harcourt, Brace, 1922.

Swingle, L. J. "On Reading Romantic Poetry." *PMLA* 86 (1971): 974–81.

Symons, Arthur. "Thomas Lovell Beddoes." In *Figures of Several Centuries*, pp. 122–29. London: Constable, 1917.

Thorslev, Peter L., Jr. *The Byronic Hero*. Minneapolis: University of Minnesota Press, 1962.

———. "The Romantic Mind Is Its Own Place." *Comparative Literature* 15 (1963): 250–68.

———. "Wordsworth's *Borderers* and the Romantic Villain-Hero." *Studies in*

Romanticism 5 (1960): 84–103.

Thurston, Norman. "The Second Language of *Prometheus Unbound*." *Philological Quarterly* 55 (1976): 126–32.

Tucker, Herbert. "Dramatic Monologue and the Overhearing of Lyric." In *Lyric Poetry*, edited by Chaviva Hôsek and Patricia Parker, pp. 226–43.

Twitchell, James B. "Shelley's Metapsychological System in Act IV of *Prometheus Unbound*." *Keats-Shelley Journal* 24 (1975): 29–48.

———. "Shelley's Use of Vampirism in *The Cenci*." *Tennessee Studies in Literature* 24(1979): 120–33.

———. "The Supernatural Structure of Byron's *Manfred*." *SEL* 15 (1975): 601–14.

Wasserman, Earl R. "The Pleasures of Tragedy." *ELH* 14 (1947): 283–307.

———. *Shelley: A Critical Reading.* Baltimore: Johns Hopkins University Press, 1971.

———. *Shelley's Prometheus Unbound: A Critical Reading.* Baltimore: Johns Hopkins University Press, 1965.

Watson, Ernest B. *Sheridan to Robertson: A Study of the Nineteenth-Century London Stage.* Cambridge: Harvard University Press, 1926.

Watson, Melvin R. "Shelley and Tragedy: The Case of Beatrice Cenci." *Keats-Shelley Journal* 7 (1958): 13–22.

Watson, S. R. "Shelley and Shakespeare: An Addendum." *PMLA* 55 (1940): 611–14.

West, Paul. *Byron and the Spoiler's Art.* London: Chatto and Windus, 1960.

White, Harry. "Beatrice Cenci and Shelley's Avenger." *Essays in Literature* 5 (1979): 27–38.

White, Newman I. "*Prometheus Unbound*, or Every Man His Own Allegorist." *PMLA* 40 (1925): 172–84.

Whitman, Robert F. "Beatrice's 'Pernicious Mistake' in *The Cenci*." *PMLA* 74 (1959): 249–53.

Whitmore, A. P. *The Major Characters of Byron's Dramas.* Salzburg: Institut für Englische Sprache und Literatur, 1974.

Wilson, James D. "Beatrice Cenci and Shelley's View of Morality." *Ariel* 9 (1978): 77–88.

Wilson, Milton. *Shelley's Later Poetry: A Study of His Prophetic Imagination.* New York: Columbia University Press, 1959.

Wittreich, Joseph A., editor. *Milton and the Line of Vision.* Madison: University of Wisconsin Press, 1975.

———. *The Romantics on Milton: Formal Essays and Critical Asides.* Cleveland: The Press of Case Western University, 1970.

———. "The 'Satanism' of Blake and Shelley Reconsidered." *Studies in Philology* 65 (1962): 816–33.

Woodman, Ross. "The Androgyne in *Prometheus Unbound*." *Studies in Romanticism* 20 (1981): 225–47.

———. *The Apocalyptic Vision in the Poetry of Shelley*. Toronto: University of Toronto Press, 1964.

———. "Milton's Satan in Wordsworth's 'Vale of Soul-Making.' " *Studies in Romanticism* 23 (1984): 3–30.

Woodring, Carl. *Politics in English Romantic Poetry*. Cambridge: Harvard University Press, 1970.

Wordsworth, Jonathan. *William Wordsworth: The Borders of Vision*. Oxford: Clarendon Press, 1982.

Zillman, L. J. *Shelley's Prometheus Unbound: A Variorum Edition*. Seattle: University of Washington Press, 1959.

Index